Cowboys & Cave Dwellers

The generous support of
Robert E. and Margot T. Linton
helped make the publication of this book possible.

To the men and women of the Four Corners

whose curiosity, determination, and sense of adventure

led to the discovery of the Basketmakers,

and to their families and descendants

whose enthusiasm and generosity

helped make our research possible.

Cowboys & Cave Dwellers

Basketmaker Archaeology in Utah's Grand Gulch

Fred M. Blackburn
& Ray A. Williamson

School of American Research Press
Santa Fe, New Mexico

School of American Research Press
Post Office Box 2188
Santa Fe, New Mexico 87504-2188
www.sarweb.org

Director of Publications: Joan K. O'Donnell
Editor: Jane Kepp
Art Director and Designer: Deborah Flynn Post
Indexer: Andrew L. Christenson
Printer: Sung In Printing Company

Library of Congress Cataloging-in-Publication Data:

Blackburn, Fred M.
Cowboys and cave dwellers : Basketmaker archaeology in Utah's Grand Gulch / Fred M. Blackburn and Ray A. Williamson.
p. cm.
Includes bibliographical references and index.
ISBN 0-933452-48-9 (cloth). -- ISBN 0-933452-47-0 (pbk.)
1. Basket-Maker Indians--Antiquities. 2. Indians of North America--Utah--Antiquities. 3. Grand Gulch (Utah)--Antiquities. I. Williamson, Ray A., 1938- . II. Title.
E99.B37B56 1997
979.2'47--dc21 96-29572
CIP

 Library of Congress Catalog Card Number 96-29572. International Standard Book Numbers 0-933452-48-9 (cloth), 0-933452-47-0 (paper).
Third paperback printing, 2000.

Cover: Basketmaker handprints at Polly's Island, Grand Gulch © Bruce Hucko. Inset: Members of the Hyde Exploring Expedition in Cave 7, December 1893. Courtesy The University of Pennsylvania Museum, neg. no. 54-139872.

Printed and bound in South Korea.

CONTENTS

J WETHERILL

Acknowledgments

THE STORY TOLD IN THIS BOOK, LIKE ALL COMPLEX STORIES, IS ONE OF MANY versions that could be recounted. It necessarily reflects our own perspectives—one of us (Fred Blackburn) deeply involved in the unfolding of the Wetherill–Grand Gulch Research Project, the other participating from a distance. Nevertheless, it could not have achieved completion without the help of many people.

First, we thank Winston Hurst for his many contributions to the research described in this book and for his help and friendship in reviewing the entire manuscript more than once for accuracy and clarity. Winston's command of the historical and archaeological record related to the discovery of the Basketmakers is encyclopedic. He went far beyond the usual role of careful reviewer and contributed to the intellectual content of the book in ways both large and small.

We especially thank Julia Johnson, who directed the Wetherill–Grand Gulch Research Project after the first year of effort. Without her organizational skills, persistence, and financial help, the project would never have gotten started, much less achieved success. We also want to recognize the invaluable contributions made to the project by Ann Hayes and Ann Phillips. All three of these core team members, and other participants too numerous to name individually, made the work not only intellectually satisfying but also fun.

We appreciate the warm support of archaeologist William Lipe for Fred's work. Not only has Lipe made major contributions to Southwestern archaeology and the understanding of Basketmaker culture, but he also has found time to guide others in the joys and frustrations of working with historic materials. And to Anibal Rodríguez, archaeological curator *extraordinaire*, whose friendship and confidence gave Fred and the Wetherill–Grand Gulch Research Project a chance at reverse archaeology, thanks again for the opportunity.

Carol Carnett, Ray's wife, read several drafts of the manuscript for this book and caught awkward phrasing, numerous redundancies, and gulfs of logic. Victoria Atkins, Fred's wife, also read the manuscript closely for content and accuracy. William Haase reviewed chapter 7 and made numerous helpful suggestions. School of American Research reviewers Eric Blinman and Curtis M. Hinsley read the draft manuscript with care and critical eyes. We thank them for their thoughtful suggestions and corrections.

Staff members of the American Museum of Natural History and the Museum of the American Indian in New York City, the Field Museum of Natural History in Chicago, and the Latter Day Saints Museum of Church History and Art and the Utah Museum of Natural History in Salt Lake City assisted the project team enormously. We are also indebted to R. G. Matson, whose book *The Origins of Southwestern Agriculture* made the task of understanding Basketmaker research much more tractable than it would have been otherwise.

We extend our heartfelt gratitude to photographer Bruce Hucko for his illuminating additions to our words. His sensitive eyes have captured many of the truths of Grand Gulch. Ira Block and the National Geographic Society, Bill Harris, Terry Moore, and John Richardson granted permission to use some of their fine photographs. Thanks are also due to the American Museum of Natural History, the Field Museum of Natural History, the Colorado Historical Society, the Denver Public Library, the Fort Lewis College Center for Southwest Studies, the University of Pennsylvania Museum, and the Middle American Institute at Tulane University for permission to publish some of the historic photographs that enhance this volume. Family photographs were offered by Eleanor Stanberry, Carol Ann Wetherill, Tom Wetherill, and the family of Emerald Flint Patrick.

Much of this book could not have been written without the help of the descendants of the early avocational archaeologists. We acknowledge the special assistance extended to the project by Katherine Ayres, Marietta Davenport, Bob Getz, Charles Lang, Jr., Charles Leslie Graham, Charles S. Graham, Robert McDaniel and the Animas City Museum, the family of Emerald Flint Patrick, Carol Ann Wetherill, and Tom, Wren, and Samantha Wetherill, all of whom opened their family photograph albums and archives. We especially mourn the recent death of Tom Wetherill, who was a good friend to Fred and an enthusiastic supporter of our work.

We owe special thanks to Jane Kepp, former director of the School of American Research Press, who acquired this book for the press, and her successor, Joan K. O'Donnell, for their thoughtful input. Jane and business manager Peter Palmieri helped us frame the original proposal. Joan helped shape the manuscript further and saw us through the publishing process. We thank them and also Deborah Flynn Post, art director, Baylor Chapman, project coordinator, and Jo Ann Baldinger, the press's in-house editor, for making the publishing experience as pleasurable as possible. Jane Kepp did a wonderfully thorough job of copyediting. Her touch has greatly enhanced the book and made it much more "reader friendly."

Over the years, in ways large and small, Douglas W. Schwartz, president of the School of American Research, has supported efforts to spread the word about the development and pursuit of archaeological research. We thank him for his confidence in our research and writing. We especially thank Robert E. and Margot T. Linton for their generous assistance in support of the publication of this book.

For both of us, writing this book on top of our full-time work commitments took many hours away from our families. We especially thank them for their understanding, patience, and good humor through the many months of writing, rewriting, and editing.

Cowboys & Cave Dwellers

The deep alcove that shelters Perfect Kiva.

1 / The Beginning

The canyon country does not always inspire love. To many it appears barren, hostile, repellent—a fearsome most waterless land of rock and heat, sand dunes and quicksand, cactus, thornbush, scorpion, rattlesnake, and agoraphobic distances. To those who see our land in that manner, the best reply is, yes, you are right, it is a dangerous and terrible place. Enter at your own risk. Carry water. Avoid the noonday sun. Try to ignore the vultures. Pray frequently.

—Edward Abbey

The hot June sun had worked its way well toward the west when we climbed out of our vehicle, slipped on our backpacks, and headed across the piñon-juniper flats of Cedar Mesa. It was just after the summer solstice in 1981, and the four of us were in the canyon country of southeastern Utah to examine archaeological sites in Bullet Canyon, one of the tributary canyons of Grand Gulch, which archaeologist Nels C. Nelson in 1920 called "a great rift in the earth, tortuous and fantastic."[1] With our two friends, we trudged for about an hour through the deep aeolian soil of the flats before reaching the edge of the canyon, where we settled in to fix a meal and eat before the sun found its home on the western rim.

It was a stunning evening. We made camp on the rimrock some two hundred feet above the canyon floor. From our campsite we looked across to a small, ancient Pueblo structure called Moon Kiva, perched high on a ledge over a precipitous drop. Above the ruin a large, flat sandstone panel displayed three circular white paintings, each about a foot across, that seemed to symbolize the moon. As we prepared our camp stew, a cooling breeze washed over us from the slope above. Later, we watched the full moon rise just above the painted "moon" symbols, now tinted rose by the setting sun.

Of the four of us, only Fred Blackburn had explored Grand Gulch before. Fred had worked in the Gulch as a ranger for the Bureau of Land Management in the 1970s, patrolling the canyons and helping protect its many archaeological sites, the long-abandoned homes of the Ancestral Pueblo, or Anasazi, people.[2]

Fred knew that the first archaeological excavations in the Gulch had taken place some ninety years earlier, beginning with the January 1891 expedition of Charles McLoyd and Charles Cary Graham. Bullet Canyon had been the entry point for the two entrepreneurs from

Durango, Colorado, who spent three months digging for artifacts to exhibit and sell back home. The only archaeological site mentioned in Graham's trip diary that can be easily identified today is the tiny sandstone structure we gazed at across the darkening chasm.

January 14, 1891

> I went up the south fork. Just above the forks in the main canon there is a small house high up with the following painting [a sketch of 2 moons with a half moon and star between them]. White paint.[3]

The artifacts McLoyd and Graham brought back from their 1891 trip piqued the interest of McLoyd's acquaintances, rancher Richard Wetherill and his younger brothers, John, Al, Winslow, and Clayton, who mounted their own Grand Gulch expedition three years later. On that trip, undertaken in the winter of 1893–94, the Wetherills discovered convincing proof that the people now known as the Basketmakers had preceded the Pueblo people in Southwestern prehistory.

As we relaxed and watched the nighthawks circle and dive in the cooling breeze, we talked about those early explorers and what they had removed from the Gulch. McLoyd and Graham, the Wetherills, and others had taken thousands of Ancestral Pueblo skeletons, preserved foodstuffs, baskets, pots, and other artifacts. Yet the present whereabouts of many of these collections was unknown, and even when their location was known their condition was uncertain. Worse, from an archaeologist's point of view, no one knew which specific sites most of the artifacts had come from. With the exception of Richard Wetherill, the early explorers kept only minimal notes. Since museum accession and curatorial practices of the time were notoriously lax as well, museum collections from the Gulch generally lacked information regarding the origin and context, or provenience, of the artifacts.

As Fred came to know the Gulch, however, he discovered that the canyon walls themselves held invaluable clues—dated signatures left by these early explorers as they made their way from site to site. Archaeologist William Lipe suggested that the signatures might be used to trace the sites in which the nineteenth-century excavators had dug:

> As much as I curse the few graffiti left by modern hikers in the Gulch, I'm thankful these pioneer archaeologists were afflicted by that human urge to record their passing. We'll keep looking for these faint old scribblings, and may someday be able to reconstruct from them the course of that first Wetherill expedition.[4]

The four of us had a chance to see some signatures two days later when we hiked back out of the Gulch. On the way to Cedar Mesa we stopped at the site called Perfect Kiva, named for the intact thirteenth-century Ancestral Pueblo kiva that still exists there. Sheltered in a relatively deep alcove carved into the canyon wall by water and wind, Perfect Kiva is a well-preserved example of the underground ceremonial chambers used by generations of Pueblo people in a tradition that continues today. *Kiva* is a Hopi word that has come into general use to describe such structures, whether they are found in an archaeological site or in a modern Pueblo village.

As we explored the alcove, or rockshelter, Fred pointed out the inscription "Wetherill 1894" carefully etched in an ax-grinding groove on a large sandstone boulder. The prehistoric Pueblo people often used a sandstone surface to sharpen their stone axes, and one of the Wetherill

Perfect Kiva Ruin, photographed in 1894.
Inset: A Wetherill 1894 inscription in lower Grand Gulch. A similar inscription at Perfect Kiva, dated January 1894, has recently been obliterated.

brothers apparently decided to use the grooves they left to indicate that he had been there, too. Inside the kiva, on the plaster wall, was the name "C. C. Graham." Fred had first seen this inscription in 1974 when he worked with the crew that repaired and stabilized the Perfect Kiva structures.

Eventually, Fred hoped to follow William Lipe's lead by using the signatures to determine both the routes of the most significant Grand Gulch expeditions and the original alcoves or rockshelters from which artifacts had been taken. Among other things, rediscovering these sites would allow archaeologists to learn more about the Basketmaker people. They would then be able to associate the artifacts with the sites and site features, establishing the artifacts' proveniences. But retracing the routes and uncovering which alcove went with which artifact would take time and the collaboration of many people. Five years after our 1981 trip, thanks to the persistent curiosity and dedicated involvement of many volunteers, Fred's dreams of tracing the routes and history of those early explorations began to be realized.

THE ADVENTURE THAT BECAME KNOWN AS THE WETHERILL–GRAND GULCH Research Project was born during another hike into Grand Gulch. Ann Hayes, a writer and avid backpacker from Boulder, Colorado, asked Fred to lead a recreational trip into the Gulch. On the afternoon of November 11, 1986, the five-day expedition began.

The backpackers would long remember those first steps into the Gulch. The sky was clear, with a smoky haze building in the southwest, the temperature pleasant as a hint of fall brought that touch of crispness perfect for hiking. Fallen cottonwood leaves lent a dash of muted gold to the drab rocks and sand of the streambed. Navajo Mountain brooded far to the south.

On the surface of the old wagon road that led into a tributary canyon and onto an outcrop of slickrock sandstone, dry potholes reminded the hikers that water in the canyon might be scarce. Beyond the slickrock, the eroded wagon trail reappeared and led the group to the canyon bottom. Climbing up and out the other side, the hikers headed south, this time following a faint cattle trail. Although cattle had not been seen in Grand Gulch since the early 1970s, in the dry climate of southeastern Utah disturbances of the land endure for years.

The remains of an 1880s cow camp in a dry alcove in Canyonlands National Park.

Nightfall found the group on the edge of one of the many natural alcoves in Grand Gulch. This site, which once sheltered Ancestral Pueblo people, was for almost a century a cow camp used periodically by the TY Cattle Company, founded in the 1880s by a cowboy named Al Scorup. Scorup got his start on this arid range by rounding up stray cattle abandoned by companies that had gone bankrupt confronting the rigors of life in southeastern Utah. He lived with his cattle year-round, nurturing their health and building up a large herd. Eventually he established line camps throughout the region and built one of the largest working ranches in the country.

At purely Ancestral Pueblo sites, it takes a trained eye to recognize the many subtle signs of earlier life. Here in the cow camp, evidence of past occupation was obvious. Familiar cowboy-era artifacts were strewn everywhere: a metal grain bin for the horses, a flour sack that still displayed a proud but faded Standard Flour trademark, a box of Ohio Blue Tip matches, swelled cans of tomatoes, peaches, and beans. The alcove also held wooden frames once used to stretch and dry the pelts of bobcats, foxes, and coyotes. Ann Hayes wrote in her journal: "We sleep that night at the Cow Camp, placing our bedrolls as to avoid the cactus barb stashes of the packrat. It's quite cold. We are lucky to be falling asleep (or lying awake) by the nearly full moon."[5]

This historic archaeological site stood in useful contrast to the prehistoric sites the group had expected to see. But camping near archaeological sites or suspected sites of any era requires more than the usual care not to damage the environment. The backpackers used no wood fires and were careful not to disturb the ground in the alcove.

The next day the group struck out along the canyon, passing more of the small alcoves that pocked the sandstone walls above the streambed and the talus—that sloping mass of eroded stone debris at the base of a canyon wall. Fred headed for an alcove he had found on an earlier visit. Cut deep enough to provide sanctuary from rain and snow, but north facing so that it would avoid sunlight most of the day, the alcove was a good setting for an ancient summer dwelling. As the hikers climbed the short slope, they could see immediately why Fred had led them there. On the floor of the rockshelter stood a semicircle of upright sandstone slabs—the remnants of a Basketmaker cist, or storage pit, originally sealed at least two millennia earlier.

In the canyon country of southeastern Utah, Basketmaker people often dug circular or rectangular storage pits in the dirt floors of shallow alcoves or rockshelters. They lined many of these cists with large sandstone slabs and usually plastered the pit walls and slabs with adobe. In the cists they could store corn and other food for long periods, carefully sealed off from hungry mice and beetles. Once they no longer used the cists for food storage, the Basketmakers buried their dead in them. Before covering the grave with stones and sand, the mourners placed a basket or two in the pit, along with a few of the deceased's prized possessions.

Although everyone on the hike had explored Ancestral Pueblo dwellings before, few had ever seen a Basketmaker site. Now the group found more of the ancient storage enclosures—but these cists lay half open and rudely exposed. They had not been opened by natural means.

Uncovered Basketmaker storage cists.

Left to right: A pair of Basketmaker sandals found along the trail; Basketmaker tray with bird and butterfly design from Grand Gulch; large incised jar photographed in situ, possibly during Cave 7 excavations, 1893.

Excavated soil still lay in a heap in front of the stones, and bits of charcoal, probably from an ancient juniper-wood fire, littered the alcove floor. Depressions could be seen in the windblown sand of the shelter floor. Were they signs of recent illegal pothunting, or had the burials in the cists been disturbed years earlier?

Emotions gripped the hikers: anger that someone might have disturbed these ancient burials, deep in protected public land; curiosity about what remnants of long-ago culture the cists had held; concern over where the artifacts taken from the graves might now be; and the keen poignancy of knowing that people had been buried here who once experienced the same human feelings they themselves felt.

As Fred pointed out, whoever had opened the burials had not finished the job. Several pristine cists remained, barely visible in the sandy soil. Close scrutiny revealed a faint inscription or signature written in a dark gray substance on the flat surface of one upright slab. Although now unreadable, the inscription appeared to have been written in an elegant script.

Examining the site thoroughly, the group decided that it must have been excavated many years before. After excavation, the pits—left open by the diggers—had partially refilled with fine, windblown sand, softening the edges of the holes but not filling the pits completely, something that might take several centuries. The incription's graceful script supported their hypothesis that it had been an early dig; the "penmanship" looked too refined to be recent. Fred speculated that they might even be looking at the remains of excavations carried out by people like Charles McLoyd, Charles Cary Graham, or Richard Wetherill.

Out of the hikers' probing curiosity arose a host of questions, some of which Fred had been asking for years. What really happened here? What had been taken from this site? Where were the artifacts now? How could the group learn more about the archaeological sites in Grand Gulch and the history of their excavation? Contemplating the fates of early explorers and their discoveries quickly became an absorbing pastime for the hikers. They also began to talk about

Cliff dwelling in an alcove up-canyon from Cave 7, Cottonwood Wash.

what they could learn by looking carefully at the evidence around them in the "outdoor museum" of Grand Gulch.[6]

Julia Johnson, a retired entrepreneur and resident of Boulder, Colorado, took particular notice. She was fascinated by the idea of returning to the Southwest some of its heritage that had been lost to collectors and museums across the country. An energetic woman with a practical bent, Julia raised still more questions: Were the Basketmaker artifacts that had come from Grand Gulch now in private collections? Were they lost to history? Or were they stored in some museum, safe but hidden away in dusty cabinets? The more the group thought about these questions, the stronger grew their determination to answer them.

The whereabouts of some artifacts were well known to archaeologists familiar with the area. Many of those collected by McLoyd and the Wetherill brothers were in the American Museum of Natural History and the Museum of the American Indian in New York City. Some of those excavated by McLoyd and Graham were in the Field Museum of Natural History in Chicago. But no one seemed to know where other artifacts might be, nor did anyone have much insight about which specific alcoves were the sources of which artifacts—either in Grand Gulch or elsewhere in southeastern Utah. So far as Fred knew, no one had even a clue where to find Cave 7, the alcove in which the Wetherills made the first recorded discovery of Basketmaker culture. Nevertheless, he was confident that with a bit of hard work in the Gulch and a research trip to the American Museum of Natural History, the hiking companions could begin to make some connections.

Out of these conversations came the germ of an idea the group came to identify by the term "reverse archaeology"—the linking of items in museum collections with their original homes. A core of people from among the hikers committed themselves to pursuing this idea. They developed a common goal: to rediscover artifacts that had been removed from Grand Gulch and other canyon systems of southeastern Utah a century earlier. With Julia Johnson's initial funding, prodding, and practical approach to action, they began.

Later, those on the hike would look back with amusement on the last night out as a portent of trials to come. Caught short of their campsite after sunset, the group trekked in darkness through an increasingly brushy, wet, confined gorge. At last reaching its far end, they found themselves inching across a narrow sandstone ledge above a large pool of cold water. One misstep and they would find themselves and their backpacks in the drink.

Somehow, everyone made it across successfully. Tired and grumpy, the hikers stumbled into camp in the dark, barely noticing their surroundings. In the morning they awoke to an array of Ancestral Pueblo pictographs and petroglyphs illuminated by the dawn. Images of deer, mountain sheep, and people in fantastic headdresses loomed above them. This must have been a special place, they felt, for the ancient dwellers of Grand Gulch. No one even noticed the faint signatures and other inscriptions left among the ancient rock art by early archaeological adventurers. That discovery would be made later.

Of the thirteen members of that 1986 expedition, five—Fred Blackburn, Julia Johnson, Ann Hayes, Bob Powell, and Carl Weil—agreed to work together on the project. Soon they were joined by Ann Phillips, an educational consultant from Boulder, whose energy and enthusiasm later helped keep them going when the project threatened to bog down. Within several months the group had drawn up a written agreement that became the basis for their quest—officially, the Wetherill–Grand Gulch Research Project.

The group's initial idea was to locate and photograph the artifacts stored at the American Museum of Natural History and then mount a photographic exhibition in southeastern Utah. In this way they would symbolically return the artifacts to their origins. Before leaving the canyon, Fred agreed to develop a proposal and a budget for photographing the known Basketmaker artifacts at the New York museum, and Julia committed funding to the endeavor.

At that early stage, the project looked relatively straightforward. As it evolved, however, it grew in both scope and membership. The original project team was later joined by photographer Bruce Hucko and archaeologist Winston Hurst, after Bob Powell and Carl Weil left the project. Joel Janetski, associate professor of anthropology and director of the Museum of Peoples and Culture at Brigham Young University, loaned his name and staked his reputation

Quail Panel, Grand Gulch.

as official "principal investigator," a role demanded by the research proposals the group submitted. Many other allies gave financial backing, sage advice, and access to historic letters, photographs, and other documents.

By the time the project formally concluded in May 1990, its members had each contributed hundreds of hours of time, significant amounts of money, and intense intellectual effort. What they gained from the effort was immeasurable—a more thorough understanding of southeastern Utah archaeology, museum practices, research methodology, and the history of Southwestern archaeology. Most importantly, they gained a deeper sense of their own abilities and of what individuals working together could accomplish.

The tortuous course of Grand Gulch and its tributary canyons.

GRAND GULCH, A SERPENTINE COLLECTION OF ARROYOS, DRAWS, AND CANYONS draining a large part of southeastern Utah, epitomizes the natural beauty and daily challenges that shaped the ancient people's lives. Hiking through the Gulch today gives one a solid appreciation of the survival skills the Basketmakers and their descendants, the Puebloans, possessed. They must have been highly inventive and hardy, too, in order to wrest a living from this harsh land.

Grand Gulch is aptly named. It makes a deep, seventy-five-mile-long cut in Cedar Mesa, creating a fissure where sheer sandstone walls tower hundreds of feet above the traveler. Depending on circumstances, visitors have either loved or hated this place. The naturalist Ann Zwinger wrote:

> To me there is an enchantment in these dry canyons that once roared with water and still sometimes do, that absorbed the voices of those who came before, something of massive dignity about sandstone beds that tell of a past long before human breathing, that bear the patterns of ancient winds and water in their crossbeddings.
>
> Here I find something of necessity. Were I to discover that I could not walk here again, something essential would be missing from my life.[7]

To Platte Lyman, however, leader of a group of Mormon settlers, the Gulch's grandeur in the harsh winter of 1879–80 must have seemed a cruel joke. Traveling east from Cedar City to found the settlement of Bluff, Utah, Lyman and his party entered the canyon in search of a passable route across southeastern Utah. Its steep defiles and rugged terrain inspired the settlers to name the chasm Grand Gulch, but they suffered there from snow, frost, deep mud, and bitter cold. Winter temperatures in this desert climate can soar from below zero in the predawn to the forties or even fifties in sheltered canyons during the day, only to plummet again as soon as the sun sinks. Lyman complained in his journal:

> The country here is almost entirely solid sand rock, high hills and mountains cut all to pieces by deep gulches which are in many places altogether impassable. It is certainly the worst country I ever saw. . . . Last night was the coldest night I ever experienced. It was impossible to be comfortable in bed or anywhere else.[8]

In summer, the sun, whose warmth is so welcome in the winter, becomes a menace. As many unprepared hikers have discovered, summer temperatures in Grand Gulch often soar to well over one hundred, especially along the south-facing talus slopes. At night, the extreme heat quickly gives way to canyon breezes, making sleeping bags a virtual necessity even in mid-August. Cooling rainstorms have their destructive side as well, for they often cause narrow canyons to become deadly flooded raceways whose waters carry everything before them in a wild rush of foam and debris. Yet unless it rains, water at this time of year is scarce. As T. Mitchell Prudden put it in 1906:

> Here is elemental life, here is genuine freedom; but these exalted states are not to be won without strict conformity to the inexorable requirements of the land. Water is often very scanty, and usually, to the uninitiated, very hard to find; and the ignorant and foolhardy can readily die from thirst.[9]

Between the extremes of blistering summer days and darkest winter nights lie the favorable means of late spring and early fall. It is then that Grand Gulch welcomes the traveler and soothes the psyche.

When Richard Wetherill and his brothers dug Cave 7, the southeastern Utah alcove that afforded the defining moment in the discovery of the Basketmaker people in 1893, he was headed for Grand Gulch, about three days from Bluff by horseback and pack train. Today, Grand Gulch is only forty-five minutes from Bluff by automobile. This magnificent piece of geology, managed by the U.S. Department of Interior's Bureau of Land Management, draws visitors with its rugged beauty, its sheltered remnants of ancient cultures, and its challenging natural environment. For those willing and able to read its signs, Grand Gulch tells a fascinating story of ancient habitation and historic exploration.

Yet the Gulch's very attractions are now under siege from both humans and nature. Arroyo cutting caused by years of overgrazing, along with high levels of visitation and deliberate looting and vandalism, is slowly but surely destroying Grand Gulch's irreplaceable resources. We risk losing the last evidence that more than two thousand years ago Grand Gulch was the home of the Basketmaker people.

CHRONOLOGY OF THE GREATER FOUR CORNERS AREA

DATE	PERIOD	DISTINCTIVE CHARACTERISTICS
A.D. 1350–1600	Pueblo IV	Large plaza-oriented pueblos in Rio Grande and western Pueblo areas; low kiva-to-room ratio; kachina cult widespread; corrugated pottery replaced by plain utility types; B/W pottery declines relative to red, orange, and yellow types.
A.D. 1150–1350	Pueblo III	Large pueblos and/or "revisionist great houses" in some areas, dispersed pattern in others; high kiva-to-room ratios; cliff dwellings; towers; triwalls; corrugated gray and elaborate B/W pottery, plus red or orange pottery in some areas; abandonment of the Four Corners by 1300.
A.D. 900–1150	Pueblo II	Chacoan florescence; "great houses," great kivas, roads, etc., in many but not all regions; strong differences between great houses and surrounding "unit pueblos" composed of a kiva and small surface masonry roomblock; corrugated gray and elaborate B/W pottery, plus decorated red or orange types in some areas.
A.D. 750–900	Pueblo I	Large villages in some areas; unit pueblos of "protokiva" plus surface roomblock of jacal or crude masonry; great kivas; plain and neck-banded gray pottery with low frequencies of B/W and decorated red ware.
A.D. 500–750	Basketmaker III	Habitation is deep pithouse plus surface storage pits, cists, or rooms; dispersed settlement with occasional small villages and occasional great kivas; plain gray pottery, small frequencies of Black-on-white (B/W) pottery; bow and arrow replaces atlatl; beans added to cultigens.
A.D. 50–500	Basketmaker II (late)	Habitation is shallow pithouse plus storage pits or cists; dispersed settlement with small, low-density villages in some areas; campsites important as well (?); no pottery; atlatl and dart; corn and squash but no beans; upland dry farming in addition to floodplain farming.
1500 B.C.–A.D. 50	Basketmaker II (early)	Long-term seasonal (?) use of caves for camping, storage, burial, rock art; San Juan anthropomorphic style pictographs and petroglyphs; camp and limited activity sites in open; no pottery; atlatl and dart; corn and squash but no beans; cultivation primarily floodplain or runoff based (?).
6500–1500 B.C.	Archaic	Subsistence based on wild foods; high mobility; low population density; shelters and open sites; atlatl and dart; no pottery.

Source: William Lipe (1993), used by permission.

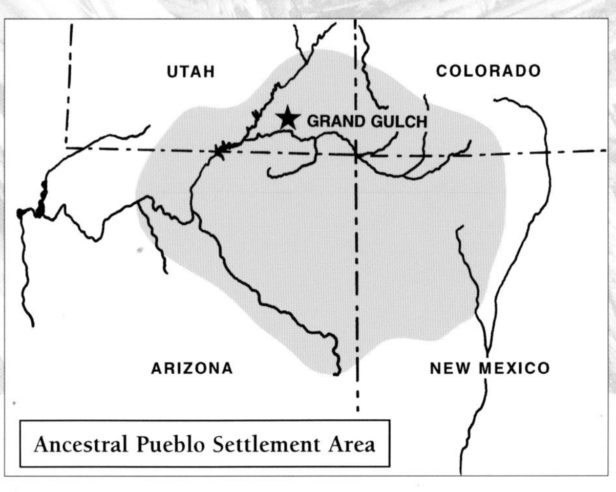

Ancestral Pueblo Settlement Area

Decorated Basketmaker baskets from Grand Gulch in the collection of the American Museum of Natural History.

WHO WERE THE BASKETMAKERS? THE SHORT ANSWER IS THAT THEY WERE THE ancestors of the Pueblo peoples who built the cliff dwellings at Mesa Verde and the graceful, symmetrical great houses of Chaco Canyon. Compared with what archaeologists know about the lives of the Pueblos, they know relatively little about the Basketmakers. An adaptable people, the Basketmakers at first lived in roughly circular pithouses dug into the earth, sometimes inside rockshelters. They apparently brought agriculture to the Southwest, focusing first on the cultivation of corn (maize) and squash. Later, as their society became more complex, they introduced beans—an important protein source—and developed pottery. Still later, they established permanent, above-ground dwellings of stone and adobe. In these later stages, the Basketmakers became what archaeologists now recognize as the Puebloan peoples, ancestors to the dozen or so Pueblo tribes of twentieth-century Arizona and New Mexico.[10]

Both archaeological research and Pueblo oral tradition, handed down in sacred myths and secular stories, confirm the general relationship of descent from the Ancestral Pueblos to the historically known Pueblo Indians. Yet despite years of study, the precise connections between specific historic Pueblo tribes and their ancestors remain unclear. Massive population shifts during the twelfth and thirteenth centuries A.D. severely disrupted Ancestral Pueblo society and obscured the lines of affiliation between prehistoric and historic groups.

The name *Basketmaker* was originally coined in January 1894, shortly after Richard Wetherill and his brothers excavated nearly a hundred skeletons from an alcove in southeastern Utah. Those skeletons belonged to an era later termed Basketmaker II by archaeologists who were struggling to organize their data in a meaningful developmental sequence. This term was formally introduced to the archaeological community and defined during the first Pecos Conference, held at Pecos Pueblo, New Mexico, in 1927.[11] Attendees at that conference originated the basic archaeological classification system still used today in Southwestern archaeology. Because evidence of an earlier "Archaic" tradition was just being unearthed when the first Pecos Conference met, the Pecos sequence began with the Basketmakers.

The Pecos archaeologists in 1927 had no way to reckon absolute dates. Neither the highly accurate dendrochronology (tree-ring dating) nor the more broadly applicable radiocarbon dating method had yet been developed. To place their finds in chronological order, they had to rely on relative dating, which was based on changes in architectural remains and pottery types observed in soil layers stratified one above the other, from oldest to youngest, at excavated archaeological sites.

The Pecos archaeologists assumed, reasonably, that because the Basketmaker sites then known revealed evidence of a relatively sophisticated people who practiced agriculture, there must have been an earlier Southwestern group who did not. Hence, they gave the name Basketmaker II to the people whose remains the Wetherills had found, reserving the term Basketmaker I for precursors whose remains had not yet been discovered. Recent research suggests that people exhibiting recognizable Basketmaker II traits lived on the Colorado Plateau at least as early as 1500 B.C. and perhaps earlier.[12]

At the end of Basketmaker II times (about A.D. 400–500), these people began to create crude forms of pottery and to use the more efficient and accurate bow and arrow instead of the atlatl, a weapon or hunting implement that combined a short spear with a throwing handle. As the culture grew in complexity, it changed in ways that led the Pecos Conference participants to name its time period Basketmaker III (today often called Modified Basketmaker).

During Basketmaker III times, families banded together to form pithouse villages. By about A.D. 700, beans had become an important part of the Ancestral Pueblo diet, improving nutrition. Because tightly woven baskets will hold liquids, the Basketmakers probably cooked squash, cornmeal, and even meat in a stew by putting hot rocks in a basket filled with water and food. Beans, however, are extremely difficult to cook in a basket because they must be boiled for hours. During Basketmaker III times, pottery making became more sophisticated, in part, some archaeologists believe, because the Ancestral Pueblos needed clay pots in order to cook beans properly.

In the early eighth century A.D., the Basketmakers began to evolve into what to our modern eyes are the more familiar Pueblo people. Archaeologists divide the Pueblo cultural sequence into five periods, from Pueblo I through Pueblo V, the historic period. Early Pueblo I people built sturdy stone and adobe houses and lived in loose clusters of family farms and small villages. By late Pueblo II and into middle Pueblo III times, their larger villages had become strikingly beautiful towns like those of Chaco Canyon or Mesa Verde, which often come to mind when we think of prehistoric Pueblo culture.

One of the strongest pieces of evidence that the developmental phases defined by the Pecos Conference indeed represent a steady cultural evolution is the kiva. In modern pueblos, the kiva is generally an underground chamber that serves as a place for religious observances and as a meeting room for the men of the tribe and sometimes the women. It seems to have developed directly from the Basketmaker pithouse, for it retains many of the elements of that earlier structure.

At the time of the first Pecos Conference, the Basketmaker I period existed only as a hypothesis. Remnants of earlier people had not yet been recognized in the archaeological evidence. Since then, archaeologists have discovered evidence of people they term *Archaic,* who made their living by gathering wild foods and hunting. These precursors to the Basketmaker II people followed ripening seeds and migrating game as the seasons changed, making their homes in base camps located at the heads of canyons where good shelter was available and water was plentiful. A few Archaic groups probably grew some corn, squash, and other crops, but they devoted relatively little energy to agriculture.

How—and indeed, whether—the Archaic foraging peoples eventually became the agricultural Basketmakers spurs intense research efforts today. Archaeologists studying the origins of the Ancestral Pueblos examine, among other things, how corn agriculture was introduced into the Southwest. Although experts agree that corn and farming technology arrived in North America from Mexico and that the Basketmakers played a major role in developing them, no one knows just how that transition took place. Did the Basketmakers move in from the south, bringing corn and corn ceremonies with them? Did they evolve from the indigenous Archaic peoples? Or is the solution to the puzzle even more complicated? The story of the Basketmakers, more than a century after their discovery, is still unfolding.

The scientific study of the Basketmakers began with the work of amateurs unschooled in the emerging discipline of archaeology. The Wetherill–Grand Gulch Research Project demonstrates that the tradition of serious amateur involvement in archaeology remains strong. Whether or not the origins of Southwestern agriculture are resolved in the near future or remain a subject of inquiry for many years, the Wetherill–Grand Gulch project has demonstrated that museums contain important evidence bearing on these and other questions—evidence that has been largely overlooked because no one knew precisely where it came from. By doing "reverse archaeology," project members have given much of that material a provenience and a more secure place in history.

This book tells several interlocking stories. It chronicles the first expeditions into Grand Gulch at the close of the nineteenth century, the explorers' gradual recognition of the early Basketmaker culture they found there, and the economic forces that caused their artifact collections to become fragmented and scattered around the country. It tells how the dedicated amateur scholars of the Wetherill–Grand Gulch Research Project rediscovered those artifact collections and unearthed much additional historical material—a story with its own share of suspense. It summarizes the results of a century of Basketmaker archaeology. And finally, it asks what the future holds in store for the Southwest's endangered prehistoric remains.

Basketmaker dart points, stone awls, and drills.

2/On the Trail of the Basketmakers

[Grand Gulch] is the most tortuous canon in the whole of the South West—making bends from 200 to 600 yards apart almost its entire length or for 50 miles and each bend means a cave or overhanging cliff. All of these with an exposure to the sun had been occupied by either cliff houses or as burial places.

—Richard Wetherill, 1897

Richard Wetherill, along with his brothers, deserves credit for "discovering" the Basketmakers. He was the first to identify them as a distinct cultural group who preceded the Pueblo people in time. But Wetherill could not have fit together the disparate clues to the Basketmakers' existence if a body of evidence had not first been gathered by others, especially Charles McLoyd and Charles Cary Graham.

In tracking down these adventurers who first sought the Basketmakers, members of the Wetherill–Grand Gulch Research Project and their colleagues located and studied not only historic signatures in the Gulch but also old photographs, notes, collection catalogs, journals, and diaries. From their investigations emerges a fascinating story of discovery, observation, supposition, hypothesis, and insight. The tale begins in the 1880s, south of Mancos in southwestern Colorado, at the magnificent ancient cliff dwellings of Mesa Verde.

Soon after the Wetherill family moved to the Mancos Valley in 1880 to farm and raise cattle, Richard and his brothers began to explore the small cliff dwellings along Mancos Canyon south of their ranch. Sometime in the mid-1880s, while reconnoitering a side canyon, Al Wetherill made a remarkable discovery. He was alone and on foot at the bottom of the canyon. As he described it later:

> I looked up and saw, under an overhanging cliff, a great cavernlike place in which was situated what seemed like a small ruined city. In the dusk and silence, the great blue vault hung above me like a mirage. The solemn grandeur of the outlines was breathtaking. My mind wanted to go up to it, but my legs refused to cooperate. At the time I was so tired that I thought later would be the time for closer investigation.[1]

Split Level Ruin.

One of the earliest photos of Cliff Palace, Mesa Verde, taken c. 1889. Inset: Levi Patrick (rear), Levi Carson(?) (front), and two unidentified men share breakfast in camp.

Fatigue and the lateness of the hour prevented Al from pressing further. Heading for home, he met his brother Richard and a local friend who were out looking for him. Relating what he had seen, he was unable to impress them, and with the demands of ranching chores, he let it slip his mind. Years later, Al Wetherill regretted that he had not kept on despite his fatigue: "Now when Cliff Palace is mentioned it always makes me feel like the nations that discovered America must feel when America is mentioned. My own discovery has become completely clouded over for not following up the lead that was offered to me."[2] A year or two passed before Richard Wetherill and Charlie Mason rediscovered the archaeological wonder.

This rediscovery, on December 18, 1888, dramatically changed the course of Richard Wetherill's life and deeply affected the lives of his family, his friends, and millions of visitors to the Southwest. While searching for stray cattle on the mesa tops southwest of the Wetherill ranch, Richard and his brother-in-law, Charlie Mason, stopped to rest their horses on the edge of the tableland overlooking Cliff Canyon. Peering across the canyon through gently falling snow, they saw a deep alcove. Tucked within the alcove, where the two could trace its dim outlines, slept an enormous ancient village, the likes of which they had never seen before. The sight nearly overwhelmed them.

In their excitement they searched for a path down, quickly forgetting lost cattle, cold, and snow. By constructing a makeshift ladder from dead tree limbs and their lariats, they made their way to the bottom of the canyon. Climbing up the talus slope on the other side, they easily entered the ruined village, which Wetherill named Cliff Palace.

The awestruck men spent hours exploring the many rooms of the ruin, picking up painted pots and other artifacts. Realizing that there must be more cliff dwellings in the area, they climbed back down into the canyon to search. For the rest of that day and part of the next they combed the nearby area and were rewarded with the discovery of two more large ruins. Wetherill later named one of them Spruce Tree House for a large fir that grew from its rubble, and the other Square Tower House for a four-story tower that dominated the village.

Returning from Cliff Canyon on the afternoon of the second day, the pair encountered some acquaintances camped out near the Wetherills' winter cabin. Excitedly, they described their finds to Charles McLoyd, J. Howard Graham (older brother of Charles Cary Graham), and Levi Patrick, who had been panning for gold and trapping along the Mancos River and digging artifacts in Moccasin Canyon.

When Richard's brother John Wetherill arrived a few hours later, he, McLoyd, Graham, and Patrick agreed to join in exploring the ruins. They soon set off on foot, carrying several days' provisions, while Richard Wetherill and Charlie Mason headed back to the ranch. The partnership that resulted from this chance meeting led the Wetherill brothers and their acquaintances repeatedly into the ancient villages of Mesa Verde to collect "cliff dweller," or Puebloan, artifacts. In his autobiography, Al Wetherill described the encounter and its results:

> They had been digging around a bit in some of the ruins of the cliff dwellings and had quite a number of articles such as pottery, woven materials, and implements, which all looked good to us. Finally, we made an arrangement with them to go on a larger scale, since we had the necessary equipment of tools and, the most important, horse power. We grubstaked them and we were to see to getting the stuff out of the cañons. . . .
>
> Brother John brought out of the canon the stuff they dug. It was a matter of packing it down there for carrying out by hand, practically a piece at a time. It was some long hard job. When he got it to the ranch, it was repacked and boxed for shipping.[3]

The discovery of Cliff Palace by Richard Wetherill and Charlie Mason has captured the public's imagination, perhaps because it feeds our own fantasies of making an important find. Yet others may well have seen Cliff Palace earlier, but not dug in it. The Utes, of course, already knew about the ruined sites because most of them lay on Ute lands. They avoided the ruins, which were considered to harbor spirits of the dead that would harm living people.

A prospector by the name of S. E Osborn may have been the first non-Indian to see Cliff Palace. In the winter of 1883–84, Osborn explored Mesa Verde; he is remembered for his description of the cliff dwellings printed in the Denver *Weekly Tribune–Republican* on December 23, 1886. In the article, Osborn described a building some six stories high and about 250 feet long that roughly matches the features of Cliff Palace.

The new partners quickly went to work on the three major sites—Cliff Palace, Spruce Tree House, and Square Tower House. Spending about a month among the ruins, they amassed a remarkable collection of artifacts, which they exhibited the following March at the Fair Building in Durango, Colorado. When the citizens of Durango showed considerable interest in their collection, the Wetherills began to levy a small admission charge to defray their costs.

Just about the time public curiosity started to wane, Benjamin Kite Wetherill, the brothers' father, showed up with a "mummy" of a child that Clayton Wetherill and Charlie Mason had discovered. Although the dried cliff dweller and Basketmaker remains are not technically mummies in the sense that they had been prepared and wrapped like Egyptian mummies, they had reached a similar state of preservation because of the extreme dryness of the alcoves in which they were found.

Sparked by the sensational exhibit of the child mummy, public interest quickly reawoke to the ancient pots, sandals, household tools, and weapons.[4] So interested were some public-spirited citizens that they tried to raise sufficient donations from their friends and neighbors to purchase the collection. When that effort failed, the Wetherill brothers moved their show to Pueblo, Colorado, where they expected to find a more sophisticated audience and perhaps a buyer.

Charles McLoyd looked after the collection in Pueblo, but when the public there expressed little interest in antiquarian relics, he took the exhibit on to Denver, where the response was more enthusiastic. It was displayed in a building opposite the Windsor Hotel on Larimar Street. A few members of the recently organized Colorado Historical Society raised money to purchase the artifacts. "A wonderful collection of Cliff-dwellers' relics is on exhibition in Denver. An effort is being made to secure them for the State Historical Society," noted *Colorado Topics* on June 7, 1889.

Society members were particularly concerned that the collection might otherwise leave the state. After some negotiation, the society purchased the collection for three thousand dollars, a large sum in those days, one that apparently figured in later charges that the Wetherills had profited handsomely from the sale of ancient artifacts. Yet considering the many hours each of the men had spent gathering the collection, and their expenses in showing it, any profit must have been small.

Principally through Richard Wetherill's efforts, Cliff Palace, more than any other single Ancestral Pueblo structure, has come to symbolize the Ancestral Pueblos and Southwestern archaeology. It was the discovery of a lifetime that led Richard Wetherill to a lifetime of discovery. Pursuit of the Ancestral Pueblos soon became his primary goal. Yet at the age of thirty, Richard bore heavy responsibilities on the family ranch. He could take up archaeology only in the winter months, when ranch duties were relatively light and the cattle were on the winter range where obvious archaeological sites were abundant.

By March 1890, Richard Wetherill and his younger brothers had searched through some 182 large and small cliff dwellings in Mesa Verde, created maps of the area, and acquired a second collection of relics. This collection was housed at the Wetherills' Alamo Ranch, which had become a small museum visited by growing numbers of curiosity seekers as word of the family's discoveries spread.

One visitor proved especially significant to the Wetherills' later work. Gustaf von Nordenskiöld, a twenty-two-year-old native of Sweden, arrived at Alamo Ranch in early July 1891, a few days after viewing the Wetherill collection in Denver.[5] The son of an Arctic explorer and scientist, the young man became so intrigued by what he saw in the collection that he abandoned his plans for touring the United States and immediately headed for Mancos to examine the ruins himself. While in Denver, he had also met Alice Eastwood, a Denver botanist who knew the Wetherills and had given him a letter of introduction.[6] Although Nordenskiöld planned to stay at Alamo Ranch for only a week or two, he soon found himself captivated by what he saw in the canyons.

Top: John Wetherill in Nordenskiöld House, Ute Mountain Tribal Park, photographed by Gustaf Nordenskiöld, 1891. Center: The Wetherill brothers in about 1893. Left to right: Alfred, Winslow, Richard, Clayton, and John. Bottom: Two of the Wetherill brothers (left, Al; right, John) in Mancos Canyon near the mouth of Soda Canyon, 1891.

Nordenskiöld recognized an opportunity when he saw it. The Wetherills took him to Cliff Palace soon after he arrived. Realizing that no one had yet written a detailed description of Mesa Verde's archaeological sites and artifacts, he set about to make his own collection of Ancestral Pueblo artifacts, with an eye to publishing his findings in a scientific treatise. Although Nordenskiöld worked in several of the Mesa Verde sites, his most ambitious project was the excavation of Step House on Wetherill Mesa. There he found burials and most of the pottery and other artifacts that he eventually took back to Sweden.

Because of his ranching duties, Richard Wetherill had little time to devote to Nordenskiöld's excavations. Nordenskiöld hired John Wetherill as foreman of the dig, and the other brothers helped when they could. Untutored in archaeology, Nordenskiöld nevertheless had received a rigorous classical education at the University of Uppsala and was a keen observer of detail. In addition to noting the locations and associations of artifacts he uncovered, Nordenskiöld carefully measured and mapped the ruins and recorded architectural details.[7]

Working with him, the brothers learned a great deal about the principles of careful excavation and thorough documentation. They learned how to use a trowel instead of a shovel to clear away the dirt and debris around an artifact.[8] They also learned in a rudimentary way about the principle of stratigraphy: unless the archaeological deposits had been disturbed, earlier cultural material would lie below the remnants of later cultures. Nordenskiöld's methods made a strong impression on the Wetherill brothers, who later emulated them when excavating in southeastern Utah.

Gustaf Nordenskiöld investigating ruins at Mesa Verde, 1891. Inset: Nordenskiöld, 1893.

Shortly after Nordenskiöld returned to his native Sweden with his collection of artifacts, he wrote a carefully constructed report on the cliff dwellings he had excavated.[9] It was the most detailed report of its time on Ancestral Pueblo culture, and until the 1960s it remained the only description of sites on Wetherill Mesa—which Nordenskiöld named in honor of the Wetherills, "who have done so much service in the exploration of these regions, and whose knowledge of the Mesa Verde has given me such valuable service."[10] While excavating Step House, Nordenskiöld even discovered a crude pot that he correctly speculated must have belonged to people from an older culture who had lived in the alcove before the cliff dwellings were built.[11]

The Wetherill brothers continued to explore the ruins of Mesa Verde, eventually assembling three large collections in addition to the one Nordenskiöld took to Sweden.[12] Two of these collections (the first and third) remain with the Colorado Historical Society. The second collection, gathered before Nordenskiöld arrived in 1891, was purchased early in 1891 by C. D. Hazzard, who worked for the H. Jay Smith Exploring Company of Jackson Park, Illinois.

According to Al Wetherill, the purchase came none too soon. With the strong encouragement of their father, the brothers had put together the second collection during the winter of 1889 and 1890. "We commenced cleaning out the debris and collecting pieces of baskets, grains and seeds, pottery, weaving, implements, and even what remained of the people themselves. . . . We tried to bring to light everything that might later be taken by the regular army of pothunters and so be scattered to the four winds."[13] A year later, expecting the same public interest in these relics that their first collection had aroused, they took the artifacts to Durango for exhibit.

> To our complete dismay, the public did not particularly care about being educated. We decided Durango was too small to be interested in anything but civic-betterment activities. . . . We went on to Pueblo and lived through a short session there, meeting indifference verging on ridicule. . . . We simply couldn't believe it. We were too young and inexperienced to know when we were licked. And we were so sure that our mission was worthwhile. . . . So with heads bloody but unbowed, we decided to take Denver by storm, sure that there we would find enthusiastic audiences.[14]

Al Wetherill's disappointment may have proceeded from his overoptimism about other people's interest in the culture of the ancients. The first collection had generated some local excitement, so Al expected even more from the second one. Yet, as historian Duane Smith pointed out in his book *Rocky Mountain Boom Town,* Durango was trying hard to be the "Denver of Southwestern Colorado." Its citizens generally took more interest in looking forward than in looking back, especially when looking back involved ancient Indians. Although they displayed interest in prehistoric artifacts as curiosities, they tended to regard contemporary Indians and Indian culture with disdain, if not with fear and hatred.

Al Wetherill reported further disappointment in the collection's Denver reception: "I shudder to think of Denver, even now. . . . It was a decided letdown to find that others did not share our enthusiasm and that, for the main part, people in the outside world cared not a thing about our ruins or their treasures."[15]

Shortly before the Wetherill brothers ran out of funds, they met C. D. Hazzard, who was looking for just the right collection of Indian artifacts for exhibition. The H. Jay Smith

EARLY ARCHAEOLOGICAL COLLECTING EXPEDITIONS

DATE	EXPEDITION/PARTICIPANTS	LOCATION
January–April 1891	C. McLoyd and C. C. Graham	Grand Gulch
Summer 1891	C. H. Green, McLoyd, and others	Grand Gulch
1892	Warren K. Moorehead and the Illustrated American Exploring Expedition	SE Utah
Winter 1891–1892	McLoyd and J. H. Graham	Grand Gulch; Red, Lake, Lost, and Deep Canyons; Colorado River
Winter 1892–1893	McLoyd, C. C. Graham, L. Patrick, W. Patrick, and John Wetherill	Grand Gulch; White, Lake, Red, Lost, Deep, and Colorado Canyons
December 1893–March 1894	Hyde Exploring Expedition	Cottonwood Canyon; Grand Gulch; Allen, Butler, Red, White, and Step Canyons
1893–1894	Charles Lang	SE Utah
1894–1895	Charles Lang	Hammond, Cottonwood, Battle, and Butler Canyons; Grand Gulch
December 1896–March 1897	Whitmore Exploring Expedition	SE Utah; Grand Gulch; NE Arizona
1897	Charles Lang	Unknown
1898–1899	Charles Lang	Canyon de Chelly; Cottonwood, Montezuma, and Allen Canyons; Comb Wash
1894–1902	T. M. Prudden	San Juan watershed

Exploring Company—which Hazzard represented and which later sent a team to Mesa Verde to collect additional items and photograph the ruins—exhibited the Wetherills' collection in 1892 at the Sixth Minneapolis Industrial Exposition and in 1893 at the World's Columbian Exposition in Chicago. Eventually, Phoebe Apperson Hearst purchased the collection (now called the Hazzard collection) for the University of Pennsylvania Museum of Archaeology and Anthropology in Philadelphia, where most of it resides today.

Caught by the lure of archaeological exploration and well tutored by the young Nordenskiöld, Richard Wetherill wanted to learn more. What were the cliff dwellers really like? How did they live? When did they leave their canyon homes? Where were their descendants? These were among the questions he and his brothers discussed late into the night with their many visitors at Alamo Ranch.

IN SOUTHEASTERN UTAH

VERIFICATION OF EXPEDITION	COLLECTION NAME AND LOCATION
Graham diary; Green catalog; signatures	Green collection, Field Museum of Natural History, Chicago
Signatures; photographs; Green catalog	Green collection, Field Museum
Articles; photographs; signatures	Moorehead collection, Field Museum
Signatures; catalog	Part of Hazzard-Hearst collection, University of Pennsylvania Museum; a few items in Phoebe Apperson Hearst Museum of Anthropology, University of California, Berkeley
Signatures; catalog	Koontz (Kunz) collection, American Museum of Natural History, New York; portion in Heye collection, Museum of the American Indian
Field records; photographs; letters; signatures	First Wetherill collection, American Museum of Natural History; portion in Heye collection, Museum of the American Indian
Article; letter; inscriptions	Lang collection at Brigham Young University, Salt Lake City
Field notes; letter; inscriptions	Ryerson-Lang collection, Field Museum
Field records; photographs; letters; signatures	Second Wetherill collection, American Museum of Natural History; portion in Heye collection, Museum of the American Indian
Letter	Stengel, "Salt Lake City furrier," unknown
Letter; field notes; inscriptions; catalog	Bixby-Lang collection. Purchased by W. J. Palmer for Colorado College; now at Taylor Museum and Denver Museum of Natural History
Field notes; letters; articles; photographs	T. M. Prudden collection, Peabody Museum of Natural History, Cambridge

WHILE THE WETHERILLS TOILED IN THE CANYONS OF WESTERN COLORADO, Charles McLoyd and Charles Cary Graham undertook the first serious reconnaissance of the archaeological treasures of southeastern Utah. On January 1, 1891, the two weary men and their equally tired horses made their way across what is now known as Todie Flats, east of Grand Gulch, searching for a way into the canyon. They were drawn by reports that untouched ancient Indian dwellings survived there in abundance. The two partners, who called themselves "Explorers of Prehistoric Ruins and Collectors of Relics," hoped to find enough artifacts in the cliff dwellings to garner a collection suitable for sale.

We know of their general route and the difficulties they faced because Graham kept a diary of the expedition—the first written account of excavation in southeastern Utah.[16] But his daily entries are agonizingly terse, each merely a line or two describing the day's major task, along with a few crude drawings of archaeological sites.

Exploring the Gulch today, we can imagine what discouraging first impressions the rugged landscape must have presented to the two explorers. Throughout most of this canyon system, vertical sandstone walls plunge a hundred feet or more before reaching negotiable talus slopes. Only a few spots offer slopes gentle enough for hikers, much less horses, to enter the gorge comfortably. The two men spent most of four days searching along the rim for a way to take their horses down. Looking below into the drainage they named Graham Canyon (now Bullet Canyon), they could see rich grasslands, shelter from the cold and wind, and Ancestral Pueblo dwellings to explore—if only they could discover a way in.

Finally, on January 4, they found an acceptable spot on the north side of Graham Canyon. First they had to build a trail. According to the diary, the two men spent another four days cutting logs and hauling stone to make a passable horse trail down from the rim. After leading the unloaded horses in, they carried their gear down on their own backs.

Turning their horses loose to graze, McLoyd and Graham set up camp and began to explore. By January 11, they were ready to go to work: "Sunday. We worked in Cliff house No. 1. Graham Canon. found 6–7 bone awls, 1 stone axe, some sandals, one bowl and small jar. Some cloth, one small coil vase with skeleton."[17]

Throughout January and February and into late March, the two men systematically explored the canyons all the way to the San Juan River, some seventy-five miles from the head of Grand Gulch. They dug artifacts in many of the largest surface ruins in the upper part of the Gulch. They braved bitter cold and snow, heavy rain, high winds, and even quicksand. Grand Gulch drains water from hundreds of square miles of the surrounding plateau into the San Juan River. Heavy spring rains quickly flood the canyon bottom, making passage all but impossible. Several times the two men were forced to stay put for a day or two because of high water.

Weather was not the only hazard. On March 5, 1891, while the men were digging in a site they called Salt Cave, falling rock badly bruised McLoyd's feet.[18] The injury was severe enough to prevent him from leaving the cave again until March 20, when the two prepared to depart the area with their booty. In order to carry their collection of pots and other artifacts to the rim, they again had to haul everything on their backs, following the trail they had constructed three months earlier. Then they transported their discoveries to Bluff, Utah, southeast of Grand Gulch, in a horse-drawn cart.[19] From Bluff, Samuel Woods, a professional freighter, packed the artifacts on to Durango, some 125 miles to the east.

McLoyd and Graham were not disappointed in their hopes for the expedition. They dug up pottery, baskets, tools, miscellaneous household implements, arrow points, articles of clothing, sandals, and many skeletons. Back in Durango they displayed the results of their efforts, and the artifacts caught the eye of the Reverend C. H. Green, who examined and bought them for three thousand dollars.[20] Green, a Baptist minister recently arrived from Ludlow, Kentucky, had developed a keen interest in what he mistakenly called the "oldest men in the world." He later sold the collection to Chicago's Field Museum of Natural History, where it resides today.[21]

FOR COWBOY ARCHAEOLOGISTS LIKE MCLOYD, GRAHAM, AND THE WETHERILLS, THE end of the nineteenth century was an exciting but difficult time in the Four Corners country where Colorado, New Mexico, Arizona, and Utah meet. Like other Americans of European descent, they saw this land as frontier territory—rough, untamed, expansive. The conveniences of Denver, the nearest major city, lay nearly 350 miles northeast across the mountains.

Earlier in the century, abundant wildlife had attracted a few hardy white men who supported themselves by hunting and trapping. In the 1860s and later, reports of gold and silver in the San Juan Mountains lured additional settlers and miners eager to make their fortunes. Small mining towns sprang from the rugged mountain terrain in Colorado and northern New Mexico, prospered briefly, then quickly faded away.

Government trapper Wash Patrick with coyote pelts, c. 1890.

By the final two decades of the century, families and their domestic animals began to appear in greater numbers as railroads and stagecoach routes took hold. These settlers established farms and ranches in the fertile valleys of southwestern Colorado, northwestern New Mexico, and southeastern Utah. A few families set up trading posts on the Navajo Reservation in northeastern Arizona and western New Mexico.

For the Indians displaced by these new arrivals—Apaches, Navajos, Paiutes, and Utes—the end of the century was a time of increasing uncertainty. Their way of life was changing irrevocably, their boundaries closing in. Friction between the settlers, eager to claim and tame the land to their use, and the Native Americans, desperate to hold on to their traditional hunting grounds and lifeways, fueled simmering tensions that occasionally boiled into outbursts of violence from both sides, generating greater prejudice against and fear of each other.

Throughout the 1870s, newspapers in Denver shrilled accusing headlines every time a real or imagined confrontation took place between Utes and whites. The newspapers' goal was to rid western Colorado of the Utes, who, through the Brunot treaty of 1873, retained most of the land there.[22] The newspapers got their opportunity in the spring of 1879 when U.S. Army Major T. T. Thornberg entered Ute territory with a contingent of about 150 men, in violation of an earlier agreement between the U.S. government and the Utes. The enraged and frightened Utes responded with force, killing Thornberg and twelve other soldiers.

The same day, another group of Utes attacked and killed Nathan Meeker, head of the White River Indian agency, and six of his employees. Meeker, who was intensely disliked by the Utes, had requested the troops to back up his attempts to force the tribe into farming, a mode of life these proud horsemen and hunters despised. They had met Meeker's efforts with contempt and strong resistance.

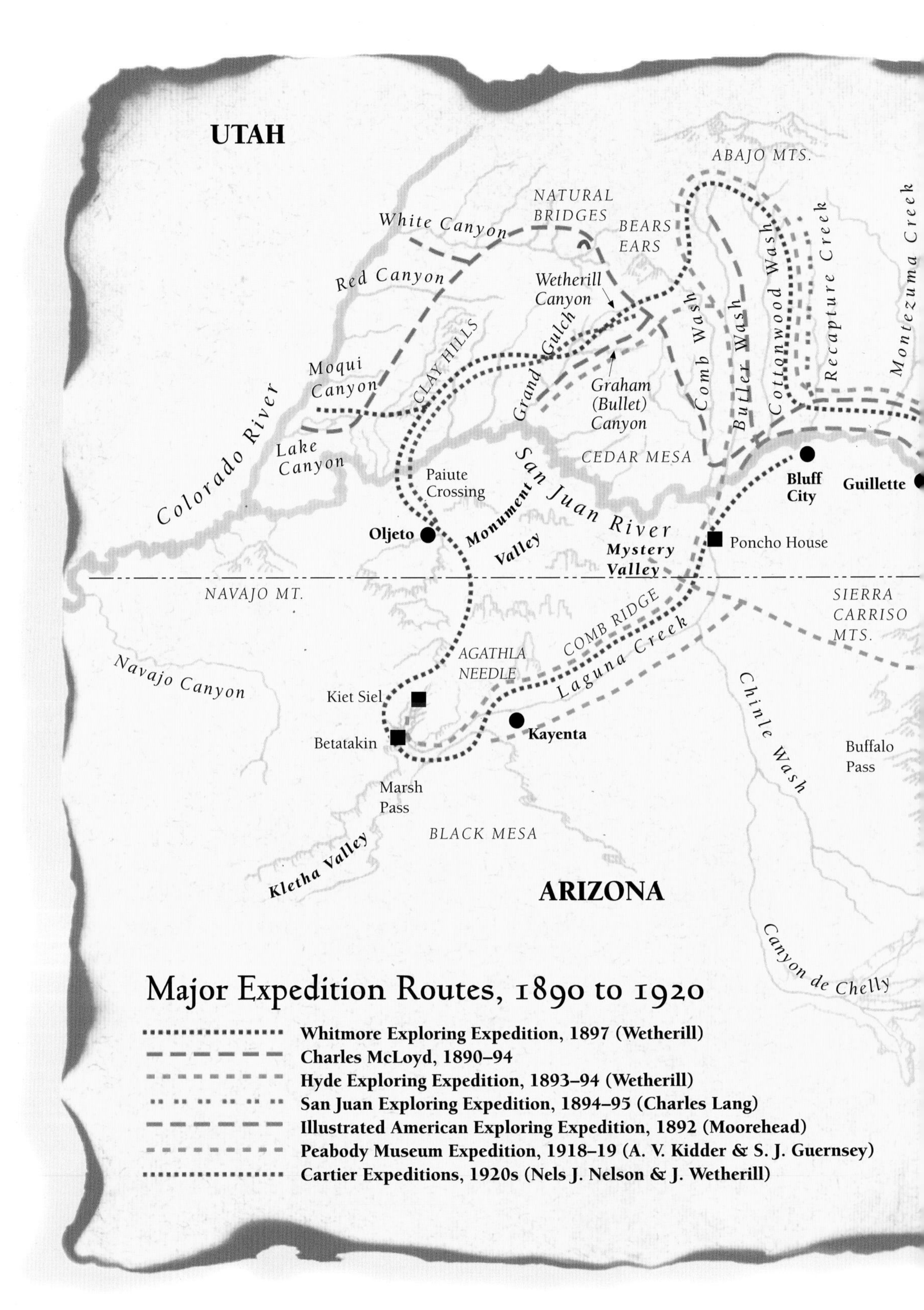
UTAH
ABAJO MTS.
NATURAL BRIDGES
BEARS EARS
White Canyon
Red Canyon
Wetherill Canyon
Comb Wash
Butler Wash
Cottonwood Wash
Recapture Creek
Montezuma Creek
CLAY HILLS
Grand Gulch
Graham (Bullet) Canyon
Moqui Canyon
Colorado River
Lake Canyon
CEDAR MESA
Paiute Crossing
San Juan River
Bluff City
Guillette
Oljeto
Monument Valley
Mystery Valley
Poncho House
NAVAJO MT.
SIERRA CARRISO MTS.
COMB RIDGE
Laguna Creek
AGATHLA NEEDLE
Navajo Canyon
Kiet Siel
Betatakin
Kayenta
Chinle Wash
Buffalo Pass
Marsh Pass
BLACK MESA
Kletha Valley
ARIZONA
Canyon de Chelly
Major Expedition Routes, 1890 to 1920
Whitmore Exploring Expedition, 1897 (Wetherill)
Charles McLoyd, 1890–94
Hyde Exploring Expedition, 1893–94 (Wetherill)
San Juan Exploring Expedition, 1894–95 (Charles Lang)
Illustrated American Exploring Expedition, 1892 (Moorehead)
Peabody Museum Expedition, 1918–19 (A. V. Kidder & S. J. Guernsey)
Cartier Expeditions, 1920s (Nels J. Nelson & J. Wetherill)

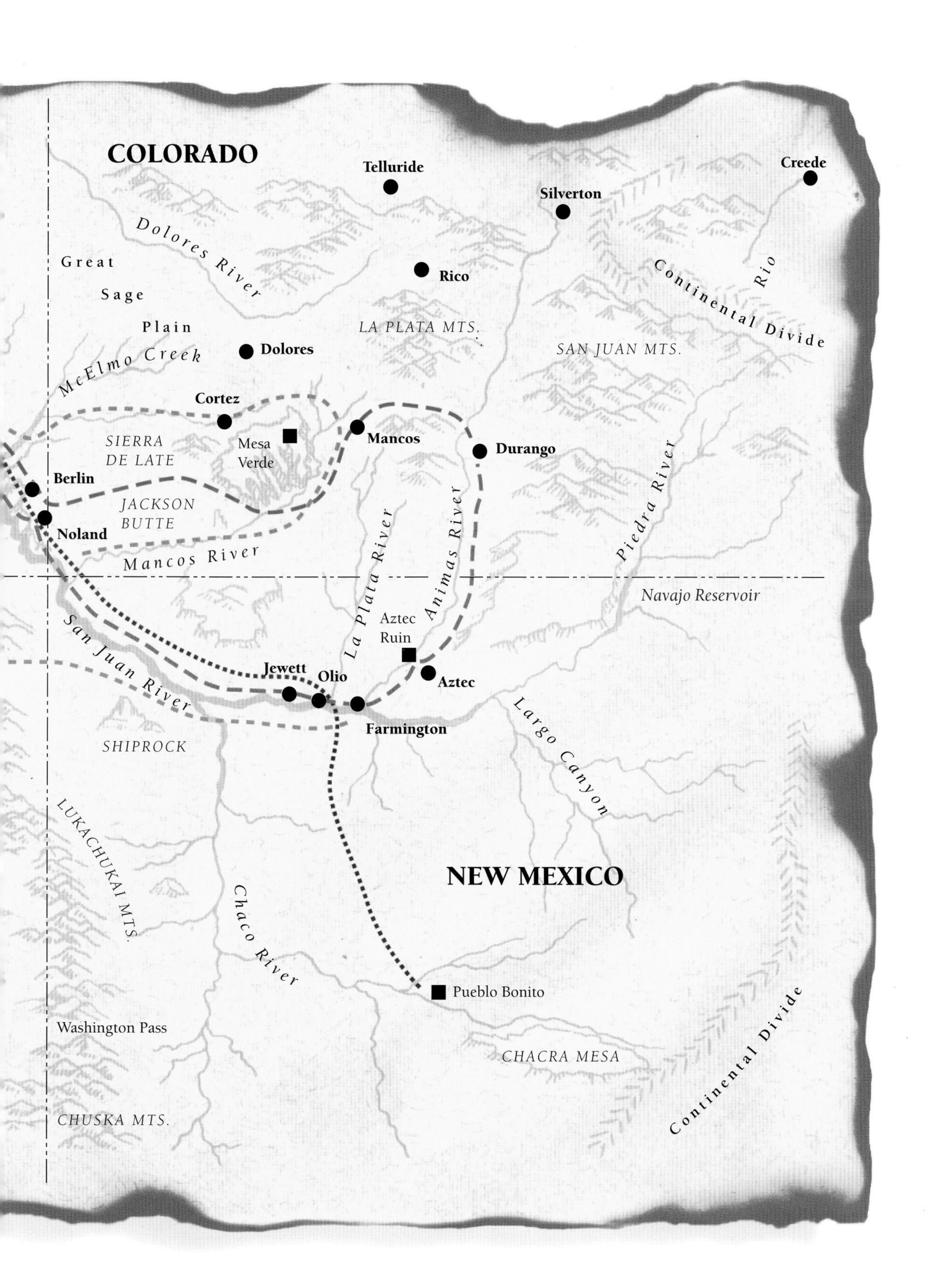
COLORADO
Telluride
Silverton
Creede
Dolores River
Great
Sage
Plain
Rico
Continental Divide
Rio
LA PLATA MTS.
SAN JUAN MTS.
McElmo Creek
Dolores
Cortez
Mesa
Verde
Mancos
Durango
SIERRA
DE LATE
Berlin
JACKSON
BUTTE
Noland
Mancos River
La Plata River
Animas River
Piedra River
Navajo Reservoir
Aztec
Ruin
San Juan River
Jewett
Olio
Aztec
Farmington
Largo Canyon
SHIPROCK
LUKACHUKAI MTS.
NEW MEXICO
Chaco River
Pueblo Bonito
Washington Pass
CHACRA MESA
Continental Divide
CHUSKA MTS.

After the killings, cooler heads soon prevailed among both Utes and U.S. officials, who quickly settled the incident. A year later, however, in the aftermath of the "Meeker Massacre," as it came to be known, the Utes lost the ultimate political battle and were removed to reservations in southwestern Colorado and northeastern Utah, east of Salt Lake City.

Although white settlers knew that many Utes faced starvation on the Colorado reservation, some, in their fear of Indians and greed for land, continued to call for the Utes' eviction even from that poor refuge.[23] "Are we in Southwestern Colorado alone to be left at the mercy of the red-skins? Let the people move in this matter . . . to remove the Southern Utes," editorialized the *Durango Record* in 1881. In Durango, the Southern Utes were generally welcome only when they came to trade. The *Durango Record* noted with obvious relish on March 7, 1890, that "it now appears that throwing open a million acres of the Southern Ute reservation is only a question of a few months."[24] Although the paper's editors were disappointed in their prediction, the Utes continued to face the threat of removal to Utah as development increased.

In southeastern Utah, Mormon settlers, responding to a mission call from their church, swelled to a significant percentage of the new settlers of the Four Corners. They began their trek during the winter of 1879–80 and, after an arduous journey across the Colorado River and through the upper end of Grand Gulch, reached the spot along the San Juan River where, in April 1880, they founded the town of Bluff. Their trip, led by Platte Lyman, came to be known as the Hole-in-the-Rock expedition because when they reached the rim on the west side of the Colorado River, they had to blast, pick, and scrape a trail down to the river some two thousand feet below through a natural break they called the Hole-in-the-Rock.[25]

In issuing its 1879 mission call, the Mormon church was attempting, in part, to create a buffer against encroachment into Utah by cattlemen from Colorado who were beginning to settle along the San Juan River just to the east. It also wanted to provide an attractive location

Men from the Southern Ute tribe at Fort Lewis, c. 1890.

for recent converts to Mormonism from the southern states, who were used to a warmer climate than they would find in the mountainous areas of south-central Colorado. The church also feared that unless it took firm control of southeastern Utah, the federal government might be disposed to settle the Utes there instead of leaving them in Colorado.[26]

Bluff City, Utah, in 1895.

Bluff, situated on the north side of the San Juan in the shadow of deep red sandstone bluffs, grew quickly, fueled by Mormon energy and a short-lived gold boom along the river. The Mormons had high hopes for the town and soon built sturdy, attractive red sandstone houses. By establishing good relations with the Navajos, Utes, and other non-Mormons, the people of Bluff prospered. Their town became a much-needed outpost for local miners and cattlemen and for the archaeological expeditions that passed through on their way to explore the region's canyons and mesas. Its merchants sold food and other supplies; the people of Bluff provided friendship and comfortable beds. T. Mitchell Prudden, who visited there in 1897, penned this description:

> [Bluff], a solitary outpost and oasis of Mormondom, exists, and even thrives in a half-hearted way . . . in the southeastern corner of Utah. This town, ninety miles from the railroad, is the metropolis of the San Juan Valley. A swiftly subsiding gold craze brought many adventurers to the valley a few years ago. But now only a few placer miners are left, struggling here and there against odds, far down the stream, picturesque and pathetic beside their rough sluices and quaint water wheels. It is from Bluff that you most conveniently enter the country of which I write, and you see no fixed human habitation, and probably no white man, until you get back, brown, tired and dusty, to Bluff again. The nearest railroad is at Mancos in Colorado.[27]

Today the town's tiny historic district reflects the expectations of the early settlers. Solid sandstone houses surrounded by stately cottonwood trees anchor each block. But here and there a once-proud dwelling stands vacant, its empty windows staring blankly outward. Since those early days of bustling commerce, the town has dwindled, victim of better opportunities elsewhere. Now it serves a different kind of traveler—tourists who use it as a base from which to embark on river trips down the San Juan or to hike into the nearby canyons.

Horse-drawn freight lines developed to carry goods between the small towns that had sprung up throughout the region. Durango, serviced by the Denver and Rio Grande Railroad, became an important commercial center for the region, with the First National Bank of Durango as its principal bank. The town grew quickly, aided by abundant lumber and coal and the lure of the region's silver deposits.[28]

First Denver and Rio Grande Railroad trains on the Ophir Loop near Telluride, Colorado, c. 1891.

Travelers reached Durango from Denver and points east through the towns of Pueblo and Alamosa. Because of the mountainous terrain, communications were difficult and slow. The trip from Denver by train took nearly two days, but when compared with the alternatives, it probably seemed luxurious. The daily train west from Alamosa to Durango even included sleeper cars, a parlor observation car, and a diner.[29] On another line, each day a narrow-gauge train pulled out of Durango heading north for Silverton and winding through the superb scenery of the Rio de las Animas and Perdidas Canyon. Part of this line is still preserved in the narrow-gauge, coal-fired trains that run daily between Durango and Silverton for the delight of summer tourists.

Miners, farmers, and cattlemen spent some of their few leisure hours exploring the endless canyons that dissected the Four Corners landscape. When they discovered the artifacts that lay hidden in the Ancestral Pueblo ruins throughout those canyons, some of the explorers—McLoyd, Graham, and the Wetherill brothers among them—took up a new line of work, digging through the ruins for antiquities to sell. Despite their high hopes, their labor yielded meager income, but it earned them a place in the history of archaeological knowledge.

THE LURE OF MONEY TO BE GAINED FROM SELLING "RELICS" PROBABLY HELPED draw Charles McLoyd, Charles Cary Graham, and others like them into digging for Ancestral Pueblo artifacts. According to Emerald Flint Patrick, a nephew of Levi Patrick, "Jack Parsons [owner of Parsons' Drug Store in Durango] put money up to go to the ruins for Wash [Washington Patrick], Levi, and McLoyd. They took three loads, wagon loads, of relics out of there. Out of the dwellings."[30] Parsons had a collection of artifacts, many of which he apparently bought from McLoyd.

Whatever its potential reward, digging for artifacts was exhausting work and, as Graham's diary reveals, dangerous as well. Besides the threat of falling rock, digging in the alcoves carries environmental health risks of which the men were probably only partly aware. In that dry climate, digging stirs up a fine dust sometimes containing the centuries-old dried feces of humans, turkeys, rodents, and other creatures, along with the fungus that causes valley fever.

Although we know a good deal about the Wetherill family, which entertained a stream of educated men and women who sometimes wrote about their experiences on tour with the Wetherill brothers, we know little about the lives of McLoyd and Graham. What information we have been able to cull from Graham's diary and other sources suggests that except for their archaeological work, McLoyd and Graham were typical of the people who settled the Colorado Plateau in the last two decades of the nineteenth century.

Charles McLoyd was a miner and rancher who lived at one time or another in Durango and in the Pine River valley near Bayfield, a few miles east of Durango. He worked for a time in the late 1880s in the mining camps of Red Mountain, between Ouray and Silverton. Charles Cary Graham came from a pioneer ranching family whose spread also lay in the Pine River valley. Many such ranches had originated to provide beef and horses to the mining camps, whose hoards of hungry miners had already hunted down most of the wildlife.

Resourceful and unafraid of hard work, McLoyd and Graham, like many other settlers, were willing to take up almost any line of employment to earn a living. Paying jobs were hard to come by, and ranchers seldom lasted long at underground mining. Injuries were high, the pay low, the work confining. More agreeable were placer mining, trapping, ranching, carpentering—at which Graham later earned his living—and digging through archaeological sites.

Members of the Green Expedition excavating Turkey Pen Ruin, 1891.

McLoyd and Graham's transformation from occasional diggers of artifacts into an archaeological collecting enterprise apparently came about because of that chance encounter with Richard Wetherill and Charlie Mason after the two had found Cliff Palace. Ever entrepreneurial, McLoyd and Graham jumped at the chance to gather even more items in artifact-rich Cliff Palace and other Mesa Verde sites.

In moving west to dig in Grand Gulch, the two men surely felt a sense of adventure, coupled with the lure of archaeological treasures. That Graham kept a diary of this first trip attests to the importance he placed on it. McLoyd apparently led the enterprise. We believe that sometime before the fall of 1890, McLoyd ran into someone who spun a story about the plentiful archaeological sites in the Gulch, and he saw an opportunity to dig still-pristine ruins. His caretaking of the McLoyd-Wetherill Mesa Verde collection when it was displayed in Durango and Denver had given him ample opportunity to meet people who knew the countryside around Bluff. He had also met freighters from Bluff, who probably knew something of the archaeological treasures that lay buried in Grand Gulch.

On their first trip into Grand Gulch, McLoyd and Graham took their cue from McLoyd's earlier experiences digging in Mancos Canyon. Because in their eyes artifacts were connected with masonry structures, they apparently excavated primarily in caves that contained cliff dwellings and overlooked the many others that held Basketmaker artifacts but no Pueblo remains. And even in caves that contained Pueblo structures, they failed to recognize that often the remains of a quite different culture—that of the Basketmakers—lay buried only a few feet below the cliff dwellings.

Like others in the Southwest at the time, however, McLoyd and Graham did differentiate between two categories of ancient Pueblo peoples—cliff dwellers and mesa dwellers, by which they meant the groups who had built the mesa-top villages. This distinction, based solely on the locations of dwellings, has not held up with time. Either the cliff dwellers and the mesa dwellers were contemporaneous Ancestral Pueblo people who preferred different places in which to live, or else they were the same people who moved between the canyon alcoves and the mesa tops.

McLoyd and Graham's artifact collection aroused the curiosity of Durango's citizenry, but no one showed keener interest than the Reverend Mr. Green. Not content merely to acquire the partners' artifacts, Green organized his own collecting trip into Grand Gulch. The expedition numbered at least seven men, including Charles McLoyd, who probably guided the others.[31] This party, later known as the Green Expedition, spent the searing month of June 1891 in Grand Gulch, adding to Green's collection.

Upon returning to Durango, Green wrote—and in 1892 printed—a seventeen-page catalog titled "A Unique Collection of Cliff Dweller Relics" to accompany his collection. The catalog listed more than four hundred items and featured two lithographs, one of an adult female mummy and one of a corrugated pot "full of shelled corn." Following the catalog in the same wrappers came reprints of some newspaper and journal articles about the cliff dwellers and an essay Green himself had written on that subject. In his essay, Green claimed that the cliff dweller artifacts were "scientifically estimated to be the oldest in the world." What evidence he might have had to support this claim he did not proffer.

Top: A collection of Basketmaker artifacts from the Green Collection, Field Museum of Natural History, Chicago. Bottom: Bob Allan of the Green Expedition excavating Turkey Pen Ruin, June 1891.

Long House Ruin, photographed by F. E. Leeka during Green's 1891 expedition into Grand Gulch. Inset: Long House, re-photographed in 1994.

Although Green's collection contained many articles from the earlier Basketmaker culture, he does not seem to have distinguished between them and cliff dweller artifacts. His catalog, which may have expanded on an earlier, unpublished one by McLoyd and Graham, did, however, distinguish between "skulls" (of unspecified type) and "natural shaped skulls"—by which he meant crania that had not been flattened at the back as Pueblo skulls often were, a result of placing infants on a hard cradleboard. Green, and by implication McLoyd and Graham, also paid relatively close attention to the associations between burials and artifacts. For example, he described item 1A, human remains, this way:

> Mummy—6 feet high, found in a cave in Graham Canon, (see cliff house No. 43), two miles below where trail enters canon. There were found with it Nos. 15, 19, 22, 26, 37, 38, 41, 42, 43, 44, 45, 52, and 54, group B [pottery and potsherds], 51 E [wooden implements], and 80, 81 I [textile fabrics].[32]

After years of trying to sell his collection, Green finally sold it to the Field Museum for two thousand dollars, a significant loss.[33] The museum got a bargain, for the collection contained the first known evidence of the Basketmaker people.

Few details are known of Green's foray into Grand Gulch; apparently he did not keep a journal. Nevertheless, several lines of evidence have enabled members of the Wetherill–Grand Gulch project to reconstruct the expedition's route and identify some of the sites in which it dug. First, the team discovered several sites in the Gulch where Green and other expedition members wrote their names. Second, banking records from Durango and Green's catalog at the Field Museum of Natural History reveal more about the expedition.[34]

Green brought a photographer along on the trip "to catch the very image of homes and fortresses that had been abandoned long ago."[35] Ten of these photographs documenting ruins in the Gulch and the expedition's campsites still exist at the Field Museum. The project team has now identified the locations depicted in them; they indicate that the Green Expedition followed McLoyd and Graham's earlier route into the upper part of Grand Gulch but did not explore its lower canyons. Using these diverse lines of evidence and input from other team members, Ann Phillips was able to piece together burial assemblages in the collection and associate them with alcoves visited by McLoyd, Graham, and Green.

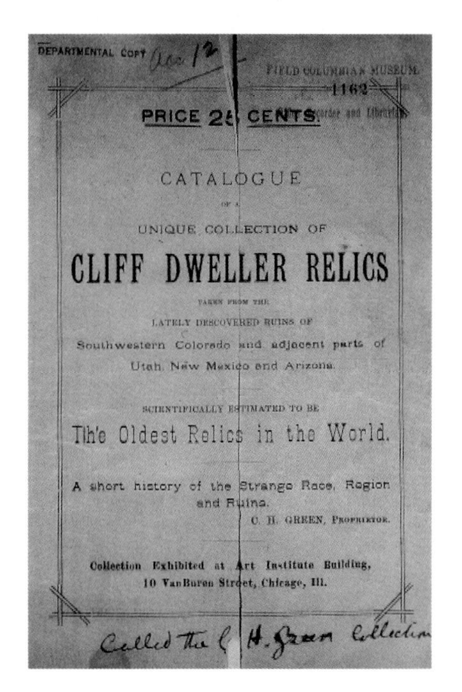
DEPARTMENTAL COPY

FIELD COLUMBIAN MUSEUM.

1162

PRICE 25 CENTS.

CATALOGUE

OF A

UNIQUE COLLECTION OF

CLIFF DWELLER RELICS

TAKEN FROM THE

LATELY DISCOVERED RUINS OF

Southwestern Colorado and adjacent parts of Utah, New Mexico and Arizona.

SCIENTIFICALLY ESTIMATED TO BE

The Oldest Relics in the World.

A short history of the Strange Race, Region and Ruins.

C. H. GREEN, PROPRIETOR.

Collection Exhibited at Art Institute Building, 10 VanBuren Street, Chicago, Ill.

Called the C. H. Green Collection

Cover of C. H. Green's 1892 catalog of "cliff dweller relics."

Charles McLoyd apparently led at least two additional expeditions into Grand Gulch and other canyons—one with J. Howard Graham, Washington and Levi Patrick, and John Wetherill, and a second one with Charles Cary Graham. The Wetherill–Grand Gulch project has turned up almost nothing about these trips, but we do know that the rancher-archaeologists amassed a large collection of Pueblo and Basketmaker artifacts. In one of the very few references to these trips, John Wetherill wrote that "the Cliff House material that came with the McLoyd collection came from White Canyon, Armstrong Canyon, and the Moki Canyon, tributaries of the Colorado River on the South. This work was done by Charles McLoyd, Howard and Charles Graham, and Wash and Levi Patrick. . . . I was with them for awhile when they were doing this work."[36]

Leaving behind the excavation practices of his first trip, on later expeditions McLoyd began to dig deeper, beneath the cliff dwellings. He and his partners uncovered thousands of Basketmaker artifacts—hunting implements, wooden and bone household tools, baskets, textiles, sandals, and robes. We estimate that the men eventually took more than two thousand artifacts from Grand Gulch sites.

Some of these items ended up in the Green collection. Others were purchased by John Koontz of Aztec, New Mexico, who then sold them to the wealthy Hyde brothers of New York. In 1895, the Hydes gave the collection to the American Museum of Natural History, where it was mistakenly renamed the "Kunz" collection. Still other artifacts acquired by McLoyd and Graham were purchased by C. D. Hazzard for display at the World's Columbian Exposition; they eventually ended up in the Hazzard collection at the University of Pennsylvania.[37]

A basket cover or plate with associated basket-weaving materials from Cave 12, Grand Gulch.

Monarch Cave, 1994. Inset: Diagram of Monarch Cave from the Illustrated American, *1892.*

In March 1892, Charles McLoyd met a man who holds the distinction of having been the first trained archaeologist to visit the ancient ruins of the Four Corners: Warren K. Moorehead of the Phillips Academy in Andover, Massachusetts. Moorehead, whose previous archaeological experience included the excavation of Hopewell and Adena mound sites in the Ohio River valley, had secured funding from the *Illustrated American,* a weekly magazine based in Minneapolis, to lead ten men on an expedition into the Four Corners region.[38] The party was to obtain a collection of artifacts representative of the cliff dwellers for Professor F. W. Putnam, curator of the Peabody Museum at Harvard University.

While in Durango, Moorehead met with McLoyd and inspected what later became part of the Hazzard collection.[39] He may also have seen the Green collection, which was still in Durango. His encounter with McLoyd excited his imagination and spurred him eagerly into the canyons of southeastern Utah. Moorehead's written impressions show his admiration for McLoyd:

> Among the ruins in the main Cañon of the Colorado, Mr. Charles McLoyd is the only person who has carried on extensive work. He has spent two winters in making photographs and drawings and in collecting objects buried in the ruins houses. Although he was accompanied by a number of men, he found the ruins so extensive that he was able to visit but one-third of them.[40]

> Fortunately, among many vandals there are a few collectors of judgment and discrimination. Such a gentleman is Mr. Charles McLoyd, of Durango, who has done scientific work of great value in the Colorado River Valley.[41]

From Durango, Moorehead's group journeyed south by horseback, boat, and wagon to the San Juan River, then pushed on to the Four Corners and Bluff. From there the party headed west and north up Butler Wash via the old dairy ("salt") road into Whiskers Draw, Cottonwood Wash, and Allen Canyon, searching out small dwellings tucked away in the alcoves. But the expedition never actually entered Grand Gulch, in part because the *Illustrated American* failed and Moorehead's funding ran out before he was able to reach it. Moorehead was personally left with the expense of bringing his group home again.

The articles Moorehead had sent to the *Illustrated American* before its demise helped build public interest in the ancient cultures of the Southwest, yet his expedition yielded little in the way of archaeological accomplishment. He brought back a few artifacts but made no significant discoveries. Above all, Moorehead missed his opportunity to identify the Basketmakers.

At some point around this time, Charles McLoyd seems to have reached the important conclusion that some of the artifacts he and his partners were digging up came from a people different from the cliff dwellers.[42] Moorehead himself, writing in the August 20, 1892, issue of the *Illustrated American,* attributed to McLoyd the following statement:

> I would divide the dwellings of the Colorado River aborigines into cliff-houses and cave dwellings. . . . The cave-dwellings are very unique. . . . In such shelters I find that primitive man dug out a number of underground chambers [cists], most of which he did not wall up or divide into rooms by partitions. . . .
>
> It is very singular to note that no pottery is found in the underground caves. In the making of textile fabrics the inhabitants seem to have been equal in skill to the cliff-dwellers. The two peoples were strangely alike in many respects, indeed, in my collection there is a striking resemblance between the objects from both class of ruins.[43]

Moorehead went on to note that the crania of the "cave-dwellers" were well shaped and not flattened as were the cliff dweller skulls.

McLoyd apparently assumed that the two cultures were coeval. He knew that in at least one alcove dug on his 1892 Grand Gulch trip, remains of the cave dwellers lay below those of the cliff dwellers.[44] Yet neither he nor Moorehead—despite Moorehead's professional training—recognized that these artifacts were fashioned by a people who predated the cliff dwellers.[45] Moorehead, of course, although he had talked with McLoyd and seen Basketmaker artifacts, had never actually dug a Basketmaker site, but only ones left by the cliff dwellers. He also lacked the years of experience examining Ancestral Pueblo artifacts that McLoyd and his partners had garnered by digging around Mesa Verde and Grand Gulch.

Charles McLoyd deserves credit for his hard-won gleam of recognition that the Basketmakers belonged to a unique culture. But it would be left to Richard Wetherill to connect the clues and realize that compared with the cliff dwellers, the Basketmakers were truly an earlier people.

Polly's Island, photographed by F. E. Leeka during the Green Expedition, 1891.

3 / The Wetherills in Grand Gulch

Grand Gulch drains nearly all the territory south west of the Elk Mountain from the McComb Wash to the Clay Hills—about 1000 sq. miles of territory. . . . The canon is from 300 to 700 feet deep—and in many places toward the lower end the bends are cut through by waters making natural bridges. . . . To enter the canon a party must be equipped with suitable pack animals and expect to spend 3 days on the road from Bluff.

—Richard Wetherill, 1897

On November 29, 1893, Richard Wetherill led a small group of men westward out of Mancos, Colorado, toward Grand Gulch, to assemble yet another collection of ancient Indian "relics." After a short stop for supplies in Bluff, Utah, the men headed north on December 11. In a letter written only six days later, addressed from "First Valley Cottonwood Creek 30 miles North Bluff City," Wetherill noted:

> Our success has surpassed all expectations. . . . In the cave we are now working we have taken 28 skeletons and two more in sight and curious to tell, and a thing that will surprise the archaeologists of the country is the fact of our finding them at a depth of five and six feet in a cave in which there are cliff dwellings and we find the bodies under the ruins, three feet below any cliff dweller sign. They are a different race from anything I have ever seen. They had feather cloth and baskets, no pottery—six of the bodies had stone spear heads in them.[1]

In these spare words, Richard Wetherill announced that he had found the material remnants of a culture totally new to the scholarly community—one that had preceded the cliff dwellers.

Richard Wetherill never wrote about his motivations for exploring Grand Gulch, but his desire for knowledge about the prehistoric Southwest undoubtedly played a leading role. From McLoyd and Graham he had learned about the wealth of sites in the Gulch. His brothers John and Al had accompanied McLoyd into Grand Gulch and the canyons of the Colorado early in 1893, and their stories may have excited Richard's interest.[2]

The artifacts displayed by McLoyd and C. H. Green in Durango must have especially captivated the elder Wetherill brother.[3] Among the familiar cliff dweller artifacts were several that looked unlike anything of cliff dweller manufacture. With his sharp eyes and intimate

Signature site in upper Butler Wash.

knowledge of cliff dweller artifacts, Richard Wetherill was unlikely to have missed seeing that some sandals were constructed rather differently from those he had seen in the cliff houses of Mesa Verde. Although made of the same materials, they lacked a notch for the little toe that cliff dweller sandals nearly always had. And skulls found in association with these sandals lacked the familiar flattened shape of cliff dweller skulls.

Rivalry with his former partner, Charles McLoyd, was, we suspect, just as important as Wetherill's intellectual motivation. In their articles for the *Illustrated American,* neither Warren K. Moorehead nor another writer, Lewis Gunkel, mentioned Richard Wetherill by name, although each referred to the Wetherill family and their knowledge of local archaeological sites. Moorehead may also have been referring indirectly to the Wetherills when he commented that "cowboys and Indians, tempted by the flattering offers made them by the traders, have despoiled the ruins of the relics easiest of access."[4] The attention McLoyd received from Moorehead, coupled with the archaeologist's veiled criticism of Richard Wetherill's work, must have rankled.

D. W. Ayres, who knew the Wetherill family, had accompanied McLoyd and Green on their expedition to Grand Gulch in June 1891, and he probably talked with Al and Richard Wetherill about what the party had found.[5] In addition, Charles Lang, a friend and partner of Richard Wetherill's, may have been in the Gulch prior to 1890 and photographed some of the cliff dwellings.[6] In the summer of 1893, Richard Wetherill entered into partnership with Lang. The *Mancos Times* carried the following advertisement:

> Lang & Witherill [sic], Photographers. Mancos, Colorado. Cliff Dwelling Views a Specialty! Rocky Mt. Views, orders by mail promptly attended to.[7]

Lang's descriptions and photographs of the Gulch likely provided all the extra incentive Richard Wetherill needed to head west in search of new archaeological riches.

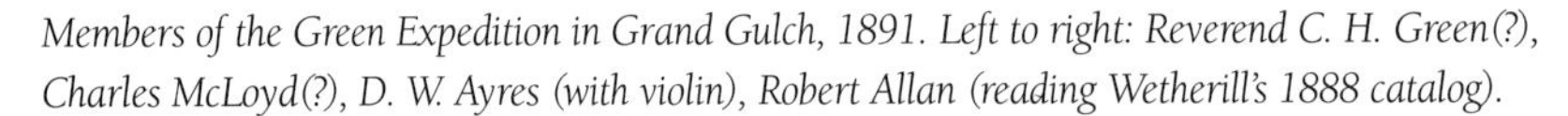
Members of the Green Expedition in Grand Gulch, 1891. Left to right: Reverend C. H. Green(?), Charles McLoyd(?), D. W. Ayres (with violin), Robert Allan (reading Wetherill's 1888 catalog).

A Charles Lang and Richard Wetherill photographic view of Spruce Tree House, Mesa Verde, c. 1892, with the photographers' stamp inset.

THE BIGGEST IMPEDIMENT WETHERILL NOW FACED WAS LACK OF FUNDS. IN ORDER to amass a sizable collection in Grand Gulch, he would need pack animals and wranglers to handle them, as well as provisions for many weeks. His opportunity came in the late summer of 1893, when Colorado state officials asked him to look after his Mesa Verde collection at the Chicago world's fair, the World's Columbian Exposition. They wanted a knowledgeable person there to greet visitors and answer questions.

This must have been an exciting time for the rancher-turned-archaeologist. His first collection, which by then belonged to the state of Colorado, was housed in the Anthropological Building at the world's fair, together with archaeological and ethnological collections assembled by such notables as W. H. Holmes of the U.S. Bureau of American Ethnology and George A. Dorsey, a student of Frederick Ward Putnam's and later an ethnologist for the Field Museum of Natural History in Chicago. The H. Jay Smith Exploring Company displayed the second Wetherill collection inside a life-size replica of Battlerock Mountain, a stark sandstone outcropping in McElmo Canyon, southwest of Cortez, Colorado. The company had built this colossus expressly for the fair.

Richard Wetherill talked to a lot of people in Chicago, but to none who would prove so important to him as the brothers B. Talbot Hyde and Fred Hyde, Jr. Wetherill had first met the pair in 1892 when they visited Alamo Ranch with their father.[8] The young men, then eighteen and twenty, respectively, were the grandsons of Benjamin Babbitt, a businessman who had made his fortune in New York City manufacturing Bab-O soap. The brothers entertained a lively interest in archaeology. As heirs to the Babbitt soap fortune, they also had money to spend. Wetherill convinced them to fund a collecting expedition into Grand Gulch during the upcoming winter, with the idea of donating the collection to the American Museum of Natural History in New York.

Richard Wetherill was determined to plan this expedition thoroughly and to record his archaeological finds in rigorous detail. After his experiences with Nordenskiöld, he probably was appalled at McLoyd's relative lack of documentation. Commenting on McLoyd and J. Howard Graham's excavations in Mancos and Cliff Canyons, Al Wetherill later noted:

> The men went to work among the buildings with a will, working in all the cliff dwellings along the main [Mancos] canyon and a short distance up side canyons, mostly in the main part of Cliff Canyon. They did not, however, keep a record of which house, room, or canyon they found the material [in]. Neither were there any photographs of the articles found, nor room positions in the building given. They did no destruction to any standing walls, but they threw the dirt and broken walls of one room into another that had already been worked. They pretty well dusted out the lower parts of Cliff Canyon. To them, all was just so much stuff to get out to market.[9]

Considering the praise that Moorehead had heaped on McLoyd's Grand Gulch excavations in his articles for the *Illustrated American,* Richard Wetherill probably felt he had to demonstrate his own grasp of scientific archaeology. Because the Hydes planned to donate the collection he made to the American Museum, he also wanted to live up to a new standard that would bear scrutiny from professional archaeologists. He had been in correspondence with Frederick Ward Putnam, who was Chief of Ethnology for the Columbian Exposition, and had a copy of Putnam's pamphlet on archaeological method.[10] He also had certainly talked with Putnam in Chicago.

After leaving Chicago in October, Wetherill journeyed to New York by way of Niagara Falls and Saratoga Springs to visit Julia Cowing, a young woman who had visited the Wetherills in

B. Talbot Hyde (left) and Frederick Ward Putnam at Mesa Verde, c. 1892.

Mancos and in whom he had a romantic interest.[11] In a letter written from Brooklyn, Wetherill proposed to Talbot Hyde the following methods:

> I arrived here night before last and will commence on Monday to outfit with such articles as cannot be procured at Durango. I send a form of work [a record sheet twelve by thirteen inches, ruled off in squares] that will meet all requirements unless something else occurs to you that would be of special interest. I find that there are none printed but I can do as heretofore, secure blanks and mark them myself in this manner—viz:

1 number of house or ruin	2 number of article	3 name of article	4 number of room
5 number of section	6 depth	7 number of floors if any	8 remarks number of room

> Every article to be numbered with India ink and fine pen or with tube paints white, red or black. Plan of all houses and sections to be made on paper or book to be ruled both ways. Drawing of article to be made on paper with numbers and name. Photograph each house before touched, then each room or section and every important article as found.
>
> I think you will find this will meet all the requirements of the most scientific but if you have any suggestions whatever I will act upon them. This whole subject . . . is in its infancy and the work we do must stand the most rigid inspection, and we do not want to do it in such a manner that anyone in the future can pick flaws in it.[12]

This plan clearly reflects the standards for documentation that Wetherill had learned from Nordenskiöld. In practice, however, his implementation fell short; he apparently never kept such a record book, although he did take notes and assemble an informative catalog.

Richard Wetherill's initial party consisted of himself, Al and John Wetherill, Charles Lang, Harry French, and James Ethridge. They headed out of Mancos by way of Cortez, then turned south for a few miles and took McElmo Canyon west toward Bluff. Wirt Jenks Billings from Denver joined the party there, along with Bob Allan, who had been part of Green's 1891 exploring party. Allan lived in Bluff, but his family raised a dairy herd on Milk Ranch Point overlooking Cottonwood Wash. He was probably suggested as a team member by Charles Lang, who had met him during Lang's earlier explorations in southeastern Utah.

In Bluff, Wetherill hired more horses and burros and bought a month's worth of supplies. On December 11, the men left the town, riding north along Cottonwood Wash, a broad, sandy drainage that empties into the San Juan River just west of town.[13] As Harry French explained in a letter years later, each member of the expedition had specific duties:

> Richard Wetherill was in charge, Alf [sic] Wetherill, cook; Charlie Lang, photographer. C. N. [Wirt Jenks] Billings kept account of everything we took out of these ruins and sent a copy with the collections to the Natural History Museum, New York City; John Wetherill had the nice job of rustling up the burros when we moved camp. Sometimes it took him a day or two to find them. Bob Allen [Allan] accompanied by one other man would take the collections in to Bluff City and bring out supplies. He made every trip as Bluff was his home and he was acquainted with the people and conditions. Jim Ethridge and myself were the two that went ahead looking for a new camp site whenever we moved. Jim had been in part of that country before, which was a help to us in locating our camps. When we made these trips ahead we would start at day break so we could make it back to our camp at night.[14]

The Hyde Exploring Expedition was an arduous venture. Except for a short reprieve in Bluff around Christmastime, the party spent four months in the field, sleeping out or in tents every night, traveling or digging in the ruins by day. Expedition members were fortunate that the winter of 1893–94 was unusually mild:

> The entire party never went into Bluff City together except Christmas 1893. While we were there, we were generously entertained by the high moguls of the Mormon Church. This was arranged by Bob Allen [sic], who was a Mormon. . . . This particular winter was wonderful for our trip. It was a mild, open winter and we had very little snow.[15]

Paradoxically, Richard Wetherill and his crew made their most significant find before even reaching Grand Gulch. After examining six other alcoves on their way up Cottonwood Creek, the men reached the alcove they called Cave 7 on December 17, discovering there clear

The Hyde Exploring Expedition leaving Bluff City in 1893. Left to right: Richard Wetherill, James Ethridge, Wirt Jenks Billings, John Wetherill.

MEMBERS OF THE HYDE EXPLORING EXPEDITION

Expedition Member	Duty
Robert (Bob) Allan	Guide/wrangler
Wirt Jenks Billings	Recorder/excavator
James Ethridge	Excavator
Harry French	Excavator
Charles Lang	Photographer
Al Wetherill	Excavator/cook
John Wetherill	Wrangler/cook
Richard Wetherill	Expedition leader

Charles B. Lang signature, Ute Cave, Allen Canyon.

evidence of the Basketmaker people. In a letter to Talbot Hyde written from Bluff on December 21, Wetherill elaborated on this exciting find: "We have only worked one Cave [,] there is hundreds of them here, but all of this class of digging is deep. . . . You would be much interested that we have now taken 90 skeletons from one cave [,] the heads are different from the Cliff Dweller."[16]

It was young Talbot Hyde who named the newly found people. The manner in which the term came about reveals Richard Wetherill's tendency to share with others the credit for his discoveries. He wrote Hyde, who was paying for much of the Wetherills' work, "We find that the basket people, or whatever you may name them, (which you should do. I named the cliff dwellers, and you should have the honor at least of naming these, since it is your expedition) . . ."[17] Hyde suggested "Basket Maker," which Wetherill thought was "more distinctive than anything I could have thought [of] for a name."[18]

Wetherill did have some reservations about the term, perhaps because basket making was a universal practice among the historically known tribes of the region. Nevertheless, he began to use the name, and after T. Mitchell Prudden and George Pepper, another professional archaeologist, used it in articles they published about Richard Wetherill's work, it caught on. The archaeologist Charles A. Amsden later shortened it into a single word, noting, "I prefer this form, Basketmaker, as the simplest form of an awkward and essentially meaningless term, for most of the world's peoples are makers of baskets."[19]

After celebrating Christmas in Bluff, the expedition apparently headed out again sometime before the end of December. We surmise this because Billings signed his name in Cave 10 (now named Fishmouth Cave) in Butler Wash on New Year's Day, 1894. Years later, Harry French reported that the Hyde expedition took many artifacts from this alcove, but Wetherill's 1894 notes make no mention of them, and the artifacts' current location is unknown. After exploring Cave 11—the location of which has yet to be rediscovered—the expedition turned west, and sometime before January 8 reached its prize, Grand Gulch.

Tree House Ruin in Ute Mountain Tribal Park. The inscriptions on the stones in foreground (detail, right) read "A. Wetherill 1.– 1.– '88" and "J. Wetherill 1–14–1890."

MOST OF WHAT WE KNOW ABOUT THE ROUTE THE HYDE EXPLORING EXPEDITION took, and the alcoves and sites it explored, comes from doing reverse archaeology. Searching through archives, participants in the Wetherill–Grand Gulch Research Project found written records few and short on detail. But luckily, members of the Hyde expedition had a propensity for writing their names on the canyon walls. Sometimes they also included the date. These inscriptions have proved to be a gold mine for historical research.

Throughout the Southwest, historic graffiti—names, messages, and dates—document expeditions, journeys, adventures, discoveries, and social occasions.[20] Sometimes they mark a homestead, a mining claim, or a camp now long forgotten. Historic inscriptions have been found on canyon walls and boulders and at archaeological sites, often well preserved because of their placement in hidden and sheltered spots. Sadly, others have deteriorated through natural processes or have been destroyed by vandals.

When readable, the inscriptions not only give us important dates but also, through their style and placement, afford insights into the personalities and characters of the individuals who recorded their moment of history. Each person had his or her preference about where to place a signature, some showing off their climbing skills by scrawling a name high on an inaccessible ledge, others incising an inscription neatly on a site feature such as an ax-grinding groove or the lintel of a doorway.

Tracking down and recording more than four hundred signatures and other inscriptions in southeastern Utah has been a formidable task and is still far from complete. The quest for relevant inscriptions has taken researchers into many of the region's major canyons. Their most intensive efforts have focused on Grand Gulch, which encompasses some seventy-five miles of main canyon and another seventy-five miles of side canyons. Because Ancestral Pueblo people lived on both sides of the gorges, research teams have been faced with exploring roughly three hundred miles of canyon in Grand Gulch alone, searching carefully in and around each archaeological site.

New pairs of eyes and different lighting conditions continually produce new discoveries. Ambient light changes throughout the day and throughout the year. The best times to examine faint inscriptions are in the early morning and evening. In winter, the sun's low angle can also improve the visibility of markings on the rocks.

It took the project team nearly five years to find and decipher the signature of H. R. Ricker, a member of the 1891 Green Expedition, in Perfect Kiva and that of Charles McLoyd in Green's Burial Cave 1. Although these sites had been examined many times by different groups in the spring and summer, better lighting conditions in the winter of 1991 finally made the names discernible. As late as July 1994, a previously unseen date was found inscribed on the wall of Cave 7. In that case, early morning light helped delineate the faint markings.

In 1992, participants in an Outward Bound instructors' workshop in Cottonwood Wash found, among debris left by contemporary pothunters, a rock bearing the finely carved name of C. B. Lang.[21] This same rock had been overlooked several times by the Wetherill–Grand Gulch team. Sometimes researchers have simply missed an entire inscription site. In 1992, hiker Jeffrey Minker found a panel in what was likely the last site excavated by the Whitmore Exploring Expedition, Richard Wetherill's second trip into Grand Gulch, in 1897. It contains the names Charlie Mason, "Wetherill," and James Ethridge, and the initials "W.E.E."

In documenting these inscriptions, it often helps to use a magnifying lens to follow the scratches. Sometimes, reversing a pair of binoculars and looking through the large end tends to pull together large, faint letters made by abrasion, charcoal, or bullet lead. Because tracing the inscriptions directly—through sheets of clear Mylar, for example—would begin to destroy them, Wetherill–Grand Gulch researchers sketch each image instead. The recorder takes care to draw only what can actually be seen and to avoid adding interpretations. Several colleagues working together help maintain everyone's objectivity.

These inscriptions have enabled us to trace the paths the different expeditions followed, the archaeological sites they dug, and the campsites they used. Together with letters, journals, maps, and photographs, they have yielded up the routes of McLoyd and Graham's 1891 expedition, Green's 1891 trip, the 1893–94 Hyde Exploring Expedition, and the 1897 Whitmore Exploring Expedition. They have also helped us identify alcoves previously lost to history, such as Cave 7.

With continued documentation of the historic inscriptions, we have high hopes of retracing other expeditions and giving provenience to additional artifacts taken from the Four Corners region. Unfortunately, signatures are a disappearing resource. We estimate that natural erosion and human vandalism have damaged or obliterated some two-thirds of the inscriptions known so far. But by correlating the still-decipherable signatures, especially those accompanied by dates, with information gleaned from letters and expedition notes, members of the Wetherill–Grand Gulch Research Project have successfully reconstructed the route Richard Wetherill and his companions took when the Hyde Exploring Expedition struck out for Grand Gulch.

After turning west at the head of Butler Wash, Wetherill's party headed for Graham (now Bullet) Canyon, following the same route to Grand Gulch that Charles McLoyd had taken three years earlier. Bob Allan may have led the team, because he knew the trail McLoyd and Graham had built into the upper reaches of Graham Canyon in 1891. On January 8, 1894, shortly after the party must have entered the Gulch, Harry French inscribed his name in Cave 14, or Perfect Kiva.

The men worked several of the alcoves in Graham Canyon on their way to the main canyon. Writing in his notes about the cultural material found in Cave 12, Richard Wetherill also dropped hints about his opinion of McLoyd and Graham's earlier excavations:

> Graham Canyon Burial Cave 1:
> Headless mummy with Sandal on feet—dug out and left by McLeod [sic].
>
> This cave is in Grand Gulch and one from which McLeod and Graham took so many mummies and baskets, several spots were left untouched. This child was in a grave 2 ft. deep around it was mummy cloth—similar to the previous. A string of black beads upon the neck. White ones upon the arms. A bag of corn meal up on top of it [see p.94] and several sandals. Found exposed on surface—dug out 1 year ago.[22]

We know from Wetherill's later summary of the 1897 Whitmore Exploring Expedition that the 1893–94 team dug in Caves 12 through 16 in Graham Canyon. The notes of the Hyde expedition itself, however—available today in the American Museum of Natural History—are not as complete as Richard Wetherill originally planned to make them. We are not sure why.

Wirt Jenks Billings apparently kept most or all of the notes. Although Wetherill put together an annotated catalog, Billings's notes and any drawings he made have since disappeared, and the notes we now have are cursory at best. Fortunately, Wetherill's summary of his second expedition into Grand Gulch contains several references to caves visited in the first, which have helped greatly in tracing the route of the first expedition.

Upon reaching the junction where Graham Canyon meets Grand Gulch proper, Richard Wetherill sent Al and John south, toward the San Juan River, to search for likely sites in which to dig along the main canyon. The rest of the party turned north, toward the head of Grand Gulch. Inscriptions bearing the same date but in widely different parts of the canyon tell us the group must have split up about January 25.

Al and John Wetherill visited side canyons and sites along the way, leaving their signatures and drawings in Step, Dripping, and Cow Tanks Canyons. They rode past the rincon called Polly's Island, past a Pueblo III site called the Grand Hotel because of its finely executed stone walls, and on past Bannister Ruin.[23] In the lower part of Grand Gulch, they found untouched Basketmaker burial caves.

Artifact assemblage from the burial of a Basketmaker child, removed from Cave 12 by the Hyde Exploring Expedition of 1893–94 and now in the collection of the American Museum of Natural History. Pictured items include four coiled baskets, one filled with piñon, parched and popped corn, and squash seeds, another holding bone needles woven together; a tanned mountain sheep skin; two large apocynum fiber bags, one filled with cornmeal; a polished mountain sheep horn; and a small fiber bag containing yellow ochre and chipped stone flakes.

Burial site and rock art panel in Cut-in-Two Cave, Grand Gulch.

The balance of the expedition team excavated several alcoves in the upper canyon, including Cut-In-Two Cave (Cave 19), from which they took buried body parts and the preserved mummy of a tall old man who had suffered a deep cut across the back and abdomen. The poor fellow had been crudely stitched together sometime before his death by means of cord made of braided human hair:

> Mummified remains of Arms and hands from elbows and legs and feet from knees showing evidence of having been cut off before burial with them was 734 [Wetherill's catalog number for the mummy]. Mummy in bottom of circular grave. Man nearly 6 ft. tall. Knees drawn up on Hands on Abdomen. Was cut in two at loins and sewed together again with hair string. (One of the most curious specimens ever found).[24]

They also dug in Rope Ruin (Cave 18), Turkey Pen Ruin (Cave 20), and Green Mask Alcove (Cave 17), so named for its striking Basketmaker painting of a green mask.[25]

Judging from the signatures and dates, it appears that upon John and Al Wetherill's return, the group packed up the artifacts, loaded them on burros, and returned to Bluff during the first three days of February. After resupplying in Bluff and resting for a short time, they headed directly for the lower reaches of Grand Gulch, where they excavated in caves near Red Man, Rope, and Water Canyons.

Richard Wetherill's letters to the Hydes and others, written in the field and in Bluff, tell much about his movements and interests. In many alcoves the party found human remains—sometimes skeletons, but more often Basketmaker "mummies" that had been well preserved by the remarkable dryness of the Grand Gulch alcoves. In a letter to Talbot Hyde on February 4, 1894, Wetherill noted:

> It is now three weeks since I left here [Bluff] for Grand Gulch. We worked in two caves two days where McLoyd dug out so many mummies [probably Cave 17 (Green Mask Alcove) and Cave 19 (Cut-In-Two)]. I sent Al and John fifty miles down the canyon to look at some caves. In the meantime, the rest of us moved seven miles up the canyon to some ruins that McLoyd worked [perhaps what is now called Split Level Ruin]. On Al's and John's return from the lower end of the canyon, they told of several caves that had been overlooked entirely by previous explorers. They dug a few minutes in each and found human remains. The next day after their return we worked in a cave that had a cliff house in it, and which had been previously worked [Cave 19 (Cut-In-Two)]. There we found nine mummies more or less perfect, one of them a remarkable specimen, and a greater find than any we have yet made. I saved all the skeletons from the first cave [Cave 7] as I thought you would want them for study, but I will not save any more; the distance is too great, but will save all skulls.

The last dated inscription that we know of for the Hyde Exploring Expedition—though it does not give the date for the end of the trip—is James Ethridge's name, which he wrote, along with "February 22, 1894," in an alcove near Rope Canyon. One of the Wetherills and Wirt Jenks Billings also left their names on the canyon walls nearby. The alcove now known as Wetherill Cave in lower Grand Gulch contains numerous inscriptions, which suggests that it served as a camp and excavation location. After having dug a total of thirteen caves (numbered 17 through 29), the Hyde expedition left Grand Gulch with its collection and returned temporarily to Bluff.

By March 14, the group was again at work in the upper reaches of Butler and Cottonwood Washes, now excavating in Double Cave.[26] Richard Wetherill described this alcove as the "Place where the Great Battle took place,"[27] a reference we find puzzling because we have found no record of any artifacts from the cave that might explain it.

By the end of March, the expedition had run out of money and credit. Wetherill had planned to push south of the San Juan, but instead laid off his men when they reached Bluff. Earlier, on February 4 and again on March 20, he had written to Talbot Hyde, urging the young man to send money he had promised. Wetherill had been unable to pay his men, and he owed merchants in Bluff several hundred dollars.

While they waited for Talbot Hyde to come through with the cash, the men took the opportunity to work some placer claims along the San Juan, searching for meager traces of gold washed down from the hills. Richard Wetherill stayed behind to continue the work he loved. On March 28 he again wrote to Hyde:

> I am in the field where I like to work and have no thought for anything else while here, but it is necessary to have supplies enough as soon as I can so that you can write a couple of articles for the *American Archaeologist*. They are anxious to have it. I told Mr. Moorehead [editor of *American Archaeologist* in 1894–95] that I would write them with your permission if you did not wish to but I think you should do it, by all means. . . . while the boys were waiting they have gone down the canyon to locate some placer claims for themselves.[28]

This letter reveals both Richard Wetherill's passion for archaeology and his constant struggle to fund it. The expedition was continually short on supplies because the Hyde brothers were slow in sending money. Wetherill's appetite for digging was such that he undoubtedly could have spent whatever the Hydes sent and more as well. He apparently contributed a substantial part of his own assets to the task, funds he could ill afford, considering the precarious state of finances back home. The family ranch was heavily in debt. Father B. K. Wetherill, in poor health, was unable to manage it, so all duties fell to the five brothers. Richard Wetherill's personal sacrifices are well documented and illustrate his deep commitment to the archaeological work he was doing, contradicting the claim some have made that he was primarily interested in excavating for the money he occasionally earned selling artifacts.

Sometime between March 28 and April 11, 1894, Richard Wetherill reassembled his expedition party, crossed the San Juan, and explored Chinle Wash. There the party visited Poncho House, a large Pueblo III site that Wetherill referred to as Long House because it was over five hundred feet long.[29] Poncho House was the Hyde expedition's last major stop before returning to Mancos.

By the end of their trip, team members had documented or excavated some thirty-three alcoves and cliff dwellings in Grand Gulch, Allen Canyon, and Butler Wash, through which they traveled on the way back to Bluff. They had made 52 pages of field notes and assembled a collection of 1,216 items, both artifacts and human skeletons. Most of these items were gathered in Grand Gulch, but 428 came from Cottonwood Wash and 71 from Poncho House. Wetherill shipped the relics to Mancos, and by April 11, 1894, he was back at Alamo Ranch working on the collection. It took him roughly two months to sort and catalog his finds before he crated and shipped them to the Hyde brothers in New York. The Hydes presented the collection to the American Museum of Natural History a year later, in the fall of 1895.[30]

Hyde Exploring Expedition members at a cliff dwelling in Butler Wash, 1894. Left to right: James Ethridge (leaning on wall), Harry French, and Wirt Jenks Billings (in window opening).

RICHARD WETHERILL'S SECOND MAJOR EXPEDITION INTO GRAND GULCH WAS A vastly different experience from the first.[31] Whereas the winter of 1893–94 had been relatively mild, now the canyon showed its harsh side. Snow blanketed the landscape, and bitter cold reigned. Forage for the animals was hard to find. Wetherill took many photographs, but because he used a "wet plate" process, they froze before they could be developed, and few survived.

On this trip Wetherill took thirteen people into the Gulch. One member of the party was his new wife, the former Marietta Palmer, whom Wetherill had met a year earlier when she and her family visited Alamo Ranch. The Palmers—Sidney LaVerne, Elizabeth Ann, and their children—were musicians who toured the Southwest, earning their living by playing concerts in the small towns and cities. LaVerne Palmer had heard of the Wetherills and their finds at Mesa Verde and became intrigued by the opportunity to explore the many Indian ruins in the area. Marietta Palmer was twenty when she married Richard Wetherill on December 12, 1896. Richard was thirty-eight. They were married in Sacramento, California, and returned to Alamo Ranch on December 30.

Richard Wetherill launched the Whitmore Exploring Expedition under circumstances rather different from those of the Hyde expedition. This time, he was driven largely by a desire to document as well as he could the culture he called the Basket Makers. He also wanted to revisit Grand Gulch before other groups, possibly better funded, could encroach on territory where "he felt he and the Hydes had prior interests."[32] Having heard in October from Charles Lang that the Field Museum was planning to send an expedition into Grand Gulch, Wetherill immediately wrote to Talbot Hyde, attempting to interest his patron in outfitting a second Utah

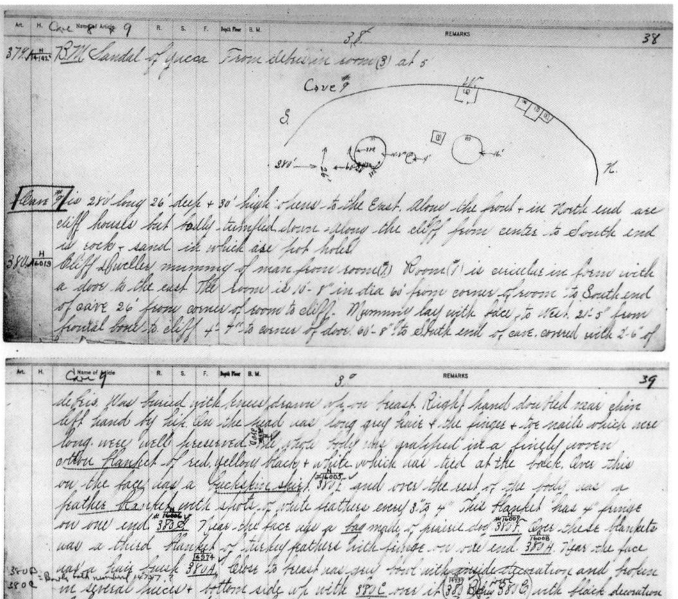

Cave 9 — 38

379 — B.M. Sandal of yucca From debris in room (3) at 5'

Cave 7 — is 280' long 26' deep + 30' high opens to the East. Along the front + in North end are cliff houses but badly tumbled down. Along the cliff from center to South end is rock + sand in which are pot holes

380 — H 16019 — Cliff Dweller mummy of man from room (7) Room (7) is circular in form with a door to the east The room is 10'-8" in dia 60' from corner of room to South end of cave 26' from corner of room to cliff. Mummy lay with face to West. 21'-5" from frontal bone to cliff 4'-7" to corner of door. 60'-8" to South end of cave. covered with 2'-6" of

Cave 9 — 39

debris. Was buried with knees drawn up on breast. Right hand doubled near chin left hand by hip. On the head was long grey hair + the finger + toe nails which were long were well preserved. The whole body was wrapped in a finely woven cotton blanket of red, yellow black + white which was tied at the back. Over this on the face was a buckskin shirt 380 E and over the rest of the body was a feather blanket with spots of white feathers every 3" to 4" This blanket has 4" fringe on one end. 380 D Near the face was a bag made of prairie dog 380 F. Over these blankets was a third blanket of turkey feathers with fringe on one end. 380 H. Near the face was a hair brush 380 A. Close to breast was [illegible] bowl with inside decoration and broken in several pieces + bottom side up with 380 C over it 380 B [illegible] 380 C with black decoration broken in many pieces + had contained corn meal.

381 — H 14366 — Jar Ring woven of black and white yucca From room (3) at center at 2'

382 — H 14143 — C.D. Sandal of yucca From room (3) at 2'

383 — H 16014 — C.D. Child From room (7) Head was 6'-7" from corner of room Child was wrapped

Above: The 1897 Whitmore Exploring Expedition's Camp 4. Left to right: Orian Buck, James Ethridge, George Hairgrove, Levi Carson, Marietta Palmer Wetherill, Teddy Whitmore, Charlie Mason, Hal Heaton, unidentified dog. Left: Marietta Wetherill's 1897 field notes and excavation plan of Cave 7.

immediately wrote to Talbot Hyde, attempting to interest his patron in outfitting a second Utah expedition.[33] Hyde wrote back that he and his brother would be unable to fund it.

Then, unexpectedly, help arrived from a Harvard student by the name of George Bowles and his tutor, C. E. Whitmore. Young Bowles was bent on adventure and had the money to pursue it with style. Wetherill suggested that Whitmore and Bowles fund an expedition to Grand Gulch. Whitmore was more than willing to approve the endeavor, and the two men joined Wetherill immediately in preparing to leave in early January 1897. The weather and an experience with some Indians near the end of the expedition were to provide much higher adventure than either of them had bargained for.

Despite her youth and relative inexperience with winter camping, Richard Wetherill's new bride, Marietta, insisted on joining the expedition team. After all, she argued, they would need someone to take notes and keep excavation records. Wetherill reluctantly agreed.[34]

The party seems to have left Alamo Ranch on or just after January 13, 1897; the ranch ledger shows that Whitmore paid his boarding charges that day.[35] On about January 18, Richard Wetherill led the party of twelve men and one woman out of Bluff, Utah, first north by way of Cottonwood Wash and then west to Wetherill Canyon (now known as Kane Gulch), where they entered Grand Gulch.

One of the Wetherill brothers had found this route during the first expedition. To Richard Wetherill, it was an improvement over the treacherous Graham Canyon route, partly because it enabled him to use horses and mules for packing, rather than burros. To Marietta Wetherill and the newcomers, it must have seemed foolhardy. On the way down, they lost one of their horses over the edge, the contents of its packs scattering on the rocks two hundred feet below. The young woman gritted her teeth and followed the others down. Later she commented, "It was so crooked that even a rattlesnake would have a hard time getting down without breaking its back."[36]

With a larger crew this time, efficiency multiplied. Not only did Richard have more people to help with the digging, but he also had Marietta to help take notes—the originals of which reveal each of their handwriting. Because Richard and his brothers were already familiar with Grand Gulch, they could focus their efforts on choosing sites and supervising the excavations.

The party stayed in the Gulch about a month, visiting or excavating some twelve sites—all of which the Wetherill–Grand Gulch Research Project has identified by tracking down signatures of the participants. James Ethridge was the only member of the expedition who dated his signatures on the canyon walls. Without those dates, project members would never have been able to trace the movements of the Whitmore expedition.

The Wetherills' notes on each alcove were accurate and detailed. Although they did not describe the party's route, it was implicit in the sequence of cave numbers assigned. By using the notes, together with Richard Wetherill's summary and site maps and Ethridge's signatures, the project team was able not only to confirm the expedition's route but also to determine the exact proveniences of some of the most important archaeological finds. The detailed site maps, which show the placement of burials and major artifacts, enabled Wetherill–Grand Gulch personnel to identify the original locations of artifacts in their alcoves with surprising precision. For example, team members pinpointed the exact provenience of the mummy someone in the Whitmore expedition dubbed "Joe Buck," which was found in Cave 9 (an alcove now known as Kokopelli and the Dancers), and of the two cliff dweller mummies in Cave 11 (Green Mask Alcove) that the Wetherills called the Prince and Princess.

MEMBERS OF THE WHITMORE EXPLORING EXPEDITION

Member	Primary Role
George Bowles	Excavation, note taking, and sightseeing; financier
Orian H. Buck	Excavation
E. C. Cushman	Care of pack animals
James Ethridge	Excavation
George Hairgrove	Kitchen
Hal Heaton	Kitchen
William Henderson	Unknown
C. C. Mason	Excavation
Clayton Tompkins	Artifact inventory and packing
Clayton Wetherill	Care of riding stock
Marietta Wetherill	Recorder
Richard Wetherill	Leader, photographer
C. E. Whitmore	Financier

J. L. Ethridge signatures, January 1894 and February 1897, Cut-in-Two Cave (Cave 12/19), Grand Gulch.

Marietta Wetherill's account of the discovery of the mummy Joe Buck provides insights into Richard Wetherill's archaeological methods. It also reveals some of the humor the party engaged in, this time at the expense of Orian Buck, who helped with the excavation:

> They dug a little ways down and found they were coming to a body. Usually after they dug the first shovelful, they saw a rim of pottery or maybe a knee, and they got the brushes out. They used whisk brooms and a finer brush and then all the digging was done with a small garden trowel in those days. Mr. Wetherill insisted on photographing and measuring before he ever started to dig. I measured from front to back then the height by holding up a stick and measuring the stick.
>
> They found this marvelous mummy in there. They called the mummy Joe Buck after one of the fellows on the trip. I don't know who did it but the boys all blamed me when Buck got mad every time anybody would say that mummy looked like him. The mummy was covered first in a plain turkey feather blanket. The warp of those blankets was yucca string, and the feathers were taken off the quill and wound around the string. That was covered with another blanket with little blue bird feathers in it. The marvel of marvels was a blanket made of cotton, beautifully woven and intricate as a design [sic] in red, black, yellow and white.[37]

For the excavators, the discovery of the Prince and Princess was probably the highlight of the 1897 expedition. In an interview given in the 1940s, Marietta Wetherill described the event:

> Under the basket was another basket and beneath that was a turkey feather blanket with bluebird feather spots. Under that was another feather blanket with yellow spots from wild canaries, perhaps. A small basket, which had a design similar to an Apache basket I have, laid at one end.

Detail of the cotton blanket in which the mummy "Joe Buck" was found.

> "Oh, she's alive!" I said when Mr. Wetherill lifted the basket from her face. I couldn't believe she was dead. You can't imagine how quickly these mummies begin to wither when the air gets to them.
>
> "She sure does look asleep, doesn't she?" Mr. Wetherill said.
>
> We called her "Princess." Her body was painted yellow and her face was painted red and her hair was long. She had sandals on her feet and a . . . necklace of shell beads. She lay in another basket a bit larger than [the] one covering her. Moisture never reached the little grave. She had just dried.[38]

Near the Princess, the Whitmore expedition crew found the mummy they called the Prince. These accumulated discoveries soon created a storage problem for the Wetherills. One night, snow began to fall in the canyon after Richard and Marietta had fallen asleep. As Marietta remembered it years later, her husband suddenly sat up and announced that it was snowing. Her mind foggy with fatigue, she pulled the blankets closer and went back to sleep. The next thing she knew, Mr. Wetherill—she always called him Mr. Wetherill, even when addressing him directly—had returned, asking, "What would you like me to do? Would you like them at your head, or at your feet?" Marietta Wetherill awoke fully to the sight of her husband holding two of the mummies they had dug up. "At the foot, Mr. Wetherill. At the foot of the bed."[39]

Decorated Basketmaker baskets in the collection of the American Museum of Natural History, probably photographed in 1906 as part of George Pepper's "Basket-Maker" exhibit.

THE HARSH WINTER WEATHER, COMBINED WITH LACK OF BROWSE FOR THE ANIMALS and the recovery of relatively few artifacts, caused Richard Wetherill to leave Grand Gulch in late February, earlier than he had planned, and head south across the San Juan. "No grass what ever was found," Wetherill wrote. "The animals subsisted on the grain fed them with the tops of brush which they picked. Before leaving there many were weak and thin."[40]

Wetherill split his party up into three groups, who agreed to meet at Marsh Pass in Arizona a few weeks later. He sent Orian Buck, Charlie Mason, and George Bowles with the strongest of the horses to Mysterious Canyon, some forty miles southwest of Grand Gulch, beyond Navajo Mountain. He and the rest of the party rested in Bluff while they prepared for the next trip.

After a few days, Clayton Wetherill, William Henderson, and Jim Ethridge headed due west for Moqui Canyon, which empties into the Colorado above Hall's Ferry. They were to look for Basketmaker remains in the canyon's large alcoves. They found that McLoyd and others had been there before them, and they unearthed little of interest in the empty Basketmaker cists.

Leaving Marietta with Bob Allan's family in Bluff, Richard and the rest of his group headed along Chinle Wash southwest toward Marsh Pass. On the way, they explored many sites that Wetherill had not seen before, including ones around Agathla Needle near Kayenta and at Moqui Rock. They also returned to Kiet Siel in Tsegi Canyon, which the Wetherills had explored in 1894, this time taking measurements of the imposing ruin and diagramming its floor plan. Unfortunately, the map Wetherill made has since been lost, although his notes survive.

In April, shortly after Richard Wetherill's party explored Kiet Siel, the three groups reunited as planned. Although the quest to Moqui Canyon had turned up little, Buck, Mason, and Bowles had brought many artifacts out of Mysterious Canyon. Sadly, the Wetherill–Grand

Gulch Research Project has so far failed to discover the current whereabouts of these items or the artifacts from Tsegi Canyon.

The men had one last excitement before heading back to the relative quiet of Bluff. Not long after the three small groups met up in Marsh Pass, Whitmore and Bowles, who had been out on a ride, failed to return as expected. The rest of the party began to search the maze of nearby canyons. In the midst of the search, an unidentified Indian approached Richard Wetherill, telling him that the two young men had been captured. The Indian demanded several hundred silver dollars as ransom, threatening dire consequences if the money was not paid quickly.

It must have rankled Wetherill to accede to this demand, but in wild, unfamiliar country he had little choice. The two Easterners could have been held anywhere. He quickly sent one of the men to Bluff to secure the ransom. By the time the rider returned with the cash and Whitmore and Bowles were released, the two had been forced to spend three full days and four cold nights atop Moqui Rock, a large sandstone outcropping near Agathla Needle.

The Wetherill family's Alamo Ranch, photographed in 1891 by Gustaf Nordenskiöld.

BY EARLY MAY, RICHARD AND MARIETTA WETHERILL WERE BACK IN MANCOS. As Richard reported in a letter to T. Mitchell Prudden on May 17:

> This expedition has been a successful one and contains material that I don't believe can ever be found again. We did not succeed in finding any more of the Basket Makers Caves South of the San Juan or about Navajo Mountain. The home of the Pah Utes. But we found a very interesting region for a desert country. Laguna Creek with two fine lakes and a fine Cliff House of 122 rooms [Kiet Siel] which was rich in Relics. . . . On the High mesa East and North of Navajo Mt. are ruins similar to those in Chaco, New Mexico.

In numbers of artifacts and human remains acquired, the Hyde Exploring Expedition was the more productive and important of Richard Wetherill's two trips into Grand Gulch. It confirmed the existence of Basketmaker culture and documented that culture with remarkable thoroughness, considering Wetherill's lack of training. His accomplishment, however, achieved recognition by the professional community only after his untimely death some years later in Chaco Canyon. In the summer of 1912, archaeologist A. V. Kidder and artist S. J. Guernsey began excavations in northern Arizona that unearthed similar Basketmaker materials. Kidder later gave Wetherill full credit for discovering the Basketmakers:

> Apparently the first application of the principle of stratigraphy to Southwestern problems was made by Richard Wetherill, when in the nineties he defined the Basket-Maker culture, and then determined, by discovering its remains below those of cliff-houses, that it represented an earlier chronological period rather than a mere local development.[41]

T. Mitchell Prudden, George H. Pepper, Clayton Wetherill, Mary Wetherill (Clayton's wife), Richard Wetherill, Jr., Richard Wetherill, and Marietta Wetherill at the Wetherill trading post at Chaco Canyon, 1899.

The Whitmore expedition, though it made no comparable discoveries, also produced artifacts of importance, and the written documentation that has survived from it is better than that from the Hyde expedition. It was Richard Wetherill's last trip to the area. Even before heading into Grand Gulch that second time, he had turned his sights south and east to the imposing buildings of Chaco Canyon in northwestern New Mexico. He had led the Palmer family there in the fall of 1895 and explored the canyon thoroughly. It was on their return trip in the early spring of 1896 that he proposed to Marietta Palmer. Later that summer, he excavated in Chaco Canyon at Pueblo Bonito under the direction of George Pepper, a student of F. W. Putnam's.

In 1898, Richard and Marietta moved permanently to Chaco Canyon to continue exploring there. To support themselves, they established a trading post on the west side of Pueblo Bonito. On June 22, 1910, Richard Wetherill was shot to death in Chaco Canyon, apparently by an angry Navajo, Chis-chilling Begay, who was convicted of his murder.

Wetherill's death brought to a close the early phase of Southwestern archaeology, when entrepreneurship counted more than scientific accuracy or accountability in unearthing prehistoric remains. Even before Wetherill's death, Congress had passed laws to protect prehistoric ruins on federally managed public lands and was creating mechanisms to begin protecting those lands. Mesa Verde National Park was established in 1906, the first national park designed specifically to protect historical resources. That same year, the Antiquities Act was passed and signed into law by President Theodore Roosevelt. By then, several groups were urging Congress to create a national park service to oversee and protect the growing numbers of federal parks and monuments. Each park operated as a separate unit until 1916, when the National Parks Act was signed by President Wilson.

The time of such men as Richard Wetherill and Charles McLoyd had passed. Their collections, for better or for worse, were stored away in museums throughout the country—ignored, for the most part, by the scientific community.

A Wetherill–Grand Gulch Research Project reconstruction of the inset 1891 photo of members of the Green Expedition excavating Turkey Pen Ruin.

4/Archaeology in Reverse

A number of years ago, Jesse Nusbaum and I were exploring cliff dwellings on the west side of Mesa Verde. We saw one that was high up on the canyon wall opposite us, and decided to look into it. But it was a terribly hard climb—up a sheer wall and across a narrow ledge, with a long drop below. But we finally made it. With great elation over our discovery and the successful climb, we peered down through an opening in the rocks at the ruin. And right there before our eyes was an upended slab of stone. On it we read these words: "What fools these mortals be. R. Wetherill."

—Alfred V. Kidder

During their autumn hike in 1986, the first partners in the fledgling Wetherill–Grand Gulch Research Project barely dreamt of rediscovering the actual sites the early explorers had dug. Their initial goal was more modest: to photograph Grand Gulch artifacts now stored in museums. They had no idea that the education of the amateur was about to begin.

Fred Blackburn thought that gaining entry to the American Museum of Natural History collections would be relatively simple. After all, in 1983 the museum had granted him access to examine prehistoric trade items that might have come from Mexico and other distant locales—shell beads and macaw feathers, for example, and crook-necked staffs. That limited objective had required only a short research statement and plan. In 1987, Fred decided to write a similar request to photograph the Grand Gulch collection.

Neither Fred nor the other project members realized what such a request meant for the museum staff. Although simple in concept, the plan would require museum personnel, who already shouldered a heavy work load, to spend more time assisting and supervising the project team than museum officials felt could be justified. The museum's short reply disappointed the project partners:

> After having reviewed the research design with members of this department and also our Public Affairs department, it is clear that a more clearly specific project, supported by a more clear-cut proposal will be necessary before we can approve your photographic documentation of the Grand Gulch collection.[1]

Fred Blackburn at Jail House Ruin, Bullet Canyon, 1993.

Now they started over. After some discussion about the project's goals, Bob Powell assisted by writing a new, more focused version of the photographic and archaeological research plan. William Lipe, an interested friend and himself an archaeologist, offered a useful suggestion for the requisite "research objectives": include a plan to review what types of cultural materials were associated with Basketmaker burials and to assess what condition those materials were in.

While the partners awaited an answer to their new and improved request, the Wetherill–Grand Gulch Research Project gathered momentum. Team members began to draw others into the effort, some for specific, short-term help, others for the duration of the project. For example, Ann Hayes's husband, Russell, helped by making available a computer and database software, enabling Fred to sort through the hundreds of museum accession records he had collected on prior visits to the American Museum. Bob Powell and Ann Phillips further refined the database, making it possible for the team to correlate specific artifacts with specific archaeological sites.

In the spring of 1988, the task of coordinating the growing project became too much for Fred, who had returned to college to earn a teaching certificate. Fortunately, Julia Johnson was able to take over as project director, relieving Fred of most of his administrative duties, and the work moved into high gear.

Team members themselves moved into the canyons, embarking on the first of many field trips required to identify and document alcoves. Vaughn Hadenfeldt, an expert mountaineering guide, supplied logistical management and support for many of the trips, which were essential in providing on-site experience for everyone. During these expeditions, team members shared ideas, discussed hypotheses, and found clues that helped them prepare for the museum documentation. Meanwhile, they waited for a decision from the director of the American Museum of Natural History.

In September 1988, seventeen months after the initial submission, the museum finally said yes, granting the team ten working days in the collections in October. Core members of the project quickly turned their efforts toward making the New York trip successful. To maximize their limited museum time, they would have to record and photograph artifacts rapidly, yet without harming them. Team members designed forms on which to record artifacts and photographs, and they rented, bought, or borrowed specialized equipment. Eastman Kodak graciously donated film. When travel and housing arrangements had been finalized, burial assemblage lists compiled from Wetherill's artifact records, and maps of New York gathered, the Southwesterners were ready to tackle the big city.

The primary team consisted of Fred Blackburn, Julia Johnson, Bruce Hucko, Winston Hurst, and Ann Phillips. Janet Ross, director of the Four Corners School of Outdoor Education, accompanied them for part of the trip. As they soon discovered, it is one thing to develop a research plan and quite another to implement it. They formulated final museum work strategies on planes and in taxis, discussions that ended only when the luggage was unloaded and they began to confront the reality of working together in an unfamiliar setting.

Fortunately, they had some help from friends. For most of the New York stay, they enjoyed the gracious hospitality of Linda Asher and Agnes Gund, friends of Julia's and Fred's. Little did the two women suspect what they had signed up for. Linda's large city apartment soon became an office and meeting place, making her almost a guest in her own home. Caught up in the team's energy, Linda soon joined the discussions too, with advice on how to conduct the research and how to survive in New York City. Julia best described the arrival:

> Desert folks are very much an oddity in New York. Winston's red tennis shoes were like neon lights. Fred with his shock of unruly red hair and hiking boots made people wonder where he was headed, or was he just coming? Bruce Hucko, our photographer, had his trunk full of camera equipment. Ann Phillips and I just stood and laughed at the scene.[2]

At the American Museum of Natural History that first morning, the visiting researchers were greeted with an encouraging smile by Anibal Rodríguez.[3] A friend of Fred's, Rodríguez was a strong supporter of avocational research in museums. Years earlier, he had passed his workdays as a potato chip salesman in the Bronx, but his curiosity about the hidden corners of the American Museum led him to volunteer many hours of labor. Over time, he had recovered many "lost" objects while helping the curators. His colleagues referred to these amazing retrievals as "Anibal's treasures." Soon his expertise and extraordinary memory brought him a full-time job in curation. With his detailed knowledge of the collections—down to the locations of specific artifacts—Rodríguez quickly became invaluable to researchers.

On their first day, the visitors strained to keep up with Rodríguez's rapid pace through the labyrinthine corridors of the museum into the deep recesses of the basement. At each stop, Rodríguez pulled out an impressive assortment of keys, unlocking elevators and doors. Excitement and anticipation grew with each opened portal. The last one revealed a small room jammed from floor to ceiling with three rows of locked storage cabinets—the vaults they had waited so long to examine.

Anibal Rodríguez with Basketmaker materials at the American Museum of Natural History, 1993.

Led by Rodríguez, the team worked its way down the narrow, darkened corridor between two of the rows of cabinets, around the end of the central row, and back up the second corridor, even smaller and darker than the first. On their left were collections taken from Chaco Canyon in the late 1890s by Richard Wetherill and George Pepper. On the right were cabinets filled with trays of artifacts collected by McLoyd and Graham and the Wetherills. As Bruce Hucko later noted, "We had to pinch ourselves. At long last within the caverns of a New York City museum, we had found the final resting place of artifacts from the caves of southeastern Utah."

Bruce set up his photographic studio in a space so cramped that it called forth every bit of talent he had. Two work tables already crowded the tiny collections room. Squeezing in one more small table for photography, Bruce filled it with lights, filters, and electric cords, leaving a small preparation area draped with textured felts and wools of varying colors. Then, as soon as he set up his tripod and looked through the lens, he discovered that the museum, far from being an inanimate object, was virtually a quivering life-form. The massive heating-cooling system shook the building as machines inhaled and exhaled for the humans inside. Long exposures suddenly posed a serious challenge. Bruce persevered, and in the end produced a series of artistically pleasing photographs that not only documented the collection but also revealed the beauty of the artifacts.

For everyone, months of planning now began to pay off in efficiency. Fred inventoried the contents of the locked cabinets, transferring artifacts to Winston, who compared their numbers with the accession records and passed them along to Bruce to photograph. Team members had to take constant care with the fragile objects, handling each one gently and wearing white cotton gloves to prevent discoloring the artifacts with the oil from human hands. Their pristine white gloves quickly turned black from a century of accumulated dust.

Fred and Winston carefully examined each artifact, many of them so delicate that a slip or sudden bump could easily damage them. The researchers soon realized that they would need to conserve some of the specimens if the artifacts were to survive. Museum staff had scheduled this collection for conservation but had not yet found time to begin the work. With Rodríguez's help, the project members lined trays with foam cushions and acid-free paper to help preserve items such as baskets and sandals. Over the years, many projectile points had been placed in the wrong drawers. When the researchers discovered the missing items, they returned them to their proper assemblages. Team members were determined to leave the collection in better shape than they found it.

Julia, Ann, and Janet spent their time examining catalogs, photographs, letters, and other papers in the museum's archives, locating and copying the many documents associated with the artifact collection. Once organized, the written archives helped make sense of the material objects and accession records.

Completing the first day's work, on October 3, 1988, Fred wrote in his journal:

> Finding minute writings on the pottery samples, it was nice to see the W of "John" [Wetherill]. It begins to be familiar. Our initial impression is that . . . many of the artifacts need care. The collection is undocumented since [Nels] Nelson [curator in the 1920s]. Our objective at this point is a systematic search and documentation by cabinet and tray to discover artifact locations.

During the ensuing days, Anibal Rodríguez continued to monitor the work carefully, but the project team apparently lived up to his standard for professional behavior. He fully understood the visitors' passion for their work. As team members later learned, Rodríguez had been instrumental in the acceptance of their research proposal. Some museum personnel had remained dubious about the Wetherill–Grand Gulch objectives and worried that letting the amateurs in might set a bad precedent. Rodríguez argued that the museum had much to gain and little to lose from the project's work and volunteered to oversee it. Without his support, the team might never have achieved its goals.

As the group completed their second day of work, the magnitude of their undertaking became overwhelmingly obvious. Their initial goal—to catalog every item, whether it was part of a burial assemblage or not—would take weeks or even months. Quickly they revised their initial plan, deciding instead to seek out and photograph only the artifacts associated with known burials.

The process evolved as they worked. The table closest to the cabinets served as a receiving area where Winston would take each specimen Fred had laid out, record it with a brief description, and match its museum acquisition number with Wetherill's catalog number and description. He then transferred the artifact and its accompanying form to another table, where Bruce would complete the form with a photographic transparency number.

After several days' experience, everyone realized that at best they would have time to gather the pieces of only one or two burial assemblages and photograph them together. In the last hour of the last day they finally allowed themselves the luxury of going back to the cabinets and making up two complete burial assemblages—one that of a young boy, the other that of an elderly man. Bruce respectfully arranged the artifacts into an artful photographic presentation. Everyone watched in awe as the humanity of these two long-dead people unveiled itself.

The child's gifts for the afterlife (see p. 55) had included the finely tanned hide of a mountain sheep, three baskets—one of which contained piñon nuts—and a burial bag made of fiber from the tough stem of *Apocynum androsaemifolium,* variously called dogbane, black hemp, or Indian hemp. The most poignant emblems of a young life lost were a large, unfinished burial bag filled with ground corn meal and a small apocynum bag containing pieces of unworked flint, yellow ochre, and a highly polished piece of horn from a desert bighorn sheep—apparently a Basketmaker child's tool kit.

The old man, when laid to rest, had likely been first wrapped in a turkey feather robe, then placed upon two carefully tanned desert bighorn hides (see p. 93). Close inspection of one hide revealed a scar from an atlatl dart that had entered the rib cage. Someone, perhaps the old Basketmaker himself, had sewn the tear with a thin sinew, nearly hiding the cut. Apocynum fiber had been used to weave a bag large enough to hold the man with his blankets and hides.

He had also worn a necklace made from large olivella shell beads, a portion of abalone shell, a disk of bone from a mountain sheep, and a finely carved tablet of red siltstone. The square tablet featured a fine-lined design highlighted in the center, with a deep line to each of the four corners. Images reflecting the four directions are relatively common in Ancestral Pueblo iconography, and the four directions and the number four are important symbols in historic Pueblo experience as well.[4]

The old man must have worn his necklace often, for the ridges of its ornaments were abraded away, leaving them polished and smooth. Those who buried him had placed a finely woven basket over or near his head. The rest of the original burial assemblage included a ceremonial crooked staff, its wood highly polished from use; a finely woven animal snare, and a bone flute. The flute, unfortunately, had been lost since the collection was cataloged, but someone substituted a similar one to complete the photograph. The wooden staff may have signified that the old man had earlier won some special status in Basketmaker society: both flutes and staffs seem to have held great ceremonial significance for the Basketmakers, and they appear often in rock art panels. At that moment, seeing these objects together again at last, the project team felt a closeness to the Basketmaker people that stunned them into silence.

WHILE BRUCE HUCKO WAS MAKING NEW PHOTOS OF ANCIENT OBJECTS, ANN PHILLIPS, searching the archives, discovered a treasure in old photographs. It seemed that in 1920, when archaeologist Nels C. Nelson was a curator at the American Museum of Natural History, he had organized an expedition into Grand Gulch. Nelson wanted to expand his knowledge of the collections for which he was responsible, and the trip was part of a much larger expedition that took him into Arizona, California, Nevada, and New Mexico. Nelson hired John Wetherill, who by that time was operating a successful trading post in Kayenta, Arizona, to guide his small party through the Gulch.

In the two weeks they spent in Grand Gulch, Nelson's group cataloged eighty sites, noting rock art and other features, mapping locations, and taking photographs. They investigated most of the sites from the Hyde and Whitmore expeditions and several of McLoyd and Graham's 1891 sites. Nelson was not, apparently, attempting to retrace Wetherill's routes but to identify pristine sites for future excavation.

Reviewing Nelson's papers, Ann Phillips was excited to learn that the curator had taken a wealth of photographs in Grand Gulch. The museum's records, however, gave no clues to where they were stored. Recognizing the importance of these historic photographs, Ann worked with Anibal and Fred to rediscover them. Eventually, Anibal found them in a fireproof vault where they had been secured because they were nitrate negatives that could spontaneously burn or explode. Fred was able to identify the Grand Gulch locations of many of the photos. He then convinced the museum that it should make a complete set of prints—the first ever—from Nelson's expedition photos.

Documentation, not artistic photography, had clearly been Nelson's goal. One particularly "good" shot, for example, depicted a Pueblo site framed neatly between the unfocused ears of

Nels C. Nelson photograph of one of his 1920 expedition's camps in a large cave in "Cartier Canyon."

his horse. Many of Nelson's photographs matched sites previously photographed by Richard Wetherill and listed in his catalog, providing a photographic record of the canyon nearly thirty years later.

Poring over records of the collections, Ann Phillips found evidence not only of Nelson's priceless photographs but also of the museum's less illustrious past, when certain collections were broken up and distributed elsewhere. Indeed, some of the Hyde expedition artifacts were missing. Ann searched the archives for hints of their whereabouts and found that some were now at the Museum of the American Indian in New York City. She also discovered why.

In the early 1900s, George Pepper, curator of anthropology at the American Museum of Natural History, was planning to leave the museum for a new institution being established by George Heye, who was amassing an enormous collection of American Indian ethnological and archaeological artifacts. Before leaving his old post, Pepper crated up many of the more interesting Basketmaker and Pueblo artifacts from the McLoyd and Wetherill collections and transferred them, in a roundabout way, to what was to become the Heye Foundation's Museum of the American Indian.[5] With the complicity of Talbot Hyde, who had donated the collections to the American Museum of Natural History, and George Heye, the artifacts left the American Museum and traveled with Pepper to the University of Pennsylvania in January 1909. Although the items had been accessioned into the American Museum and given numbers corresponding to the numbering system in use there, Talbot Hyde apparently still considered them his property.[6]

Pepper received a temporary appointment at the University of Pennsylvania as assistant curator of American archaeology, a position apparently underwritten by George Heye. Later Pepper transferred to the new Museum of the American Indian, Heye Foundation, taking the collection with him. He seems to have been enticed into this arrangement by the opportunity to work for Heye, who wanted to acquire artifacts collected by McLoyd and the Wetherills in order to close some of the gaps in his collection. As Pepper noted in a 1908 letter to G. B. Gordon, curator of the Department of Archaeology at the University of Pennsylvania:

> Mr. Heye is also to be congratulated. He has been working for a definite object. He has worked hard in an endeavor to make a collection that would be of use when the proper time came. Step by step he has increased the usefulness of his material by filling in culture gaps and rounding out the series of tribal artifacts as opportunities were presented.[7]

Pepper's actions, the project team discovered, occasioned one real museum tragedy. In splitting the collection, apparently Pepper or someone under his direction cut in half a beautifully designed, woven cotton blanket that at one time had covered the mummy the Wetherills called Joe Buck. Half is now at the American Museum of Natural History, the other half at the Museum of the American Indian. Seeing firsthand something of the ethics of early museum administrators and curators, project members gained a new appreciation for Richard Wetherill and his efforts at careful documentation.

The project team had already known that some artifacts from Wetherill's and McLoyd's collections resided at the Museum of the American Indian—though they hardly suspected why. Earlier, they had attempted to gain access to the collections, without success. Despite Winston's credentials as an archaeologist and museum curator, neither the project's research intent nor its experience with collections meant much at this museum: "We are seriously concerned with your description of yourselves as 'avocational archaeologists,' which is most often a euphemism for a collector who has not been trained in the discipline."[8]

Considering the checkered history of the beginnings and later management of the Museum of the American Indian, the irony of this response did not pass unnoticed by the project team.[9] Nevertheless, they were disappointed by the rejection. Eventually, however, persistence gave them a small victory. The museum granted the team just two days to document and photograph burial assemblages, an opportunity the group took advantage of during their second week at the American Museum of Natural History. Mary Purdy, curator at the Museum of the American Indian and an avid Southwestern archaeology buff, agreed to shepherd the group through the collections, intervening as Anibal Rodríguez had done at the American Museum.

Although their visit to the Museum of the American Indian was short, team members were able to view many items from Grand Gulch, including baskets, gaming pieces, and the other half of Joe Buck's blanket. Unfortunately, they were able to document very little of the museum's Basketmaker collection. On a later trip, Ann Phillips went through the archives at the Museum of the American Indian and located some valuable papers, including the document that finalized the sale of part of the Wetherill collection to George Heye.[10]

To date, the Wetherill–Grand Gulch project's photographic and written documentation at the Museum of the American Indian has not been completed because of lack of funding. In the meantime, the museum's collections have been transferred to the Smithsonian Institution's new National Museum of the American Indian, to be built on the Mall in Washington, D.C.; the collections are closed for research pending a detailed inventory. As a result, there is much left to be learned about early exploration in southeastern Utah.

Winston Hurst at the American Museum of Natural History, 1988.

DOCUMENTING THE COLLECTIONS AT THE AMERICAN MUSEUM ESTABLISHED THE team's credibility with museum officials and paved the way for future visits. Winston Hurst evaluated their efforts:

> I think we did well, considering the circumstances. . . . We need to keep our own standards impeccably high and beyond reproach because, as I've argued before, we are the little kid on the block, and we'll have to work harder to prove ourselves.[11]

Shortly after the museum visit, David Hurst Thomas, director of the American Museum of Natural History, wrote Fred:

> I regret that we did not have a chance to get together during your brief visit to New York City. . . . I have, however, spoken at length with Mr. Anibal Rodríguez and Ms. Barbara Conklin, both of whom were extraordinarily impressed by the professionalism shown, and thoughtfulness of those involved in the Wetherill–Grand Gulch Project. I have gone over the artifact forms you and your team have filled out. I too am extremely impressed with the careful work that was conducted. It will provide not only a baseline for your continuing research, but will also provide a useful collection management tool here at the American Museum.[12]

Team members were delighted to get such a letter. Their careful planning, hard work, sacrifice, and commitment had paid off, not only in work accomplished but also in recognition from the professional museum world. Exhausted, the five friends flew home—but on the way they could not refrain from making plans for additional canyon expeditions and a trip to Chicago's Field Museum of Natural History.

The media soon learned about the project. Articles appeared in the *Boulder Daily Camera* and Salt Lake City's *Deseret News*, which the Associated Press picked up and republished throughout the Southwest.[13] Project members began to get more requests for speaking engagements and more offers of help from other avocationals and professionals—more of both than they could comfortably handle.

Many people asked, "When will the artifacts be returned to Utah?" Of course, returning the artifacts was an impossibility. Museums, after all, hold on to their collections like a snapping turtle to its prey. Besides, return of the artifacts would require a facility appropriate to maintain them, which did not then exist in southeastern Utah.[14] The Wetherill–Grand Gulch Research Project could, however, return the artifacts symbolically by assembling a collection of photographs, historical documents, and other information in a locally maintained archive.

Earlier, project members had fantasized about holding a Basketmaker symposium in Blanding, Utah, a town near Grand Gulch that is home to the small Edge of the Cedars State Museum. Now they could begin to plan such an event. The project team would not only present its own work but also invite professional archaeologists to share their latest Basketmaker research. Winston Hurst, who at the time was curator at Edge of the Cedars, suggested donating the project's collected papers to the museum, making them readily accessible to scholars and other interested people. The team could even deliver the archive to the museum ceremonially during the symposium. Confidently, they set a date—May 1990—allowing plenty of time, they hoped, to complete museum visits and compile all the documents.

As they soon learned, crowded work schedules became even tighter as the self-imposed deadline loomed near. They also needed more funding in order to host the symposium. Julia Johnson undertook the task of writing a grant proposal to the Utah Endowment for the Humanities. The prospect of funding from the endowment helped the project gain additional support from private donors. Preparing for the symposium and finishing other project tasks soon turned into enormous commitments. All felt the strain of spending less time with their families and greater demands on their money, patience, and good nature as they began to learn what volunteer work really meant.

In the months that followed, Julia wrote several grant proposals, organized the symposium, and worked with Ann Hayes on logistics for the upcoming trip to Chicago. Somehow she and Fred both found time to present papers at Mesa Verde National Park in December 1988, during the one-hundredth-anniversary celebration of the discovery of Cliff Palace. Ann Hayes collaborated with archaeologist Dale Davidson of the Bureau of Land Management on a "Save the Signature" brochure that alerted Grand Gulch visitors to the importance of preserving the historic inscriptions. Ann Phillips took on the massive task of correlating documents with collections, indexing photographs, and organizing the project's accumulated information for the new archive. She also struggled through the hundreds of sheets of artifact forms, matching them to artifact photographs.

Fred continued his effort to document signatures in Grand Gulch, develop a data base to manage the information, and create a map of inscription locations. Bruce, Winston, and Fred worked together relocating the alcoves and ruins originally photographed on glass plates. Bruce undertook to rephotograph the sites with his four-by-five-inch view camera and to prepare a photographic exhibit for the symposium. In the field, assisted by volunteer Owen Severance, Winston worked on the quest to relocate Cave 7, site of the Basketmaker discovery.

D. W. and Marie Ayres, c. 1865.

Mr. and Mrs. Charles Lang, Jr., Los Angeles, 1920s.

Charles Leslie Graham in Albuquerque, 1992.

SOME OF THE MOST SATISFYING WORK PROJECT PARTICIPANTS ACCOMPLISHED WAS research on the family histories of the early explorers. They contacted as many descendants as they could locate, tracking down relatives of D. W. Ayres, Charles Cary Graham, Charles Lang, and Al, Clayton, and Richard Wetherill. They not only turned up invaluable information for the project but also forged some lasting friendships. In return, some of the families got reacquainted with their own histories.

Fred was particularly keen to find out more about D. W. Ayres, a judge and a respected member of Durango society who had accompanied the Green party into Grand Gulch in 1891. Ayres had also worked with Richard Wetherill in Mancos Canyon and helped found the Durango Archaeological and Historical Society.[15] Fred's mother, Sylvia Blackburn, introduced Fred to her friend Kathryn Ayres, a lifelong resident of Durango and a granddaughter of D. W. Ayres.

Together, Fred Blackburn and Kathryn Ayres looked through diaries, bibles, and letters, searching for information about her grandfather's life. Because Fred was attempting to identify all the people in the photographs taken on Grand Gulch expeditions, he hoped to find a photograph of the judge. Though they discovered letters, Ayres's signature, and his birth and marriage dates, for a long time they failed to turn up even one photograph. Eventually Kathryn Ayres located a photograph of her grandfather and his wife taken shortly after their marriage in 1864. Fred found a second one in the glass-plate print collections at the Field Museum in Chicago.

Studying the photograph found in Chicago, Kathryn Ayres recognized a mandolin that had been in her father's home. Comparing details in the two photos, she and Fred then realized that D. W. Ayres had been "watching" the two of them the entire time from the living room wall.

Among numerous old paintings was a portrait of a distinguished, balding man who resembled the figure in both photographs. It was signed "D. W. Ayres 1892" and appeared to be a self-portrait. In the early 1890s, Ayres had taken ill and spent many days convalescing, during which time he apparently painted his own likeness.

Historical research often brings wonderful surprises. In 1976, Helen Sloan Daniels, a Durango resident who had worked with Earl Morris on nearby excavations in the late 1930s, published the diary of Charles Cary Graham. Reading Daniels's preface to the diary, Ann Hayes noticed the following: "I was acquainted with Mr. Graham and his daughter Agnes, now Mrs. Frank E. Schalles of Albuquerque. After her father's death she found his penciled diary and . . . knowing my interests, gave me a copy."[16]

Ann thought the original diary might still exist and attempted to contact Mrs. Schalles. She learned that although Mrs. Schalles had died, her brother, Charles Leslie Graham, still lived in Albuquerque. She tracked down his phone number and passed it on to Fred, who soon called the old gentleman—a little nervously. Graham turned out to be extremely gracious and willing to share what he knew. He mentioned that he had albums of family photographs and that his son, Charles S. Graham, kept the original of Charles Cary Graham's diary in Houston. Fred immediately called the grandson, who generously made a photocopy and sent it along.

Bruce Hucko interviewed Charles Leslie Graham and copied photos of his father and other members of the family. Then Bruce asked to take a portrait of Charles Leslie. He snapped the shutter on what was to be the last portrait of the son of Charles Cary Graham. Charles Leslie Graham died a few months later.

As team members discovered, searching out family members in mobile America can be exacting. And once found, not everyone is eager to share family history. At first, no trace could be discovered of Charles B. Lang's whereabouts after he left Bluff, Utah, in 1905. Then Winston found a brief note in some papers of Kumen Jones, a former resident of Bluff, indicating that Jones and his wife had made a visit to Los Angeles in 1932 and stopped off to see their "good friend" Charlie Lang.

Armed with this information, Winston contacted Gary Shumway, a history professor at California State University at Fullerton and a former resident of San Juan County, Utah. Shumway suggested contacting Donald Ray, an investigative reporter who was teaching a journalism class for the University of California at Los Angeles. For her class project, Sandy Zimmerman, a student in the class, volunteered to trace the family history of Charles Lang and attempt to find any living relatives. She soon discovered that Charles Lang, Jr., the son of Charles B. Lang, still resided in Los Angeles.

Charles Lang, Jr., born in Bluff in 1902, is a distinguished cinematographer with many important motion pictures to his credit. He won an Academy Award in 1933 for *A Farewell to Arms,* was nominated for sixteen other films, and continued to make movies until the early 1970s, when he filmed *Bob and Carol and Ted and Alice* and *The Love Machine.* Sandy Zimmerman attempted to contact Mr. Lang numerous times but had little success in ferreting out details about his father. Lang, initially reluctant, soon refused to talk at all, contending that he had no portraits and or other information about his family.

Finding this hard to believe, Fred tried to contact Lang on his own. The group had learned early on that "nothing" seldom meant that no information existed, but rather signaled that family members were suspicious of the Wetherill–Grand Gulch project. Fred, too, met a blank wall. Charles Lang, Jr., insisted that he had nothing to share about his father; during one of Fred's calls he even hung up, saying that he wished no further involvement with the Wetherill–Grand Gulch Research Project or anyone who was part of it.

Realizing that he had to establish a foundation of trust, Fred continued to inform Mr. Lang of new discoveries regarding his father and periodically called him for brief, one-way offerings of information. Fred studiously avoided asking Lang anything about his family. As a member of the San Juan County Historic Commission, Winston Hurst sent Lang a letter explaining the importance of his father's contribution to early Utah archaeology. In 1992, four years after the first of Fred's phone encounters, Fred's and Winston's persistent efforts finally paid off. Charles Lang, Jr., granted them a one-hour, face-to-face interview.

In mid-March, the two colleagues lifted off from the Durango airport into a crystal blue sky, only to land in a smoke-laden Los Angeles under National Guard watch.[17] They had arrived just after the riots that followed the acquittals of the Los Angeles Police Department officers accused of beating Rodney King. As they worked their way through traffic in the neighborhood where Lang lived, helicopter gunships flew overhead. Sirens screamed. For two men accustomed to the relative quiet of canyon country, it was as if they had alighted on some huge movie set.

Shortly after 5:00 P.M. they pulled in at Lang's house and were greeted at the door by a tall, handsome man whose features, speech, and bearing belied his ninety years. For the interview he led them to a narrow study furnished with antique furniture and mementos of a long and productive career.

Charles Lang, Jr., they learned, was aware of his father's archaeological quests in Utah. He sketched out his father's life and recounted stories of his days in Utah. When his family reached Los Angeles in about 1906, his father had joined the movie industry as a film cutter. At the age of fifty-five the elder Lang contracted polio, and Charles, Jr., left law school to help the family. The event propelled him into a career in cinematography. In addition to telling family stories, Lang brought out his photograph album, which held pictures of his parents in Bluff. Most generously, Mr. Lang allowed Fred and Winston to photograph the album. Precisely one hour into the interview, the meeting ended.

Sandy Zimmerman later helped Fred and Winston find the graves of Charles Lang, Sr., and his wife, Gertrude, in Forest Lawn cemetery. It was a particularly poignant time, because funerals were being held for some of the dead from the riots. But after years of frustrating search, the two had at last trailed Charles Lang west from Allen Canyon, Utah, to his final resting place.

Research into family histories led not only to some surprising successes but also to enduring friendships. In 1988, Fred discovered that Tom Wetherill, the grandson of Al Wetherill, lived in Farmington, New Mexico. Fred thought Tom might be willing to share information about the Wetherill family. For some time, project members had wondered where the records of the Wetherills' Alamo Ranch might reside. They were particularly interested in finding the ledger in which Benjamin Kite Wetherill recorded ranch activities, hoping that it and family letters would help them trace some of the ranch's many visitors. Fred and his wife, Victoria Atkins, invited Tom, his wife, Wren, and their daughter, Samantha, to Fred and Victoria's home in Cortez, Colorado, to discuss the project. Their visit began a lasting friendship.

Because Tom was at first unsure how legitimate the project might be—and leery because of earlier attempts to profit from the Wetherill name—he brought only a few pictures, but he also brought the Alamo Ranch ledger. As it turned out, Tom owned not only the ledger but also most of the rest of the family's memorabilia. During his youth, he had lived with Al Wetherill, and he had inherited the mementos when Al died.[18] Impressed by the project team's dedication to gathering the Wetherill family history, Tom gave the project full access to the family archives. Learning that it was Wren's birthday, Victoria baked a birthday cake for dessert.

Tom cherished fond memories of his grandfather. Seeing this, Fred encouraged him to present a paper at the 1988 Wetherill Symposium at Mesa Verde National Park, which was being organized to reassess the role of the Wetherills at Mesa Verde and elsewhere in the Southwest. Although he is a very private person, Tom read a moving essay entitled "A Personal Assessment of the Wetherills."

Tom Wetherill at the Alamo Ranch, 1993.

After the symposium, the project team planned a weekend to review the archives at Tom and Wren's home. Julia, Ann Phillips, Fred, and Victoria descended on Farmington in search of missing pieces of the Wetherill story. Among the papers they discovered the only register listing early visitors to Mesa Verde; it contained signatures of many characters whose inscriptions the researchers had been documenting in the canyons. The handwriting of Al Wetherill, John Wetherill, Charles Lang, D. W. Ayres, Gustaf Nordenskiöld, James Ethridge, Harry French, Talbot Hyde, H. Jay Smith, and many others stared boldly at them from the yellowing pages.

They also found correspondence that filled in gaps in the archives at the American Museum of Natural History, personal letters between John and Al Wetherill explaining the Basketmaker discovery, and a worn and creased map of the Four Corners, dated 1893 and marked by Al Wetherill with trails and notes.[19] Day quickly turned to night before they finished leafing through Tom Wetherill's paper treasure.

All too quickly, it seemed, the day arrived to catch the train for Chicago and the Field Museum of Natural History—January 6, 1990. At the Field Museum, the team would see the collections made in 1890–91 by McLoyd and Graham, which were later purchased by the Reverend C. H. Green and then resold to the museum, and the 1894 collection made by Charles Lang. The team's research goals were clear, its questions confident. Thorough preparation, recent discoveries, and solid experience at the American Museum of Natural History had transformed a group of naive enthusiasts into a collections SWAT team.

Fred and Winston met in Monticello, Utah, on a warm winter morning and drove to the whistle stop at Thompson, Utah, where they boarded the train. As the pace of life seemed to slow—trains have that effect—the two settled in to share ideas and reflect on the project's progress. Late that evening, Julia, Bruce, and the two Anns joined them at Denver's Union Station. They quickly caught up on Fred's and Winston's latest findings and theories and pitched right in with their own. Unable to sleep for excitement, the entire team worked late into the night as the train rocked its way across Kansas and Nebraska. Outside, clusters of street lights appeared and faded quickly from sight as the train passed one small farm town after another.

They could not help thinking back to Richard Wetherill's own train trip to Chicago and the time he spent shepherding his collection at the World's Columbian Exposition of 1893. It must have been a special time for him in many ways. Not only was Chicago a vigorous city with a way of life vastly different from that of the ranch back in Mancos, but the exposition was also a treasure trove of American Indian archaeological and ethnological artifacts. It contributed many of the initial collections that today make the Field Museum such a crucial source of information about American Indian life. Now, nearly one hundred years later, the six researchers were headed for the same setting in which Richard Wetherill made his proposal to the Hyde brothers.

The team had less than a week to document and photograph the collection, and they had to abide by museum rules that forbade them to work through lunch hours—something they had been able to do at the American Museum of Natural History. In addition, the Field Museum's cooling and heating system shook the structure even more violently than anything they had experienced in New York. But they were happy to discover that the collections of Charles Lang and C. H. Green had recently been well curated. Dry materials lay on acid-free papers and cushioning foam. The curatorial area was separated by floor levels with metal plankway grating, which made it possible to see collections above and below each level. All items were easy to find, and the curators knew where both collections and individual items were located. With assistance from museum staff members Christine Gross, William Grew Mullins, and Janice Klein, the project team was able to move quickly.

Prior to the trip, Ann Phillips had worked long hours to assemble lists of the articles in the Green catalog that had been found together in burials. Green's pamphlet, like most others of the time, grouped similar objects together—pottery, baskets, ornaments, and so forth—rather than listing them as burial assemblages. Because of this practice, without Ann's lists the task of reassembling associated objects would have been an organizational nightmare.

Once again, project members found that artifacts had gone missing from an early museum collection. Especially frustrating was the loss of over one hundred projectile points McLoyd and Graham had found at a single Grand Gulch site. In 1906, the museum apparently gave the points to T. R. Roddy, a trader who owned a store dealing in Indian curios across the street from the Field Museum, as part of an exchange. Museum records indicate that Roddy periodically traded items with the museum. In any case, the points are no longer part of the Green collection and appear to be permanently lost. That Graham and McLoyd discovered so many points within two or three days of searching at one site meant something extraordinary must have happened there in prehistoric times. Winston had hoped that the artifacts would provide important clues to at least one prehistoric conflict and the people who participated in it.

Fred's searches in the photographic collection at the Field Museum helped confirm the route of the June 1891 Green Expedition in Grand Gulch. But first he learned a useful lesson about the reliability of historical archives.

Looking through a worn album of photographs of the Southwest, he noticed a shot that was unmistakably of Perfect Kiva Ruin in Graham Canyon. Yet the caption read, "Cliff Dwellings Canyon de Chelly." A photograph of Jail House Ruin in Grand Gulch was also labeled "Cliff Dwelling Canyon De Chelly," and a pictograph panel in Grand Gulch called Quail Panel was labeled "Mesa Verde Pictographs." These things happen. Photographs might not be labeled until years after a collection is donated, and then by someone who has never visited the place where the pictures were taken. A researcher must be extremely careful to verify the identity of each historic photograph, never fully trusting what is written in collection inventories and indexes.

Inspecting the photograph of Perfect Kiva closely, Fred noted that the alcove's wall carried some sort of inscription, but it was not the one he was used to seeing—Harry French's signature from the Hyde expedition, dated January 8, 1894. French's signature was evident, for example, in a later 1894 photograph of Perfect Kiva in the Hyde expedition archives at the American Museum of Natural History. Using a magnifying lens, Fred was able to make out two names on the wall not visible in the 1894 images: H. R. Ricker and Henry Knowles. French's signature was not yet there.

Fred was so intrigued by his discovery that he nearly missed the nine other photographs accompanying the one of Perfect Kiva. With excitement, Fred realized he was probably viewing photos taken during the Green Expedition to Grand Gulch, which would make them the earliest known photographs of Grand Gulch sites. He later learned that Ricker had owned a candy store in Durango and probably accompanied C. H. Green to Grand Gulch in June 1891. Henry Knowles, a local cowboy, may have been part of the group, too, but because he tended cattle in the area, he could easily have written his name there at a different time. Fred's examination of records at the First National Bank of Durango revealed the photographer to be F. E. Leeka, who was also listed in a newspaper article as accompanying the Green Expedition.

The project team later used copies of these photographs on field visits into the Gulch to identify the Green Expedition campsites. Not surprisingly, they turned out to be some of the same locations mentioned in Charles Cary Graham's diary of his and McLoyd's 1891 explorations. Green, apparently, was intentionally revisiting and photographing sites from which the artifacts in his collection had been taken. His photographic plate numbers neatly match the numbers assigned to the sites in his catalog.

The mystery of the seeming disappearance of Ricker's and Knowles's inscriptions from the 1894 photographs was solved later, when Fred examined the print from the Hyde expedition

Perfect Kiva today and (inset) in 1891, photographed by F. E. Leeka of the Green Expedition.

more closely. The two names had been painted out so they would not show up in the print. Perhaps Richard Wetherill wished to imply that the site was pristine when he dug there.

For Bruce Hucko, photography at the Field Museum posed a new challenge. Not only did he have to contend with vibrations from the ventilation system, but he also had to shoot many artifacts through the glass of antique display cases in the public halls—cases that had been permanently sealed and could not be opened. Only by using extreme ingenuity could he avoid getting distracting reflections from the glass.

After five days of frenzied effort, the group left Chicago in the evening, worn out but happy. Everyone struggled for comfort in the hot, enclosed train. Somehow the trip back seemed twice as long as the journey to Chicago. But they were on the final stretch now, both literally and figuratively. They had only four months left to complete their preparations for the May symposium. Bruce, Julia, and the two Anns disembarked in Denver. Six hours later, the wide open spaces of southeastern Utah welcomed Fred and Winston home.

IF PLANNING FOR THE BASKETMAKER SYMPOSIUM NOW BECKONED URGENTLY, SO did hypotheses the Wetherill–Grand Gulch crew had developed concerning the routes of McLoyd and Graham. They could hardly wait to get back into the Gulch.

More than ever they had to function as a team. While some members prepared for a trip into the canyons, Julia took on planning, coordinating, and grant writing for the symposium. Throughout the winter of 1989–90 she seemed to spend most of her time on the telephone, checking and rechecking details of the event. May 1990 was approaching faster than anyone dreamed possible.

In April, Fred led a group of project members, with several new volunteers, back into Grand Gulch. Armed with copies of historic photographs, journals, and expedition notes, they aimed to seek out campsites and archaeological sites they had tentatively identified during their documentary research. Starting down an unnamed canyon, they first tackled a site Fred had never visited before but which he believed must be there if he was reading Graham's diary correctly. The diary reported a small, unnamed canyon that came in from the east in the central portion of Grand Gulch. Finding the ruin there would confirm Fred's hypothesis about McLoyd and Graham's cave numbering system.

Climbing through a brush tangle and up loose, boulder-filled debris, the group at last spotted the site they were looking for. There above them, perched on a ledge at the entrance to a small alcove, stood a sandstone wall about ten feet high and several feet thick. Impressed by its size, a member of the group named this Pueblo III structure the Great Wall Site. To reach it meant climbing a steep incline of loose talus that covered the slope in front of the group. Vaughn Hadenfeldt, who could always be counted on to reach the unreachable, climbed easily to the site and then lowered a belay line so the others could follow.

They all quickly saw that they were not the first to sit at the top of the slope. A log jammed below the doorway of the ancient structure showed grooves from a rope no longer there. On the rock face above the climbers was a clear charcoal inscription: "McLoyd and Graham January 1891." Apparently the grooves in the log had been created by a rope sliding over the surface as the men lowered themselves out of the ruin. Fred had truly learned to interpret the subtle clues of Graham's terse diary.

Leaving the Great Wall Site, the documenters turned their attention to an alcove that appeared in one of the photographs from the Field Museum, which they thought might have been taken during the Green Expedition in 1891. Ironically, it was also the alcove where the Wetherill–Grand Gulch Research Project had first taken form. This time, nearly four years of experience in looking at canyon inscriptions, combined with close study of diaries, letters, and catalogs, paid off immediately. The team found that the wall they had slept under in November 1986 displayed not only hundreds of prehistoric paintings but also the signatures of some very familiar characters from archaeological history. First someone spied the name Green inscribed in bullet lead, tucked in among the brightly painted rock art designs. In short order the group also sighted the names of Charles McLoyd, D. W. Ayres, and the Wetherills. The signatures, especially Green's, confirmed one of the most important deductions the team had made in Chicago—that the unlabeled historic photographs at the Field Museum were indeed from the 1891 Green Expedition.

The research trip into the Gulch bolstered the group's confidence on the eve of the symposium, but it also consumed precious time. The push to complete everything on deadline now went into overdrive. Ann Phillips spent eighteen-hour days compiling the archive of papers, photographs, and documents that was soon to fill ten milk crates. Ann Hayes pitched in wherever the need was greatest, and Bruce Hucko hurried to put the finishing touches on his photographic exhibit.

Members of the Wetherill–Grand Gulch Research Project documenting signatures at the Great Wall Site.

Photo taken in 1891 by F. E. Leeka of Quail Panel in Step Canyon, where members of the Green Expedition inscribed their names.

All along, one of the team's central goals in planning the symposium had been symbolically to return to Grand Gulch the documentary collection they had compiled. They would do so by formally conveying the documents to Edge of the Cedars State Museum, the museum nearest the Gulch. It had the facilities to care for the collection, which in turn would augment the museum's value to the community. But just a few weeks before the symposium, park manager Steve Olsen notified Julia that he lacked the authority to accept the collection. He would have to ask permission from his superiors, and, as he explained it, there was simply too little time to do the necessary paperwork.

Project members were dumbfounded. After all the hurdles they had surmounted, here was bureaucracy at its worst. Julia, however, knew how to handle the situation. She approached it head on, making a few well-placed phone calls to Utah state officials. The problem quickly vanished, and preparations continued unabated.

As the day approached, Julia and the others began to wonder where everyone would sleep during the two-day symposium. Blanding, Utah, after all, is a very small town. When the weekend finally arrived, five hundred people showed up at the town's high school, most of them avocational historians, archaeologists, and canyon hikers with a deep personal commitment to Grand Gulch. Miraculously, they all managed to find accommodation nearby. The people of Blanding pitched in to provide breakfasts, lunches, and snacks for the multitude. At times it seemed as if the entire population of Blanding had turned volunteer.

It was an emotional and rewarding time for the Wetherill–Grand Gulch team. The crowd's enthusiasm for knowledge about the Basketmakers was astounding. Suddenly the countless hours and the high price seemed well worthwhile. The audience sat through two days of papers in which project members and professional archaeologists announced the fruits of their research. At the end, team members walked onto the stage of the Blanding High School auditorium with the tangible evidence of four years of research. Catalogs, letters, diaries, maps, and photographs seemed to fill the space. The crowd stood and applauded.

James Parker, Utah state director for the federal Bureau of Land Management, presented the project crew with the agency's highest award for a volunteer group:

> We are pleased to present to your Wetherill–Grand Gulch Research Project participants the Bureau of Land Management (BLM) national award for exemplary voluntary service contribution to conservation and management of cultural resources of the nation's public lands.

Julia Johnson later received a second honor for her work in organizing and administering the symposium:

> The Utah Humanities Council presents a 1991 Award of Merit to Julia M. Johnson in recognition of the exemplary quality of the project "Basketmaker: Grand Gulch, Past, Present, Future" and its contribution to public humanities programs in Utah.

With the Basketmaker symposium and the presentation of the archives to the museum, the Wetherill–Grand Gulch Research Project was officially over. Yet the group still had a few loose ends to tie up. First, the location of Richard Wetherill's Cave 7, site of the Basketmaker discovery, was still to be discovered, as was the trail into the Gulch that McLoyd and Graham had engineered. Second, each of the fifteen symposium participants had prepared a paper, but what was to be done with them?

Immediately after the conference, participants met to decide how to publish the papers. The BLM graciously offered to fund a symposium volume. The group persuaded Victoria Atkins, who is a BLM archaeologist in Colorado, to serve as editor. Volunteerism had not ended along with the symposium. Kathy Hurst, Winston's wife, offered to copyedit the volume, and Lisa McClanahan of Salt Lake City volunteered to format the chapters and design the book. Many others chipped in with time, effort, and money to see the book into print. It appeared in November 1993 under the title *Anasazi Basketmaker: Papers from the 1990 Wetherill–Grand Gulch Symposium.*

Finally, there was the matter of a possible exhibition based on the symposium. The Utah Museum of Natural History was interested in hosting an exhibit on the Basketmakers that would feature artifacts from Grand Gulch, historic papers and photographs, and material on historic preservation. The exhibit at the Utah Museum of Natural History, designed and implemented under Winston Hurst's guidance, opened in 1996 as the museum's contribution to Utah's statehood centennial celebration.

Left to right: Ann Phillips, Julia Johnson, and Ann Hayes with Johnson's 1991 Award of Merit from the Utah Humanities Council.

The Wetherill–Grand Gulch Research Project inscription documentation team near Step Canyon, 1990. Front row, left to right: La Plata, Wally Mauck, Bob Powell, Ann Hayes, Ken Evans, Ann Phillips; back row, left to right: Bill Harris, Kim Hurst, Fred Blackburn, Vaughn Hadenfeldt, Winston Hurst, Ken Douthett, Marge Quist, Maddy Goldhawk, Tom Goldhawk.

ALTHOUGH THE WETHERILL–GRAND GULCH RESEARCH PROJECT HAS RUN ITS course, its spirit of inquiry lives on. Some members of the project team continue to seek pieces to historical puzzles still unresolved. New leads come in as people around the country learn about the project's achievements.

For example, in October 1993, Karen Dohm of the Smithsonian Institution's National Museum of Natural History contacted Fred about a mummy that had recently been donated to the museum. It had initially been part of a collection given to Westtown College in 1896 by William C. Allen. Allen had made a complete provenience record of the fifty-six artifacts he collected but had lost his documentation in an exotic variation of "the dog ate my homework." His letter noted: "My original list was much more satisfactory. . . . But the burros got into camp the day before we started for civilization and got away with the list—so this one is the list from recollection."[20]

Allen's list of sites included Fortified House, She House, and Turkey Track House in Acowitz (Lion) Canyon, a tributary of Mancos Canyon on the Ute Mountain Ute Reservation. His artifacts were items such as corn cobs, handprints in jacal, metates, jar rings, and pottery that could easily have been collected from piles of dirt that other excavators had left behind. The mummy, which according to the catalog was a "man [of] fine preservation," was, Karen Dohm suspected, not from near Mancos Canyon at all. To her, it looked like a Basketmaker mummy, a surmise she confirmed by having a small portion of the mummy's covering radiocarbon dated. The result, about A.D. 226, placed the man's life squarely within the late Basketmaker II period.[21] Considering the mummy's association with the Mancos Canyon artifacts, it is entirely possible that it was sold or given to William Allen by the Wetherills. Allen had, indeed, signed the Alamo Ranch register in 1896.

Two months later, an article by David Roberts in *Smithsonian* magazine, marking the centennial of Richard Wetherill's discovery of the Basketmakers, opened new sources of information.[22] Upon reading the article, Jonathan Batkin, director of the Wheelwright Museum of the American Indian in Santa Fe, New Mexico, told Bruce Hucko and Fred about a collection of Ancestral Pueblo pottery and other artifacts he had seen at the Taylor Museum in Colorado Springs when he had directed that museum. As he remembered it, the collection was called the Bixby-Lang collection, but it had no accompanying documentation, and Batkin had not known who Charles Lang was until he read the *Smithsonian* article.

This news helped resolve a mystery that had arisen during the project team's 1990 visit to the Field Museum in Chicago, when Ann Phillips discovered a copy of a catalog describing a collection gathered by Charles B. Lang. At the top of the catalog, Paul S. Martin, former curator of archaeology at the museum, had written, "I have not been able to find any of the articles on this list. If the museum ever received these things, they are not catalogued and have not turned up yet."[23]

Project members had dubbed this the "Lang Mystery Collection." Except for the catalog, it had altogether disappeared. Fred strongly suspected that the Lang Mystery Collection and the collection at the Taylor Museum were one and the same, and he quickly arranged a visit to the museum. With help from Cathy Wright, Taylor Museum director, Fred determined that the Bixby-Lang collection had been donated to Colorado College at the turn of the century by General William J. Palmer, who had purchased it from Lang in Salt Lake City. In the 1970s, the collection was transferred to the Taylor Museum, but the catalog was lost in the transfer, so the collection had no provenience information.

Luckily, Ginny Keifer, acting curator of the Tutt Library at Colorado College, was able to track down the missing catalog in the library collection. Although the catalog, typed on a different typewriter, was minus a page, and the artifacts were listed in a different order from the way they appeared in the Field Museum's copy, this clearly was the right catalog. Moreover, it contained handwritten marginal notes proving that the artifacts had come from sites in southeastern Utah. Although they were all ancient Pueblo rather than Basketmaker finds, the artifacts answered one more riddle—the whereabouts of one of Lang's missing collections.

Reuniting Lang's artifacts with their places of origin gave Fred and the rest of the now "unofficial" Wetherill–Grand Gulch team a well-earned sense of satisfaction. Thanks to their efforts and the spirited help of hundreds of people like them, new riches of information would be available as archaeologists continued to explore Basketmaker culture and pioneering archaeological work in the Four Corners.

Ancestral Pueblo granaries, Grand Gulch.

The Art and Artifacts of Grand Gulch

Reassembled burial goods from an elderly man's grave in Grand Gulch, excavated by McLoyd, Graham, and the Patrick brothers, c. 1892, including a yellow stone disk with a central perforation, a string of olivella shell beads, several baskets, sacks, sticks, and flutes.

String bag from Grand Gulch, part of the 1892–93 Koontz collection.

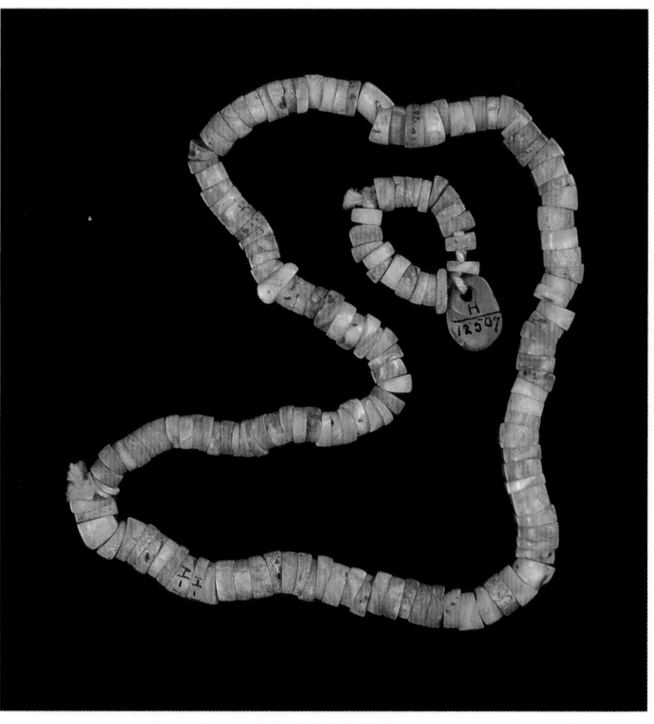

String of Spondylus (spiny oyster) beads and a small string with a turquoise pendant, from the McLoyd/Graham/Koontz collection in the American Museum of Natural History.

Cornmeal was found in this unfinished apocynum fiber bag by the Hyde Exploring Expedition in 1893–94 near Burial Cave 1 in Bullet Canyon.

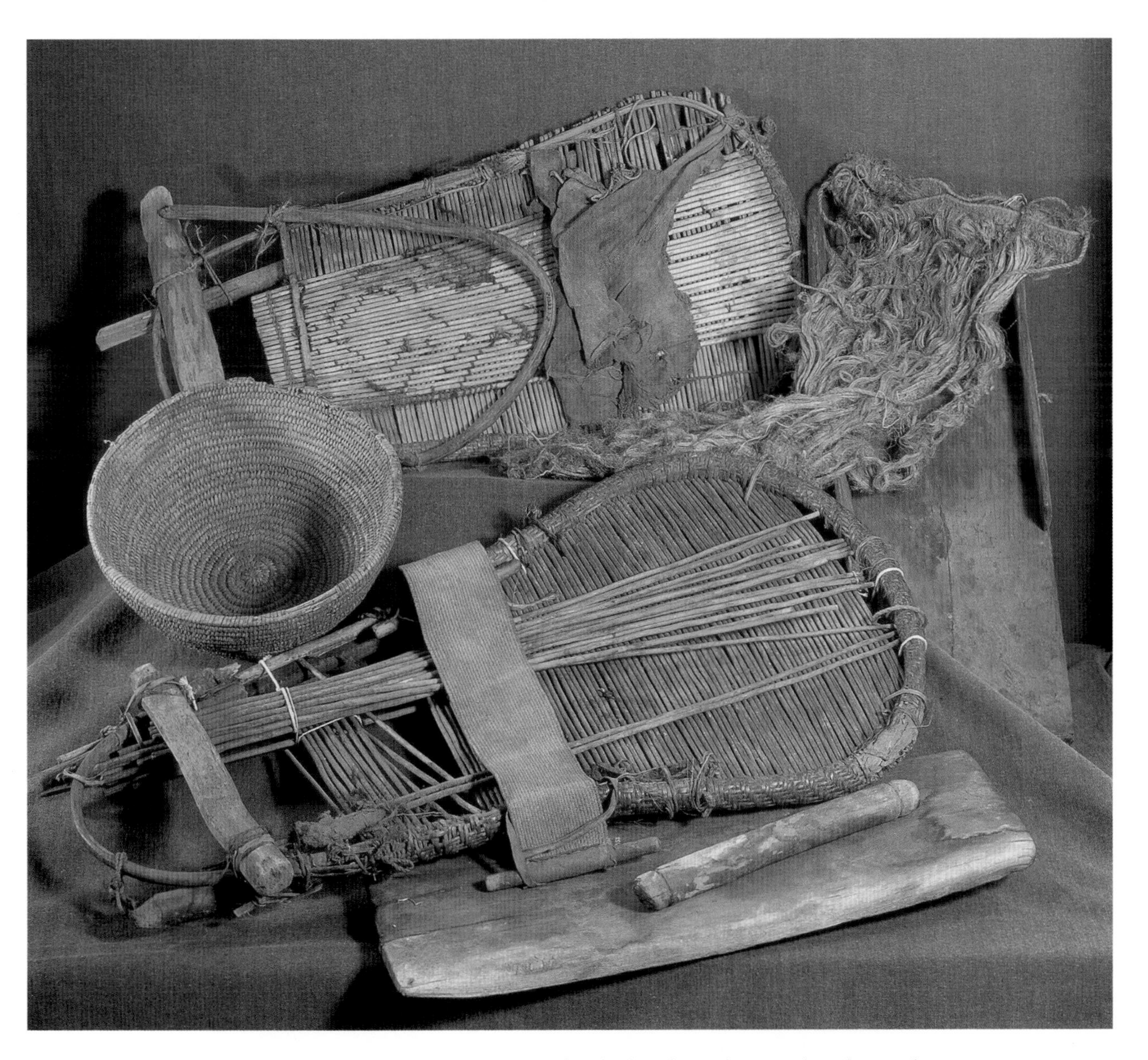

Cradle boards, basket, and associated items found in burial caves by McLoyd, Graham, and Green during their 1890 and 1891 expeditions in Bullet Canyon, now in the C. H. Green collection of the Field Museum of Natural History.

Detail of Basketmaker cradle board.

Woven sandals of yucca and apocynum fiber from the McLoyd/Graham/Koontz collection in the American Museum of Natural History. The heels on two of the sandals are worn through; the third, with red and natural yucca-fiber toe fringe, is perfectly preserved and has never been worn. The child's sandal at right has a leather toe ring.

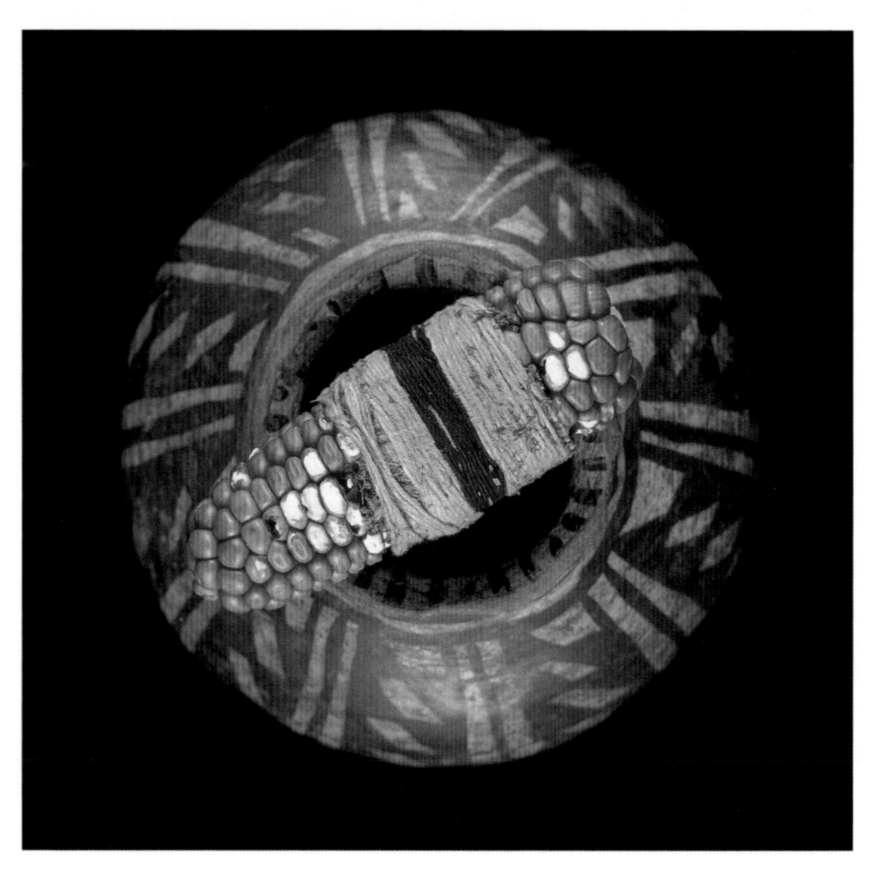

Ear of golden corn wrapped with black and white twine over bluebird feathers rests on a Mesa Verde Black-on-white kiva jar. Excavated by Charlie Mason in Cave 2, Grand Gulch, during the 1897 Whitmore Exploring Expedition.

Yucca-fiber basket woven from a single yucca plant. Found in Cave 26 by the Hyde Exploring Expedition in 1894, the basket was filled with red and yellow corn kernels and surrounded by ears of blue corn.

Blue macaw and bluebird feathers bound to yucca-fiber twined strings, found in Cave 31, Allen Canyon, by the 1894 Hyde Exploring Expedition.

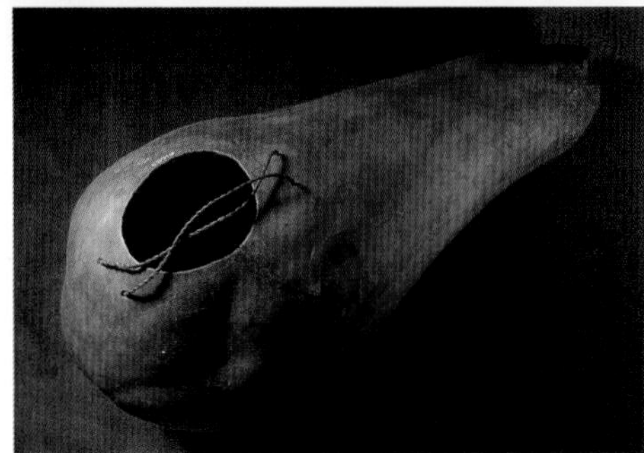

Large gourd container with cordage handles, used to carry water.

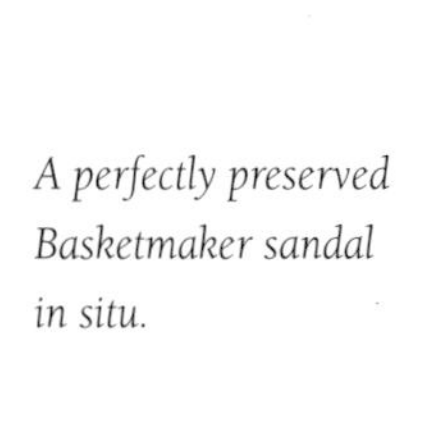

A perfectly preserved Basketmaker sandal in situ.

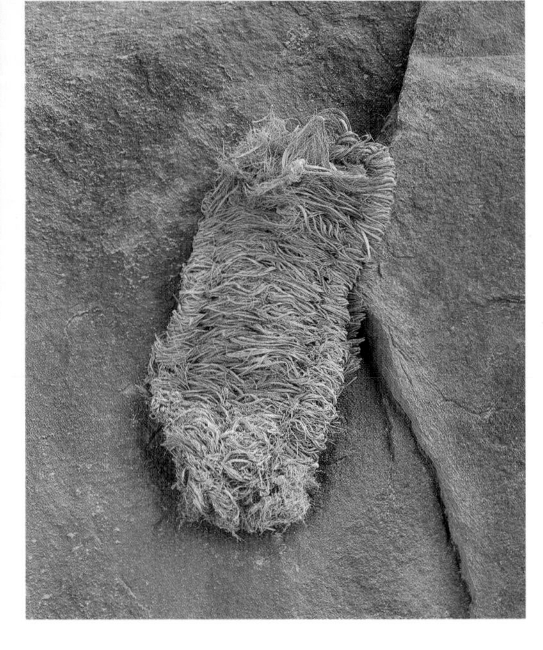

The Basketmaker-era Big Men Panel, Grand Gulch.

Basketmaker handprints at Polly's Island, Grand Gulch.

Moon Kiva, Cedar Mesa.

Detail of the Big Panel, Grand Gulch.

Bighorn Sheep Panel at Indian Creek, southeastern Utah.

Kokopelli figure and Basketmaker granary, Grand Gulch.

5/Rediscovering Cave 7

Ninety-seven skeletons were taken from this cave. Many of the men showed evidences of having been killed, as spearpoints were found between the ribs and arrowpoints in the backbones. One case where the hip bones were pinned together with a huge obsidian spearpoint shows that no small amount of force was used to bury a point of that size into two inches of bone.

—Richard Wetherill, 1896

Two riddles still had the Wetherill–Grand Gulch team stumped at the time of the Basketmaker symposium in May 1990. The more important, and the more difficult to solve, was the whereabouts of Cave 7, the site that had enabled Richard Wetherill to proclaim the discovery of the Basketmakers. The other was the location of the trail Charles McLoyd and Charles Cary Graham had built with logs and stone to get their horses into Graham Canyon. Even after the symposium, team members could scarcely rest until they scratched these last two itches.

The quest for Cave 7 had, indeed, begun many years earlier. Archaeologist Jesse Nusbaum, superintendent of Mesa Verde National Park for most of the years between 1921 and 1946, was among the first to try solving the puzzle. Nusbaum correctly deduced that Wetherill's Hyde Exploring Expedition of 1893–94 had dug ten alcoves before entering Grand Gulch. Mistakenly, he thought these sites were all in Butler Wash. He also missed the mark in identifying Cave 7. As Nusbaum wrote in 1950:

> In the prodigious cave site in the tilted east face of Comb Ridge, inscribed as "HEE No. 10" (Hyde Exploring Expedition Cave Site 10) . . . they [the Hyde expedition] completely looted the Southwest's largest known Basket Maker II cave site in nine days; December 23, 1893–January 2, 1894. In all, 90 burials, mostly mummified, were found, covered with baskets and with other accompaniments. It was here that Richard Wetherill recognized that the skulls of those buried with baskets were not deformed like the cliff dweller skulls; and that this culture underlay the later cliff dwellings. Due to the prevalence of baskets with these burials, he named them Basket Makers.[1]

"A small house 200 yards south of house number 7" in Cottonwood-Whiskers Wash, described by Richard Wetherill in 1893.

Nusbaum was probably misled in part by a 1947 letter from Harry French, who by then was the last surviving member of the Hyde Exploring Expedition. Nusbaum had written to French requesting information about the route the expedition had taken in Butler Wash. He received the following reply:

> We camped at Butler Wash, Utah, the last week of December 1893, and a day or two in January 1894. We took out quite a large collection from this place, but I do not remember how many mummies. We found very well preserved pottery, skulls, arrow heads, baby boards, feather cloth, spear heads, small beads, and an unusual large amount of turkey feathers.[2]

From this information, Nusbaum convinced himself that "H.E.E. No. 10" was the site of the Basketmaker discovery, partly because he had already decided that the discovery had taken place in Butler Wash. Because of research carried out by the Wetherill–Grand Gulch project, we now know that French was certainly describing the excavations in Cave 10, but that Cave 10 was not the site of the Basketmaker discovery.

William Lipe in Grand Gulch, 1995.

Another archaeologist who took up the cause of locating Cave 7 and other sites dug by the early explorers was William Lipe. Lipe had studied Basketmaker sites throughout southeastern Utah in the 1960s, 1970s, and 1980s and was intimately familiar with the Grand Gulch alcoves. He had examined the papers of Nels C. Nelson, the curator at the American Museum of Natural History who had trekked into Grand Gulch in 1920, as well as Richard Wetherill's notes and catalogs. By the late 1970s, Lipe was able to identify nearly all twelve of Wetherill's 1896–97 sites, but he had not yet tackled the sites of the 1893–94 expedition. Lipe's accomplishments, however, set the stage for the Wetherill–Grand Gulch Research Project.

The Wetherill–Grand Gulch team took its first step toward unraveling the route of the 1893–94 Hyde Exploring Expedition during its 1988 visit to the American Museum of Natural History. Every evening during those ten hectic days, after a short break for dinner, team members reassembled to share experiences, plan the next day's work, and argue over their theories

The interior of Fishmouth Cave, Butler Wash, and (inset) a Hyde Exploring Expedition inscription ("HEE") from 1893–94 in the cave.

Winston Hurst in Cave 7, 1993.

concerning the expeditions and their routes. On one such evening, Winston Hurst, who had been putting together clues from statements in Wetherill's catalogs, convinced his friends that most of the first eleven alcoves the Hyde expedition had dug, including Cave 7, lay in Cottonwood Wash or along its tributaries. Winston's hypothesis was a genuine breakthrough.

Once back in Utah, Winston led the long and often frustrating search for Cave 7, assisted by Fred Blackburn and by Owen Severance, an avocational archaeologist with a superb knowledge of southeastern Utah's many canyons. The first obstacle the three faced arose from a letter Richard Wetherill had written, describing Cave 7 and placing his campsite in "First Valley, Cottonwood Creek."[3] But no one now living knew where First Valley was located. To complicate matters, the project team knew only in rough outline the route the Hyde expedition had taken out of Bluff toward Grand Gulch. Where, in that labyrinth of fissures, was First Valley?

In retrospect, the task should have been easier. By Cottonwood Creek, Wetherill must have meant the upper part of Cottonwood Wash, the same area where the team already believed Cave 7 lay. All they had to do was to search systematically, alcove after alcove, in upper Cottonwood Wash until they found one that matched Wetherill's description of Cave 7. But a combination of time, confused memories, and mislabeled photographs led the team along a more circuitous path.

For one thing, many geographical place-names had changed over the years. Graham Canyon, named after Charles Cary Graham, was now known as Bullet Canyon. Willow Springs had become Johns Canyon, and the former Epsom Wash was now Comb Wash. Moreover, accounts of the discovery of Cave 7 conflicted with one another. Some writers placed Cave 7 in Butler Wash, to the west of Cottonwood Wash. Richard Wetherill's brother John, who had participated in the original discovery, reminisced in a 1930 letter that Cave 7 was in Hammond Canyon, a northwestern branch of Cottonwood Wash.[4] Alcoves abound in all of these canyons, so that even with a detailed description of the site, finding Cave 7 promised to be like trying to find one special oak in a forest.

Confusion over the whereabouts of Cave 7 only increased when the Wetherill–Grand Gulch researchers turned up several of Richard Wetherill's photographs that might have been taken in Cave 7. Unfortunately, the pictures' labels were not always accurate. In his book *Richard Wetherill: Anasazi,* Frank McNitt had included a photograph of a place he identified as Cave 7, Grand Gulch, from the 1897 Whitmore Exploring Expedition. The large number of skeletons and artifacts in the photo suggested that it might in fact have been Cave 7 from the

Hyde expedition, but the image showed little of the cave and none of its setting. To make matters worse, project members had a copy of another photograph from the McNitt collection showing the same site from a different angle but labeled "Cave 10, 1893–94 expedition."[5]

Looking for hints in Richard Wetherill's letters and notes, Winston found a fairly detailed description of the length of the cave and its orientation. He suggested that the team systematically explore the area around Cottonwood Wash and Allen Canyon, in the hope that Charles Lang, who had accompanied the 1893–94 expedition, might have returned to Cave 7 when he excavated several alcoves in Allen Canyon in 1895. Wetherill's description seemed to fit the drawing Lang had made of an alcove in Allen Canyon he called Battle Cave. If nothing else, Winston reasoned, the team could proceed by a process of elimination, carefully examining every alcove they could find.

While they explored, they carried Lang's notes and maps, which easily led them to the caves Lang had excavated but revealed nothing that closely fit Wetherill's description of Cave 7. Turning south and west, the searchers continued canyon by canyon, cave by cave. Over many months they searched Hammond Canyon, North and South Whiskers Draw, and the drainages of Cottonwood and Butler Washes, getting some assistance from research groups organized by the College of Eastern Utah's White Mesa Institute, the Colorado Archaeological Society, and several school groups as well.

In many of the caves these teams discovered signatures of the Wetherills and their compatriots. Some signatures also carried dates—especially those of James Ethridge, who had accompanied both of the Wetherill expeditions. Slowly but surely, the team was able to eliminate alcoves from the list of possibilities while also assembling a growing catalog of historic signatures and other inscriptions on the alcove walls. Fred, Winston, and Owen were able to establish small segments of Wetherill's route during the Hyde Exploring Expedition, gradually narrowing the search.

Drawing by Charles Lang, c. 1895, of "Battle Cave" ("Burial Cave, No. 1," Allen Canyon).

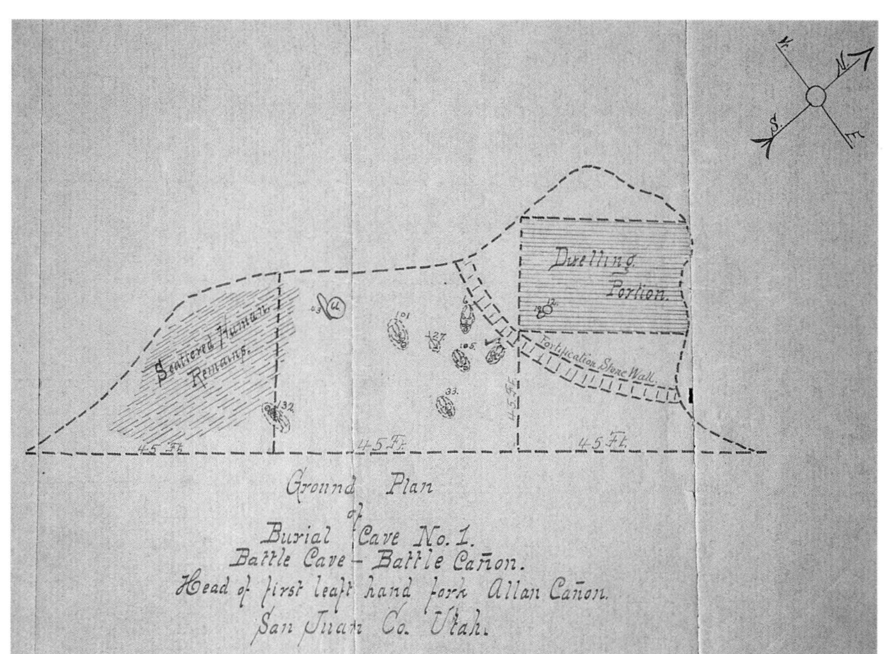

In Butler Wash they found the signatures of Wirt Jenks Billings and Harry French, both members of the Hyde expedition, in Cave 10. These were dated December 31, 1893, and January 1, 1894. Cave 10 is an imposing alcove in Comb Ridge, overlooking Butler Wash to the east. It was once called "Giant's Cave" for its size, and later Fishmouth Cave because when viewed from Butler Wash it looks like the open maw of a largemouth bass.[6] This find confirmed that the Hyde expedition had returned to Bluff with artifacts from Cave 7 before heading out again shortly after Christmas.

The project crew next found the date January 8, 1894, in Graham Canyon, where Harry French had inscribed his name on the back wall of Perfect Kiva. This suggested that the Hyde expedition had crossed Comb Ridge near the head of Butler Wash and ridden west into this tributary of Grand Gulch sometime between January 1 and January 8.

But even as they made slow gains in tracing the Hyde expedition's footsteps, the three team members remained puzzled over the whereabouts of First Valley. Modern maps were of little help because none of them identified a valley by that name. Maps from the 1880s were full of errors, generally showed only the major drainages, and seldom identified side canyons or other small features.

Winston, a lifelong resident of southeastern Utah with extensive knowledge of its history, turned to the writings of local historian Albert R. Lyman. Lyman had grown up in Bluff and worked as a cowhand in the area during the 1890s. He later wrote several books and left copious notes about the history of southeastern Utah. In an interview given in 1973, shortly before his death, Lyman disclosed that "First Valley is where you go over from the head of the Butler [Wash] and enter the first valley you come to on the mountain."[7]

The phrase "on the mountain" confused Winston at first, because local residents generally used it to refer to the Elk Ridge uplift, which overlooks the canyon system. But as he inquired further about the name, Winston discovered that many local people also used it loosely to refer even to the lower slopes of Elk Ridge. Lyman's unpublished writings affirmed that First Valley was a tributary of upper Cottonwood Wash, on the southern slope of Elk Ridge.

They also revealed that First Valley had been the site of an incident involving Willard Butt, an early dairy herder, and a Ute Indian named Whiskers. Rancher Butt was alone at his dairy one day when old Whiskers showed up, pulled out a rifle, and ordered the farmer to give him dinner. The farmer quickly complied, and to his great relief, Whiskers left pacified.[8] Because of this incident, First Valley, the first of several small valleys north of the head of Butler Wash, is now called Whiskers Draw. The team's first visit to Whiskers Draw had failed to locate Cave 7.

Having established the location of First Valley, Winston, Fred, and Owen returned to the still vexing problem of identifying which of the alcoves in First Valley was Wetherill's Cave 7. That would take many more hours of exploration, some outside help, and a bit of luck. Although they had not reckoned on the search taking so long, they were encouraged that at least they already knew of many alcoves that were *not* Cave 7, some of which contained historic signatures.

BY THE END OF MAY 1990 AND THE BASKETMAKER SYMPOSIUM, THE THREE MEN HAD come tantalizingly close to locating Cave 7. The final piece of the puzzle fell into place three months later. In August, Allesandro Pizzati, archivist at the Museum of Anthropology and

Archaeology of the University of Pennsylvania, sent Fred some photographs he believed to be from the Wetherill expeditions and requested help in identifying the people pictured in them. Two of these photographs finally surrendered the key to discovering Cave 7.

The label of one, matching McNitt's "Cave 10," read "Excavating Cave 7." In it, posing with shovels and artifacts, were members of the 1893–94 Hyde Exploring Expedition—faces Fred and Winston by then knew well. On the wall behind them were inscribed "IAEE," the initials of Warren K. Moorehead's "Illustrated American Exploring Expedition," and "C. Lang" in large, clear letters. The second photograph carried the label "First Camp in First Valley Cottonwood," the very place from which Richard Wetherill had written his letter of December 17, 1893. A third photograph revealed John Wetherill excavating a large corrugated pot, an artifact of the Pueblo occupation in Cave 7, labeled as such.

With the first of these photos, Fred now had in his hands an image of a large portion of Cave 7 that the team could use to identify the alcove when they finally saw it. Comparing this shot with the one in McNitt's biography of Richard Wetherill, he realized that McNitt's photograph had indeed been mislabeled. It showed not the Cave 7 of the 1897 expedition but the Cave 7 excavated in 1893. Its mate in McNitt's collection, too, was mislabeled as Cave 10 of the 1893–94 expedition, rather than as Cave 7. Examining the label on this second print more carefully, team members discovered that someone had written the number 10 on top of an original number 7.

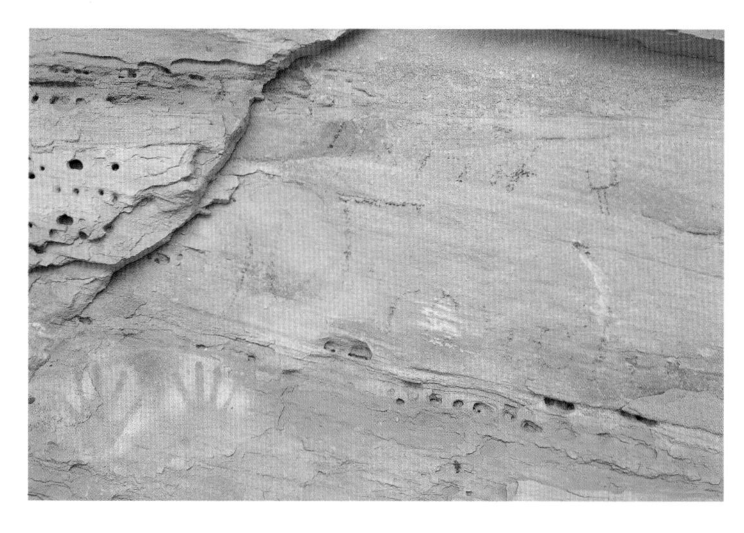

Harry French inscription from Cave 7, dated December 12, 1893.

The photographs from the University of Pennsylvania, which were slightly different from other known photographs taken during the Hyde expedition, also demonstrated that either Charles Lang, the Hyde expedition's photographer, or perhaps Lang and Richard Wetherill together had taken two sets of negatives of the alcove. Fred and Winston had now seen prints from both sets.[9]

Armed at last with photographs of the alcove, Winston and Owen began searching South Whiskers Draw for Cave 7. They soon found the remnant of an alcove that looked very much like the one in the photo. To their disappointment, it had been nearly washed away by flooding induced by overgrazing. Near this alcove Owen discovered Harry French's signature, dated December 12, 1893—just five days before Richard Wetherill wrote his first letter of the expedition. If this was not Cave 7, they were very close to it.

Hyde Exploring Expedition excavating in Cave 7, December 1893. Foreground: Wirt Jenks Billings. Background, left to right: James Ethridge, Harry French, Al Wetherill, Robert Allan, John Wetherill. Inset: Wetherill-Grand Gulch re-photograph of the 1893 HEE scene in Cave 7. Standing at right: Fred Blackburn, Winston Hurst.

The three men continued to search. Although at first the eroded alcove seemed to match Wetherill's description, it failed to match the photographs. Late one afternoon in September, Winston and Owen returned once more to explore Whiskers Draw. Owen took Winston to examine some signatures in a hidden alcove he had visited once before—the only alcove in Whiskers Draw they had not examined closely. As Winston entered the alcove, he immediately recognized the scene in the photograph. Several hundred yards away, at the head of the small box canyon, a beautiful little cliff dwelling sat just inside another shallow alcove. Unaccountably, Richard Wetherill had only briefly mentioned this tiny gem, perched like the guardian of the canyon.[10]

Two days later Fred received a postcard. "Bingo!" was all it said. Fred needed no signature to understand that the card, postmarked in Blanding, had been sent by Owen. The one word revealed that at long last Cave 7 had yielded the secret of its whereabouts.

Several weeks later, with family and friends, Fred, Winston, and Owen converged on Cave 7 to savor their success and also to document, measure, and record what they had found. Cave 7 itself was nearly covered with bushes and small trees. Working down ancient steps into a tangle of oak brush, chokeberry, and snowberry, they rounded the gentle curve of the canyon wall and stepped into the alcove that had so long eluded them.

There before the group lay the remnants of the small cliff dwelling that Richard Wetherill had mentioned in his letter of December 17, 1893. It was heavily eroded by time and the effects of nearly a century of artifact removal. The "IAEE" and "C. Lang" inscriptions so evident in the photograph were gone—obscured by natural erosion and later graffiti. Yet every angle, curve, and crack in the back of the alcove could be matched against the photograph from the University of Pennsylvania museum.

While the group measured the alcove and surveyed its features, Fred documented two signatures left by James Ethridge, one of them dated December 20, 1893, three days after Richard Wetherill first reported finding skeletal remains. Thanks to Ethridge's propensity to leave his name and the date, it was possible not only to affirm the photograph's authenticity but also to trace a crucial step in the route of the Hyde Exploring Expedition.

In July 1994, while revisiting Cave 7 with Ray Williamson and his wife, Carol Carnett, Winston found a second date inscribed in the sandstone—December 22. That inscription must have been made just before the Hyde party left for Bluff to celebrate Christmas.

Why did the project team devote so much effort to rediscovering Cave 7? First, the alcove is the site of the discovery of the Basketmakers. Second, knowing the location of Cave 7 places the artifacts and other materials taken from the cave back into a context they had lacked for a hundred years. Finally, and most important, artifacts and skeletons found in the cave offer tremendous insights, even a century later, into Basketmaker life and times. As the project team learned in 1988 when it examined the Hyde expedition collections at the American Museum of Natural History, the archaeological items from Cave 7 were still virtually complete and in good condition. Archaeologist Christy Turner has gone so far as to suggest that Cave 7 may be one of the most important sites in North American archaeology.[11]

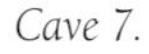

Cave 7.

In excavating Cave 7, Richard Wetherill observed:

> The number of skeletons found at one level and in one place would suggest a sudden and violent destruction of a community by battle or massacre. Many of the skulls were broken, as well as the ribs, and the bones of the arms and legs. In the backbones of two different skeletons we found the ends of spear points firmly embedded; in one case the break in the bone was partially healed, showing that the person must have lived for some time after the wound was inflicted. . . .
>
> We found one interesting group, a mother with an infant on each arm, and another lying on her breast with its head under her chin. There are warriors, "mighty men of valor," with ten or twelve spear points laying [sic] near; younger men with bone tools near them, and the unwarlike counselors or priests, with decaying baskets originally filled with food, or possibly tools of trade.[12]

In the early 1980s, Christy Turner had examined the skeletal remains from Cave 7 as part of a study he was conducting of violence in the prehistoric Southwest.[13] In the late 1980s, Turner returned to the American Museum of Natural History to study them in collaboration with Winston Hurst. Their detailed analysis of the bones confirmed Richard Wetherill's observations that the skeletons showed signs of violent attack. Some bones seemed to have sustained damage far beyond that normally seen in battle. Many of the skulls displayed fractures and other damage that suggested they had been bludgeoned, perhaps with a wooden club.

Although study of the Basketmaker remains from Cave 7 is far from complete, at a minimum the skeletons demonstrate that extreme violence was not unknown in Basketmaker society. Such finds are comparatively rare, but Basketmaker skeletons from other locations, such as some discovered by archaeologist Earl Morris in Canyon de Chelly and several other examples unearthed by McLoyd and the Wetherills, verify that the violence witnessed in Cave 7 was not an isolated event.

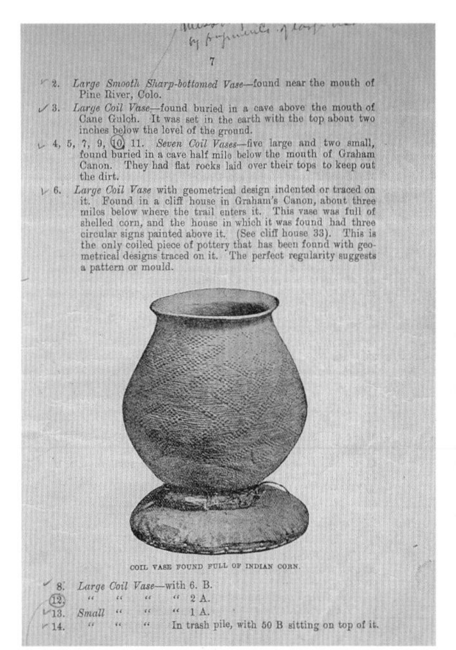

7

2. *Large Smooth Sharp-bottomed Vase*—found near the mouth of Pine River, Colo.
3. *Large Coil Vase*—found buried in a cave above the mouth of Cane Gulch. It was set in the earth with the top about two inches below the level of the ground.
4, 5, 7, 9, 10, 11. *Seven Coil Vases*—five large and two small, found buried in a cave half mile below the mouth of Graham Canon. They had flat rocks laid over their tops to keep out the dirt.
6. *Large Coil Vase* with geometrical design indented or traced on it. Found in a cliff house in Graham's Canon, about three miles below where the trail enters it. This vase was full of shelled corn, and the house in which it was found had three circular signs painted above it. (See cliff house 33). This is the only coiled piece of pottery that has been found with geometrical designs traced on it. The perfect regularity suggests a pattern or mould.

COIL VASE FOUND FULL OF INDIAN CORN.

8. *Large Coil Vase*—with 6. B.
12. " " " " 2 A.
13. *Small* " " " 1 A.
14. " " " In trash pile, with 50 B sitting on top of it.

This large patterned corrugated jar—shown (left) in the 1892 McLoyd and Green collection catalog—was located by the WGGP team in the Field Museum's collections (right).

NEARLY AS GREAT A MYSTERY AS THE LOCATION OF CAVE 7 WAS ANOTHER THAT would go unsolved for almost two years after the "official" end of the Wetherill–Grand Gulch Research Project. Where was the trail that Charles McLoyd and Charles Cary Graham had constructed into Grand Gulch on January 9, 1891?

Even before the Wetherill–Grand Gulch project started, Fred had begun to gather information about the caves McLoyd and Graham had dug on their 1891 trip. In 1974, he had assisted with the archaeological stabilization of Perfect Kiva ruin in Bullet (Graham) Canyon. During this work, he discovered several historic inscriptions in the alcove, including the signature of C. C. Graham. Then, in 1976, Fred met Helen Sloan Daniels, who had just published Graham's diary.[14]

Fred began working with Helen Daniels in an attempt to match each Grand Gulch location mentioned in the diary with an inscription. Soon he was able to identify a few of McLoyd and Graham's sites with places he knew—Perfect Kiva, Jail House, Green Mask Alcove, and Moon Kiva. Yet it was not until 1988 that the Wetherill–Grand Gulch team succeeded in thoroughly documenting the Perfect Kiva alcove.

During that trip, team members discovered that C. C. Graham's signature, inscribed in charcoal on the kiva's plaster wall, also included a date—January 11, 1891. The four-inch-high letters had been partially covered by the urine varnish of wood rats nesting in the kiva. With the aid of a flashlight, the researchers could clearly make out both the date and the signature. Interestingly, this is the only known signature from McLoyd and Graham's expedition with a complete date. It establishes conclusively that McLoyd and Graham's Cave 1 is the alcove containing Perfect Kiva.

In each cave he explored, McLoyd seems to have staked his archaeological claim by signing his name.[15] Altogether, the Wetherill–Grand Gulch project discovered more than fifty McLoyd or Graham signatures inscribed using charcoal, knives, or, most commonly, bullet lead. Linking these signatures with the evidence contained in Graham's diary, project members have now traced the origins of many of the artifacts the two men took from the canyon.

For example, by carefully following Graham's diary and matching the entries with alcoves and other natural and cultural features along the route, team members were able to show that the site people now call Jail House was the cliff dwelling that McLoyd and Graham first visited on Monday, January 12, 1891.[16] According to Graham's diary, the two early explorers called it Cliff House 2: "In the afternoon worked in house no. 2. Graham C. got two coil jars, one of them with designs, 2 bone drawing knives, 1 wooden knife, 1 wooden dipper, the large coil jar was full of shelled corn in perfect condition."

The project team confirmed its identification by finding McLoyd's signature on the back wall of one of the small houses in the alcove.[17] Later, when Ann Hayes located the Reverend C. H. Green's catalog in Chicago's Field Museum of Natural History, she noticed that one of the few items pictured in it was a corrugated Pueblo pot full of shelled corn. Green described it this way:

> Large Coil Vase with geometrical design indented or traced on it. Found in a cliff house in Graham's Canon, about three miles below where the trail enters it. This vase was full of shelled corn, and the house in which it was found had three circular signs painted above it. (See cliff house 33). This is the only coiled piece of pottery that has been found with geometrical designs traced on it. The perfect regularity suggests a pattern or mould [sic].[18]

Jail House Ruin (Cliff House 2) in Graham Canyon, photographed by F. E. Leeka for the 1891 Green Expedition. Inset: WGGP re-photograph.

Searching the Green collection in the Field Museum, the project team found the jar itself, as well as a wooden ladle, a large hatchet, and some other tools associated with it—all artifacts that had been excavated by McLoyd and Graham and then sold to Green. The Jail House site, too, was clearly recognizable from Green's description of the three circular symbols. Each is about a foot and a half in diameter and painted in white pigment; the pictograph's meaning is unknown. Matching these ancient objects with their place of origin emerged as one of the project's first big successes in reverse archaeology.

Locating the trail McLoyd and Graham built to get themselves and their pack animals into the canyon was an important part of documenting the pair's movements. Although Graham's diary indicated that the trail began on the north side of Graham Canyon, somewhere between the sites of Perfect Kiva and Moon Kiva, evidence of the route was scarce. In 1990, while searching the rim between the two archaeological sites, Bob Powell had discovered two rock cairns that seemed to mark the head of a trail. He also traced out the upper part of the trail but did not follow it to the bottom. Since then, the rock cairns had been scattered, perhaps by hikers ignorant of their meaning.

In March 1992, Fred mounted a concerted effort to document the original trail in its entirety. He and archaeologist Marietta Davenport, great-granddaughter of Richard and Marietta Wetherill, led a group of explorers into Graham Canyon on an expedition sponsored by the White Mesa Institute of the College of Eastern Utah. They started by carefully inspecting the canyon walls between Perfect Kiva and Moon Kiva.

Marietta Davenport, great-granddaughter of Richard and Marietta Wetherill, in Grand Gulch, 1993.

As they crisscrossed the area between the sites, their eyes alert to tiny details, the group soon found the scattered cairns and then isolated traces of a trail—here logs or stones supporting a large boulder, there a switchback or two. In the bright sun, the bare, hewn ends of the logs gleamed white from years of exposure to sun and weather. Slowly but surely, as the crew members worked down the slope and their eyes became accustomed to seeing faint evidence, the trail gradually took shape. After several hours of intense searching, they were able to follow the entire trail.

Standing on the north side of Bullet Canyon, today's visitor might well marvel at how McLoyd and Graham managed to get their horses to the bottom without killing either the animals or themselves. The trail drops precipitously in several places, affording only poor footing. Humans with backpacks find the trip a challenge. For horses, it looks impossible.

BY TRACING MCLOYD AND GRAHAM'S TRAIL INTO GRAND GULCH, FINDING CAVE 7 and the explorers' routes, and documenting the museum collections, the Wetherill–Grand Gulch team and their associates had resolved most of the major open questions about early archaeological exploration in southeastern Utah. In doing so, they gained a deep appreciation for the efforts of the early Southwestern explorers.

How are we to judge the contributions these explorers made to Basketmaker archaeology? Theirs is a mixed story. Although they dug important sites and assembled large collections for museums, in their enthusiasm for artifacts they also destroyed crucial evidence for future generations of archaeologists. Richard Wetherill has generally received credit for first recognizing and characterizing the Basketmaker people, yet his analysis depended on the physical labor and intellectual contributions of his brothers, on his association with Nordenskiöld, and especially on the previous excavations and insights of Charles McLoyd and the brothers Charles Cary Graham and J. Howard Graham. By 1893, McLoyd and the Graham brothers clearly understood that the people they called the cave dwellers, who constructed the large underground chambers, were different from the cliff dwellers.

The first clue that they recognized a difference came in the 1892 catalog written by C. H. Green, which noted: "There were three distinct races, Mesa, Valley, and Cliff Dwellers perhaps contemporaneous. The cliff dweller is characterized by a perpendicular artificial flattening of the back of the head . . . the Mesa or tableland dwellers had natural skulls."[19]

Green's understanding of the artifacts and skulls in his collection undoubtedly depended heavily on the observations of McLoyd, who seems to have been the organizer and intellectual leader of the expeditions in which he participated in southeastern Utah. Although Green posited the existence of three groups, rather than two, he did distinguish between the artificial flattening of cliff dweller skulls and the undeformed skulls of the mesa dwellers.

The people Green termed the mesa dwellers were those McLoyd and Graham named "cave dwellers" in a catalog they wrote in 1892 to accompany the second McLoyd collection (the 1892 Hazzard collection).[20] That catalog described artifacts and human remains taken from the Colorado River drainage and its tributaries. In numerous places throughout the catalog, the two distinguished between cave dweller skulls and cliff dweller skulls. For example:

> Group A, 24. A cliff-dweller's skull buried in a cave in Lake Colorado River drainage and its tributaries.
>
> Group A, 25. Cave-dweller's skull found in same cave as No. 24, Group A. This skull was found in a room that had been excavated in the clay bottom of the cave, and was about six feet below the surface. The underground rooms had been filled in, and the cliff-dweller's [sic] had constructed stone houses over them.[21]

By the time he compiled the catalog for his third collection in 1893 or 1894, McLoyd clearly understood the stratigraphic relationship between the cave dwellers and the cliff dwellers. He summarized his findings in the prefatory material of the catalog:

> Some of the skulls in this collection were obtained from underground rooms, that have been excavated in the clay bottoms of the caves. The largest of these rooms are as much as twenty two feet in diameter; they have been filled in with ashes and other refuse, and the stone

Cliff houses constructed over them. The heads taken from these rooms are of natural form, never having been changed by pressure.

No skulls of this shape are found in the stone Cliff-houses that are in the same caves, and no flattened skulls are found in the underground rooms.[22]

The contribution made by McLoyd and C. C. Graham to the discovery of the Basketmakers was summed up in a 1966 article by archaeologist M. Edward Moseley:

> McLoyd and Graham were cognizant of the differences [between Basketmaker and Pueblo artifacts] and interpreted the material as evidence of the existence of two prehistoric populations. . . . The explorer-collectors made no statement about the temporal relation of the two groups. They were, however, explicit about the differences between the two cultures, noting distinctions in skull form, architecture and material remains.[23]

The research carried out by the Wetherill–Grand Gulch project supports Moseley's interpretation. Although McLoyd and Graham failed to appreciate that the Basketmakers lived before the Pueblo people, they certainly recognized the existence of a people different from the pueblo dwellers, and they even commented on the stratigraphic relationship between the two. We must also credit McLoyd and the Graham brothers for understanding the importance of associations among the artifacts they uncovered. For example, although they grouped artifacts according to type in their catalogs, they took care to cross-reference each artifact with others found in the same location. Perhaps it is not too extreme to say that without the work of McLoyd and the Grahams, Richard Wetherill might never have achieved the synthesis that led to his "discovery" of the Basketmakers.

IN FAIRNESS, WHAT JUDGMENT DOES HISTORY PASS ON THE WETHERILLS? By digging more than two hundred archaeological sites in Mesa Verde, Grand Gulch, and Chaco Canyon, and by taking hundreds of visitors to enjoy them, Richard Wetherill and his brothers introduced their neighbors and the rest of the world to the archaeological riches of the Four Corners. By showing that the prehistoric Pueblo groups had built their stone and adobe dwellings atop the remains of another, earlier people, Wetherill established that there had been an evolution of cultures in the prehistoric Southwest. His discoveries and deductions helped to dispel the notion, then prevalent in anthropological circles, that American Indians had inhabited the Americas for only a few centuries.

Yet from the beginning, the Wetherills had their detractors, mostly because they supported themselves partly by selling artifacts. Nevertheless, the brothers quickly grasped the importance of taking excavation notes and keeping collections from any one area together for later scientific examination. As Al Wetherill noted many years later:

> The cliff-dwelling work was much more exciting than hunting gold (and I have done both), because we never knew what we might find next. We had started in as just ordinary pothunters, but, as work progressed along that sort of questionable business, we developed quite a bit of scientific knowledge by careful work and comparisons.[24]

This view of the Wetherills is supported by the opinion of Eleanor Stanberry, granddaughter of Levi Patrick, who told Fred Blackburn in 1995, "I really think Levi, McLoyd, and Graham split with the Wetherills and Mason because they only wanted to take out relics and sell them,

John Wetherill excavating a large yucca-fiber wrapped jar in Cave 7, December 1893.

while Wetherill became an amateur archaeologist and wanted to excavate scientifically."[25]

Richard Wetherill was singled out for criticism in the early days of American archaeology, perhaps because he attracted the most attention. Some of his greatest detractors were archaeologists from the East Coast who had never visited southeastern Utah and who failed to appreciate the significance of his discoveries. They either ignored him or considered him an untutored charlatan.

Some years after Wetherill's death, Alfred Vincent Kidder, the archaeologist whose excavations eventually vindicated the rancher's assertions, told the story of one of his Harvard professors, who insisted that Richard Wetherill "had taken his undeformed skulls, baskets and sandals and had segregated them from the rest of his Grand Gulch collection to create a myth 'of an early basket race.'" This he did, the professor claimed, in order to "increase the sales value of his collection."

Only in 1914, when Kidder and Samuel J. Guernsey confirmed the existence of the Basketmaker people by digging in northeastern Arizona, was the record set straight. Kidder later recalled: "As soon as Guernsey and I got into the caves of the Monuments area and Marsh Pass we found exactly the same sort of Basket Maker remains Wetherill had described."[26] Had Richard Wetherill's excavation methods and documentation been as rigorous as Kidder's—the methods of a Harvard-trained professional—no later confirmation would have been necessary.

Disparagement of Richard Wetherill and his brothers has persisted over the years. For example, in a history of Southwestern archaeology published in 1979, one National Park Service archaeologist essentially ignored Richard Wetherill's discovery in Cave 7 and attributed to a 1902 article by George Pepper the first suggestion that the "Basketmaker material represented an earlier development than that of the Pueblo."[27] Yet it was well known that Pepper had based his article almost entirely on Richard Wetherill's notes and had illustrated it with photographs taken by Wetherill. At the least, discounting Wetherill's contributions distorts the history of American archaeology and the substantial role avocational archaeologists have played in it.

To many professional archaeologists, Richard Wetherill's name is synonymous with "pothunter" or "looter." In a paper written in the early 1980s about a site in Grand Gulch that had been looted in the late 1970s, one archaeologist used the Wetherill name to conjure up images of pillage and plunder. "Not since the work of Richard Wetherill during the early to mid 1880's [sic] has the Turkey Pen Ruin site been subjected to such looting and wanton destruction."[28] Such allegations might fit McLoyd and Graham's excavation style better than Richard Wetherill's. Although Wetherill dug as deep as eight feet in Turkey Pen Ruin, McLoyd and Graham had already cleaned out most of it in 1891, leaving little record of their work.

The attitudes of some current archaeologists seem to arise from misconceptions about Wetherill's methods and from the mistaken belief that he kept no data about the archaeological sites in which he dug. They also stem from the knowledge that, in keeping with common practices of the 1890s, Wetherill sold most of the artifacts he excavated. The finds went primarily to museums or to individuals who donated them to museums, which at the time had relatively low standards for provenience information. As anthropologist Douglas Cole has described it, even collections of ethnographic materials were often purchased with poor documentation of their origins. Sometimes old museum records reveal nothing more than the name of the tribe from which a collection was obtained, and at other times, merely the geographical region.[29]

When judged by today's standards, Richard Wetherill's archaeological methods leave a lot to be desired. Yet his best work approached the professional standards of his day. The discipline of archaeology was in its infancy, and even the professionals were just learning to measure and record every detail of a site and to use stratigraphy as a guide to the relative age of cultural material. Richard Wetherill was always open to instruction, whether it came from Frederick Ward Putnam or young Gustaf von Nordenskiöld.

In deducing that the Basketmaker people must have lived much earlier than the cliff dwellers because their remains were buried well below those of the cliff dwellers—under a layer of soil devoid of cultural material—Wetherill was using, in a rudimentary way, the principle of stratigraphy. Although professional archaeologists such as Putnam understood and advocated the use of stratigraphic principles, in which each successive layer downward represents

Hyde Exploring Expedition excavations in Butler Wash, 1893.

an earlier time period, the stratigraphic method of excavation was not fully developed in the Southwest for another twenty years. In 1914, the archaeologist Nels Nelson used the technique while excavating San Cristóbal ruin in the Galisteo Basin south of Santa Fe.[30]

Richard Wetherill was a keen observer of archaeological evidence, but he also made use of an important analogical tool in interpreting his data—ethnographic information about living tribes. He reasoned from his considerable firsthand knowledge of local Navajos and Utes, and from his observation of the Hopi people, to infer the substance of the Basketmakers' daily lives. Ethnographic analogy is a powerful technique that archaeologists have put to considerable use since Wetherill's time.[31] In attempting to explain Basketmaker burial pits, which were bell-shaped holes in the floor, lined with plaster and often covered with a large stone, Richard Wetherill suggested:

> Originally they may have been intended for caches since both the Pah Ute and the Navajo use the same thing for the storing of grain—near their fields, but digging into some high spot where the water will all drain away.
>
> I believe it is the custom of the present Indians to build a fire inside and pretty thoroughly bake the linings of the cache. This of course would drive out all the moisture and make a safe granary.[32]

Wetherill also made effective use of the camera, a tool that has become indispensable to modern archaeologists. Struggling with cumbersome eight-by-ten-inch glass plates and a large portrait camera, he documented as many of the ruins as he could. The photographs he and Charles Lang took of the sites they excavated provide a crucial record of Grand Gulch archaeology. Wetherill was fully aware of the impact photographs could have and used them to the best of his ability. Although his photographic record is agonizingly slim, the Wetherill–Grand Gulch Research Project found the surviving images invaluable for identifying sites and tracing artifact proveniences.

Whatever his shortcomings as a researcher may have been—and his records fell woefully short even of his own expectations—Richard Wetherill made a far greater effort than other early excavators to document his finds. For example, in his notes from both Grand Gulch expeditions, Wetherill continually referred to the way others before him had already emptied many of the alcoves in which his group dug. If it were not for the historical record that Richard Wetherill left us, meager as it is, we would have much to mourn in the clean sweep the Wetherills and others made in Grand Gulch and other canyons of southeastern Utah.[33]

Because of the earlier excavations by McLoyd and Graham and the Green party, the Wetherills mostly found isolated artifacts in Grand Gulch. They excavated few complete burials with the full artifact assemblages so crucial to archaeological interpretation. But Richard Wetherill's experience in Cave 7 had taught him that burials could be found at great depth. He dug deeper in the alcoves of Grand Gulch than his predecessors had done and found artifacts, burials, and tool assemblages overlooked by McLoyd and Graham. He also dug in alcoves they had missed. In addition, he was able to find significant materials in lower Grand Gulch below Collins Canyon.[34]

Today we wish that Richard Wetherill had retained all of the artifacts he and his crews dug in southeastern Utah and elsewhere, and kept them together. We are fortunate that so many of his collections found their way into museums, with a paper trail pointing the way, but many objects remain unaccounted for. For example, the Wetherill–Grand Gulch Research Project has so far been unable to locate the current home of artifacts the Hyde expedition took from Cave 10 in Butler Wash and from Laguna Creek and Mysterious Canyon, south of the San Juan. These may have been sold to individuals and become dispersed over time. Or they may exist as nearly complete assemblages in some museum collection as yet undiscovered by the project.

Perhaps typical are some items dug from Green Mask Alcove (the Hyde expedition's Cave 17). The Alamo Ranch ledger of March 18, 1894, notes that Robert K. McNeely paid one hundred dollars cash for artifacts from that site. In 1895 McNeely donated these artifacts, which included a mummy and associated materials, to the University of Pennsylvania.

Richard Wetherill even sent some of his Basketmaker finds to his friend Gustaf Nordenskiöld:

> Enclosed find shipping receipt for box of 12 skulls of the Basket Makers we call them that because they made no pottery and did not make houses but lived as the Indians now do except they made their caches in the caves in the Cliffs and buried their dead there as well as using these places for storage.[35]

To most people today, trafficking in artifacts that belong to the public seems reprehensible as well as illegal. But at the turn of the century, both public attitudes and the law were quite different. Only with the passage of the Antiquities Act in 1906 did the removal of artifacts from public lands become a crime.[36] By then, people had begun to realize how important artifacts and their on-the-ground associations were in reconstructing the lifeways of earlier cultures.

All in all, we can laud Richard Wetherill's attempts to amass a thorough, documented collection of Basketmaker and Pueblo artifacts. R. G. Matson, for example, in his comprehensive book on Basketmaker culture and the origins of Southwestern agriculture, notes the "essential correctness of Wetherill's deductions about the Basketmaker culture."[37] Seen through contemporary eyes, Wetherill's methods were rudimentary. For his own time, however, he was well ahead of his Southwestern colleagues and even ahead of some academy-trained archaeologists. Better than most of his peers he grasped the subtleties of Basketmaker culture and the way it related to the later Pueblo people.

One of the ironies of these early excavations in southeastern Utah is that archaeologist Warren K. Moorehead explored Cave 7 in the spring of 1892, nearly two years before Wetherill entered the alcove. Some member of Moorehead's party left the initials "IAEE" on the alcove wall. We wonder how Richard Wetherill felt about digging in Cave 7 directly under his predecessor's inscription. If he paid any attention to it, he gave no indication in his writings.

Richard Wetherill's finds in Cave 7 and other sites were of signal importance to American archaeology. Although his archaeological methods were crude and his lack of formal training impeded his acceptance by professional scholars, he exhibited curiosity, a love for the ancient dwellers of the Southwest, and a strong desire to understand them. Richard Wetherill used his considerable observational powers and his native intelligence to launch the study of the Basketmakers, an endeavor that even today produces surprising new findings to excite archaeologist and layperson alike.

The Corn Panel, Grand Gulch.

6/Basketmaker Research after Wetherill

The method of burial observed in this cave, the natural or undeformed condition of the crania, and the nature of the mortuary offerings, all present features foreign to the normal cliff-house culture of the region. . . . [T]he finds in this cave agree very closely with those made in Grand Gulch, Utah, by the Wetherill brothers and assigned by them to an older culture which they named "Basket Maker."

—A. V. Kidder and S. J. Guernsey,
Archaeological Explorations in Northeastern Arizona

The search for the Basketmakers turned scholarly in the summer of 1914, when archaeologist Alfred V. Kidder and artist Samuel J. Guernsey began excavating in northeastern Arizona.[1] The pair not only confirmed the Wetherills' earlier discoveries but also established a firm foundation for the later development of archaeological method and theory in the Southwest.

Kidder and Guernsey made their headquarters at the Kayenta, Arizona, trading post of John and Louisa Wetherill. Although John Wetherill is seldom mentioned in books about early American archaeology, he maintained an active interest in the subject throughout his life.[2] From Kayenta, he and Louisa hosted many professional archaeologists, and sometimes John guided them through northeastern Arizona and southeastern Utah. His younger brother Clayton guided Kidder and Guernsey.

They began work in Sayodneechee Canyon on the east side of Monument Valley, finding many small Pueblo storage structures and excavating six small cliff houses. The most important site they dug, however, was a shallow cave, or rockshelter, where they found four jar-shaped Basketmaker burial cists carved out of the hardpan soil in the cave's floor. The men excavated thirty-two full or partial skeletons with associated artifacts. Although nearly all of the baskets originally covering the bodies had decayed away, enough remained to confirm that these people had been buried in the manner of the Basketmakers. What was more, none of the skulls was flattened, and no pottery was present in the lower layers of soil.

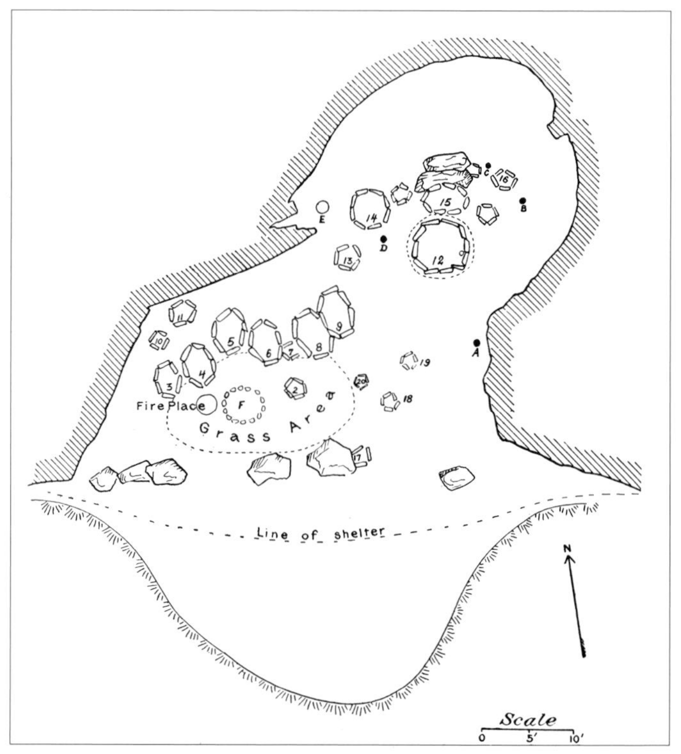

Interior and plan of Kidder and Guernsey's Cave 2, Kinboko Canyon.

Later that summer, water sources in Monument Valley dried up, and Kidder and Guernsey were forced to relocate. At the suggestion of Byron Cummings, a fellow archaeologist who happened to be visiting the Wetherills at the time, they moved to Marsh Pass, southwest of Kayenta.[3] The change of venue proved fortunate for Basketmaker research. Now explicitly interested in finding more Basketmaker material, the two came across a large rockshelter, which they called Cave 1, where Kinboko Canyon opens into Laguna Creek. Cave 1 contained storage and burial cists similar to those in Sayodneechee Canyon. Unable to complete their investigations by summer's end, Kidder and Guernsey returned to Marsh Pass in 1915 to excavate. As they had hoped, they discovered a wealth of new Basketmaker material.

Cave 1 held nearly sixty cists that apparently had functioned originally as storage containers. Of these, about twenty had been converted into burial cists. According to Kidder and Guernsey, "[Burial] offerings were numerous and varied, but the one standard gift to the dead seems to have been coiled basketry; wherever we found burials at all well preserved they were always accompanied by at least one such basket."[4]

The next rockshelter they excavated in Kinboko Canyon—Cave 2—contained twenty-two cists, slab lined and carefully made. Typically, these cists were oval in outline and roughly four and a half feet long, two and a half feet wide, and eighteen inches deep. The cists clearly had served as storage containers; none had been used as a burial pit. One unusual cist, a circular pit some five feet in diameter and three feet deep, had been neatly roofed with four log rafters, each about four inches in diameter, covered with small sticks, cedar bark, stones, and adobe.[5]

About ten feet inside the drip line of the rockshelter, Kidder and Guernsey also discovered an elliptical area roughly ten by twenty feet over which bundles of grass had been spread. In their later writings, the two suggested that Cave 2 "was without doubt domiciliary, for it contained a considerable amount of ash and other debris; furthermore, no burials were found in it with the exception of parts of the skeleton of a very young baby."[6] Accepting Kidder and Guernsey's judgment that Basketmaker people had used this rockshelter as a living space, archaeologist R. G. Matson suggested in 1991 that the large grass-lined area might once have been a lightly covered pithouse.[7]

Cave 2 was also noteworthy for the many paintings on its walls. There were "square-shouldered human figures in white paint, handprints in red, and curious geometric designs also in red."[8] Kidder and Guernsey suggested that because human figures like these appeared in areas of Basketmaker occupation but not elsewhere, they were definitely Basketmaker in origin. Later research has confirmed that anthropomorphic figures in the style described by Kidder and Guernsey are indeed typical of Basketmaker rock art.

In the three dry rockshelters they investigated in Arizona, Kidder and Guernsey found not only burials and an astonishing array of artifacts but also the remains of well-preserved foodstuffs. It became clear that people of the culture now known as Basketmaker II gathered acorns, piñon nuts, and fruits and cultivated corn and squash.[9] The two archaeologists found no beans, however, and only a few animal bones—which puzzled them, because they did find deerskin, mountain sheep hide, prepared sinew, and parts of bird skins and feathers. They were unsure whether the Basketmakers had domesticated turkeys.

Kidder and Guernsey found a few skin robes and fragments of robes made of fur cloth. To manufacture the fur cloth, Basketmaker artisans wrapped strips of the skin of rabbits or other small animals around twisted yucca cords and then wove the fur strings together with twined yucca cords to make robes. Such fur robes were the Basketmakers' primary warm garments in cold weather. They also made a few robes in a similar way from the skins of small birds, still holding the downy feathers. From leather they made bags, robes, sandals, and cradle lashings. The two archaeologists also discovered a type of string skirt, a tasseled sash, and a G-string.

Among the artifacts were many sandals, which the two described in considerable detail and for which they created a four-part typology: yucca-leaf sandals (whole leaf or crushed leaf), cedar-bark sandals, cord sandals (plain sole or reinforced sole), and hide sandals. As Kidder and Guernsey noted, the sandals were quite unlike those of the cliff dwellers.

The excavations turned up a remarkable assortment of household items. There were infants' cradles, some with rigid frames and others manufactured more flexibly of crushed and shredded cedar bark.[10] Cedar bark also appeared in the form of torches, sandals, padding, and even bags. Among their most interesting finds, Kidder and Guernsey uncovered several small, cleverly made brushes of plant fiber that had apparently been used as hairbrushes. Entangled among the bristles were strands of human hair.

The two also found many examples of the Basketmakers' trademark craft, basketry. They excavated whole coiled baskets and many more fragments in different shapes and sizes. The most common form was a shallow tray ranging from three inches to three feet in diameter. From fragments, they could discern large carrying baskets constructed with wide mouths and narrow bottoms, as well as small, neatly made baskets with restricted openings. To Kidder and Guernsey, the most interesting basket was one that started small at the bottom, flared outward near the upper part, and closed in again at the top. On the sides were two carrying loops. The entire inner surface of the basket and part of the exterior were thickly covered with piñon gum, leading the two to believe that it had once been used to carry water. All of the baskets were made with a two-rod-and-bundle foundation. Kidder and Guernsey were unable to identify the source of the rods, but the bundles were generally made of yucca fibers.

Kidder and Guernsey found no items of cotton, an absence confirmed by later archaeological expeditions. Twine and rope were generally made of yucca fibers or from apocynum. The Basketmakers also used human hair to make all kinds of string. The archaeologists found several bundles of hair, stored away and ready to be used for making twine.

Along with baskets, the Basketmakers specialized in making finely crafted bags, which they wove from apocynum strings over warps of yucca or apocynum. Kidder and Guernsey found bags of many different sizes, used to hold all manner of items. They were decorated by weaving red, black, or natural (yellow-brown) string in horizontal bands around the bag. The two also excavated several bands woven of human hair or hair and apocynum. They speculated that the bands had been used as headbands, burden straps, or even cradle carriers.

One of the most important tools the Basketmakers possessed was the atlatl, or throwing stick, which they used in hunting and as a weapon. An atlatl consisted of a slender stick some two feet long, with a stop at one end and loops or a hand grip at the other. When preparing to throw, the atlatl user placed the butt end of his spear against the atlatl stop and held the throwing stick by putting his first and second fingers between the loops. The third and fourth fingers served to steady the throwing stick, while the spear was held with the first and second fingers and steadied with the thumb. The atlatl in effect served to lengthen the thrower's arm, increasing his throwing power. It was an effective weapon that served the Archaic and early

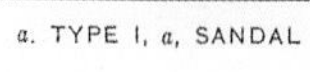

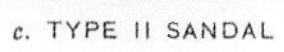

Clockwise from top: Types of Basketmaker sandals identified by Kidder and Guernsey; water-carrying basket; atlatl in the collection of the Middle American Research Institute.

Basketmaker II peoples for centuries until the bow and arrow were introduced in late Basketmaker II times.

Kidder and Guernsey unearthed several atlatls. The most complete example came from a burial cist and had become somewhat bent and twisted. Yet its smooth finish demonstrated the great care that the Basketmakers characteristically put into making their implements. Of special interest was a small piece of carved white limestone that lay in the soil just below this atlatl. Originally, it had been tied to the bottom of the atlatl a few inches toward the butt from the finger loops. Kidder and Guernsey speculated that the stone, which weighed about an ounce, might have helped improve the balance of the atlatl. Recent experimentation has shown that such stones serve no useful function in improving the atlatl's balance or range, but instead quiet the sound made during the throw.[11]

In considering the relationship between the Basketmakers and the Pueblo people, the two archaeologists asked, "Was the Basket Maker culture the product of a people inhabiting the region before the coming of the Cliff-dwellers, and later on displaced by them; or was the Basket Maker the prototype of the Cliff-dweller, and did a gradual growth take place in the region from the Basket Maker . . . to the Cliff-dweller?"[12]

They favored the second hypothesis, but unlike the Wetherill brothers, Kidder and Guernsey had no clear stratigraphic evidence that the Basketmakers were not coeval with the cliff dwellers. Because they wisely chose to argue solely from the evidence, they left the question open for further research. The next two summers of fieldwork resolved the issue beyond a doubt.

In 1916 and 1917, Samuel Guernsey worked alone in the Marsh Pass area. A. V. Kidder, meanwhile, began excavating in New Mexico at Pecos Pueblo, southeast of Santa Fe—the first season of a fourteen-year project that would establish him as a leading Southwestern archaeologist. In Marsh Pass, Guernsey started with Sunflower Cave, a site the two archaeologists had partially excavated in 1915.

They had named the cave for its spectacular yield of twenty-six wooden objects, carved and painted to resemble sunflowers, and two leather "sunflowers" in an unusual pottery bowl. The sunflowers all derived from the cliff dweller culture, but the 1915 excavations had also uncovered evidence of Basketmaker occupation. In 1916, Guernsey soon found seven Basketmaker cists that unquestionably lay beneath cliff dweller debris. With this discovery, the question of Basketmaker precedence was settled for the scholarly world.

Guernsey excavated twelve additional caves in 1916 and 1917, including one known as White Dog Cave, in which he found abundant Basketmaker remains. White Dog Cave was named after a mummified white dog, resembling a small collie, that had been buried with a man. Guernsey also discovered a smaller black and white dog, more like a terrier, buried with a woman. Both dogs were probably killed and buried along with their owners.[13]

The combined evidence from Guernsey and Kidder's four summers of work laid a firm footing for future Basketmaker research. In addition to confirming the Wetherills' earlier finds, the two described in systematic detail a rich lode of cooking implements, hunting tools, foodstuffs, clothing, adornment, and art from which their colleagues could begin to glimpse the Basketmaker way of life. One question Kidder and Guernsey could not answer, however, was where the Basketmaker people had lived.

CLEARLY, THE BASKETMAKERS SPENT NEARLY ALL THEIR WAKING HOURS OUTDOORS, but harsh weather must have forced them into shelter from time to time, especially to sleep. From the evidence they had at hand, Kidder and Guernsey could only suggest that "the Basket-makers lived mostly in perishable structures built in the open, and . . . resorted to caves for temporary shelter in severe weather."[14] For reasons that remain unknown, by the time Guernsey completed his research at White Dog Cave, the two had retracted their earlier speculation that Cave 2 of the 1915 field season had served as a habitation site. They urged that "a rigorous search . . . be made for 'pre-pueblo' habitations and graves in locations where they may be expected to be found protected from moisture."[15]

Over the next two decades, other archaeologists, including Jesse Nusbaum and Earl H. Morris, accumulated a growing body of evidence about the Basketmakers.[16] But not until 1938, when Morris and Robert F. Burgh excavated two rockshelters along the Animas River north of Durango, Colorado, did anyone find clear evidence of Basketmaker II houses.

Morris learned of the Falls Creek rockshelters from Durango residents I. F. Flora and Helen Sloan Daniels, both amateur archaeologists and members of the Colorado Archaeological Society.[17] After seeing a few artifacts dug from the cave and determining that they were very like Basketmaker artifacts he had previously dug in Mummy Cave in Arizona's Canyon del Muerto, Morris returned the following year with Burgh to dig the two Falls Creek sites.[18] The work they did there and at nearby Talus Village in 1940 occasioned key advances in Basketmaker research.

Carved wooden items from Sunflower Cave, Marsh Pass.

The most important of their finds were the remains of Basketmaker houses at all three sites. After uncovering evidence of what appeared to be house floors at the Falls Creek rockshelters, Morris was convinced that the caves had been used for habitation. As he wrote to his friend A. V. Kidder early in the excavations, "I have not yet been able to prove that side walls or roofs ever existed. But in any event we have long occupied Basket Maker II living quarters."[19] He was perplexed at not finding any post holes that might have held posts to support the roof. Not until he and Burgh excavated Talus Village two years later was Morris able to confirm that their earlier finds were indeed houses, and to learn why they lacked support poles.

Although none of the thirty-five house floors at Talus Village was complete, one had part of an original wall still intact. The Talus Village people had not used posts to build a frame but instead laid logs on the bare earth around the edge of the pit, securing them with adobe and then placing successive tiers of logs above the first row to make a cribbed roof. Similar cribbing was used later, in the Pueblo period, to roof kivas. Most Southwestern archaeologists believe that the kiva was originally derived from the Basketmaker pit house. This hypothesis dovetails closely with the Pueblo view that kivas represent the place of emergence of the Pueblo people.

Dotting the house floors were small slab-lined cists, some of them covered with beehive-shaped clay structures. Some house floors also yielded evidence of jar-shaped cists and simpler earth basins. Most floors contained heating pits, which Morris and Burgh surmised the Basketmakers had used by heating rocks in fires outside and then carrying them into the house with sticks.[20] House 1a, the largest and most complete house floor discovered at Talus Village, measured some twenty-seven feet in diameter at floor level—a relatively comfortable living space for an extended family. If kept dry, the storage cists in the house's floor would have protected the family's food from spoiling and from being carried away by mice or packrats.

Basketmaker pithouse floor with stone retaining wall, excavated by Morris and Burgh at Talus Village.

Enough wood remained from House 1a to determine by tree-ring dating that it had been constructed about A.D. 330. Wood from other houses at Talus Village dated as early as A.D. 150, and the north shelter at Falls Creek yielded a date of about A.D. 50.[21] These dates were the first well-substantiated ones for the Basketmaker II culture, and they showed that archaeologists had been right in believing, on the basis of tree-ring evidence from Pueblo and Basketmaker III sites, that Basketmaker II dated to A.D. 500 and earlier.[22] Although A.D. 500 has held up as the date for the transition from Basketmaker II to Basketmaker III, even today archaeologists have yet to determine the earliest dates for Basketmaker II culture.

Analyzing the house remains and artifacts they uncovered, Morris and Burgh demonstrated that contemporaneous communities of Basketmaker people in widely separated locations shared many traits in common but also displayed cultural variability. For example, they recognized a new type of sandal, different from those reported elsewhere. These specimens were twilled from tule, the stalks of native bullrushes, and had "two rows of side loops . . . caught with a crisscross lace over the foot."[23] Among the baskets from the Durango sites, some were made by using a one-and-a-half-rod-and-bundle foundation rather than the two-rod-and-bundle foundation employed farther west. As Morris noted in a letter to Kidder, even before he began to excavate, "There seems to be something peculiar about the Durango district. This stuff appears to vary in certain respects from the standard run of Basket Maker II material."[24]

Because some of the Durango Basketmaker traits, such as cribbed roofs and the presence of heating pits, were similar to features of early Mogollon sites in southeastern Arizona, Morris and Burgh hypothesized that the Mogollon and the Basketmakers both evolved from an Archaic culture called the San Pedro Cochise, whose remains have been found in what is now southwestern New Mexico and southeastern Arizona.[25] In other words, the two suggested an origin for the Basketmaker people that lay outside the San Juan region.

Morris and Burgh did not published their monograph on the Falls Creek sites until 1954. A few years later, Frank W. Eddy carried out a series of archaeological "salvage" excavations in northwestern New Mexico impelled by the construction of Navajo Reservoir. His discovery of Basketmaker sites this far southeast of Durango greatly expanded the known area in which Basketmaker II people had lived. Eddy and his team worked in three out of sixteen Basketmaker sites along the Pine River, which flows into the San Juan east of the Animas.[26] Eddy called them *Los Pinos phase* Basketmaker sites. He dug two additional Los Pinos phase sites even farther east along the San Juan.[27]

Unlike Morris and Burgh's sites along the Animas, these Basketmaker dwellings had once stood in the open, not far from the rivers, rather than in rockshelters. The people who lived in them probably cultivated corn and squash on the nearby floodplains, where there was a steady source of water. Each site consisted of several randomly arranged pithouses. Los Pinos phase Basketmakers constructed their roughly circular houses on a cribbed wooden framework, laying river cobbles against the logs to hold the cribbing in place. Several of the houses had antechambers attached. Most house sizes ranged between three hundred and five hundred square feet, but two houses were much larger. From analysis of the artifacts and the house structures, Eddy was able to show that the Pinos phase people were culturally very similar to the Durango Basketmakers, and he also identified some new similarities between the Basketmakers and the early Mogollon people to the south.

View of a Basketmaker rockshelter.

Ironically, many of the modern construction projects that either destroy or cover up archaeological sites have also been sources of vital information about Southwestern prehistory, thanks to federal and state laws that require whoever is responsible for the project to survey the affected area and excavate important sites. Frank Eddy's research along the Pine River and the San Juan still serves as a fine example of the fruit such projects can bear.

By 1960, archaeologists had accumulated enough data on Basketmaker sites throughout the Four Corners country to begin asking questions that could be answered only on a regional scale. Where, for example, did the Basketmaker people choose to locate their houses, their agricultural fields, and their work sites? Such questions have to do with a people's *settlement pattern,* a subject that can tell us much about the ancient economy and about a group's relationship to the land and climate.

In the early 1960s, William Lipe investigated some sites on the Red Rock Plateau in southeastern Utah, west of Cedar Mesa.[28] He found that the Basketmakers there displayed cultural traits very similar to those found in Marsh Pass and Grand Gulch. Basketmakers in all three areas used two-rod-and-bundle, noninterlocking-stitch methods to weave their baskets, which distinguished them from the Durango and Los Pinos Basketmakers to the east, who used one-and-a-half-rod-and-bundle construction.

Among other things, Lipe was bent on figuring out Basketmaker II settlement patterns by combining information about habitations, campsites, and burial sites. In Moqui Canyon, which slices through the Red Rock Plateau and joins Glen Canyon some twenty-five miles west-northwest of Grand Gulch, he found a total of nine Basketmaker II sites. Three of these were in rockshelters, which Lipe classified as habitation/burial sites, the first to be discovered outside of Durango.[29] Four sites appeared to be campsites, and two were storage areas. Because of the stone projectile points, chips, manos, and grinding slabs found at the campsites, Lipe suggested that they were used as bases for gathering, hunting, and processing food. The four campsites lay near sand dunes that at the time of excavation supported abundant stands of Indian rice grass. Perhaps the processing sites had been chosen to take advantage of this food resource.

In the 1970s, Lipe teamed up with R. G. Matson to study Basketmaker settlement patterns on Cedar Mesa.[30] Using a fundamental survey technique—tramping across the landscape—they identified 132 Basketmaker II sites, which they grouped into five broad types: habitation sites, campsites, stone tool preparation sites, and two classes of "limited activity" sites, one displaying a greater number of tools than the other. Lipe and Matson were able to date several of the sites they discovered on the survey, through both tree-ring and radiocarbon methods. These dates indicated that Basketmaker people had lived on Cedar Mesa between about A.D. 200 and 400.

Lipe and Matson classified some fifty-two sites as habitations on the grounds that they displayed more surface features than other sites. Although the survey revealed clear signs of pithouses in only about half of the habitation sites, Lipe and Matson argued on the basis of other evidence that most of the rest probably contained pithouses as well. The geographical distribution of the known pithouses led the two to conclude that they were grouped in well-dispersed villages. Furthermore, the habitation sites tended to be located away from the canyon rims at relatively high elevations in the densest piñon-juniper zones.

Lipe and Matson's research demonstrated the importance of microclimate in areas that are marginal for agricultural. The higher elevations on Cedar Mesa, like those in many other parts of the Southwest, receive more rain and snow than do lower elevations near canyon rims, which often receive less than the yearly twelve inches of precipitation required to support corn. Lipe and Matson discovered that sagebrush valleys on Cedar Mesa, which have deep soil suitable for agriculture, held relatively few habitation sites. Contrary to what one might expect, these valleys are cooler at night than the surrounding higher elevations, and so they are less suitable for agriculture. Sagebrush tolerates severe cold better than piñon and juniper. Lipe and Matson reasoned that the Basketmaker II people chose higher elevations as favorable spots for their fields and then situated their houses nearby.

They also found, in contrast to the pattern for habitation sites, that the Basketmakers' limited activity sites and campsites lay scattered over a much broader range of elevations. Many campsites appeared in areas with little agricultural potential but with an abundance of other resources, particularly Indian rice grass.

In the mid-1970s, around the time Lipe and Matson were engaged in their Cedar Mesa research, a team of archaeologists working on Black Mesa, north of the Hopi villages in northeastern Arizona, discovered clear evidence of Basketmaker II occupation. Theirs was a "contract" archaeology project headed by George J. Gumerman, who been contracted to survey and excavate sites in advance of coal mining on Black Mesa. Gumerman's crews unearthed important new information about Basketmaker II settlement patterns.

Altogether, the Black Mesa team identified more than one hundred Basketmaker II sites, of which they excavated thirty-five. The sites spanned the known range of Basketmaker types, from those displaying only a few artifacts to groupings of up to a dozen pithouses, which the excavators classified as villages.[31]

Woven yucca-fiber basket filled with corn kernels, found in Cave 26 by the Hyde Exploring Expedition, 1894.

Some pithouses, unexpectedly, had been constructed by digging a few feet directly into the friable bedrock. Considering the investment of labor required to construct these residences using only handheld stone tools, the builders must have intended them to be relatively permanent. Presumably the Basketmaker II farmers of Black Mesa returned to the same habitation sites and campsites season after season. In contrast to Cedar Mesa, which is cut by relatively deep canyons, Black Mesa features broad, shallow washes that enable people to practice floodplain farming. Rather than having to rely on rainfall to water the cornfields, Black Mesa farmers might have been able to receive some portion of the seasonal rains as they streamed off the mesas and flooded the cornfields positioned in or along the washes.

The study of Basketmaker II habitation sites and settlement patterns throughout the 1960s and 1970s confirmed that similar Basketmaker II traits were broadly distributed across the Four Corners region. It also validated Morris and Burgh's and Eddy's earlier finding that when cultural traits were scrutinized closely, significant differences existed between eastern and western groups.

Metates from Talus Village.

IN AN ATTEMPT TO UNDERSTAND MORE ABOUT THE BASKETMAKERS' USE OF ROCKSHELTERS, Francis Smiley and several of his colleagues on the Black Mesa project excavated Three Fir Shelter, northeast of Black Mesa.[32] There, along with clear evidence of habitation, the archaeologists found surprisingly old corn. Radiocarbon dating of some samples of corn and other plant material from the site produced dates ranging from 560 B.C. to 150 B.C.—an unremarkable result. But dates obtained from two other corncobs revealed that those ears had been harvested about 1900 B.C.[33] This is still the earliest well-documented date for corn on the Colorado Plateau, and it leads us to a question that has preoccupied archaeologists for years: In the origins and evolution of the Basketmaker people, what was the role played by the inception of agriculture?

Ever since the discoveries of the Wetherills and McLoyd and Graham, archaeologists had known that the Basketmakers cultivated corn. Yet until relatively recently, they had insufficient data to tackle the important questions of how and where agriculture came into the Southwest and how it evolved. Did the Basketmakers immigrate from the south, bringing corn along with them and displacing or assimilating an earlier Archaic people? Or did the Archaic people of the Southwest take up corn agriculture, after living for millennia by hunting and gathering, and evolve into what we know as the Basketmakers? Were corn and the secrets of its cultivation traded into the area like the olivella and abalone shells sometimes found in Basketmaker sites? Unlike many seeds, corn requires growers to have some minimal instruction in how to plant and tend it. For example, someone who is used to planting amaranth by scattering seeds or shaking the seed head over the ground would have no idea that corn must be planted six inches deep or more in order to thrive.

Corn and corn agriculture have a long and honored history in the Southwest. Traditional Pueblo Indians, even in this era of supermarkets and abundant, relatively cheap food, maintain a reverential attitude toward corn. They say, "We *are* corn." Until the twentieth century, Pueblo ceremonial life, mythology, and everyday affairs were structured around the cultivation of corn. Even though corn plays a much diminished role in the diet of today's Pueblo Indians, the memory of its earlier importance lives on in their traditions.

Samples of corn found in Basketmaker caves.

The transition from dependence on gathering and hunting to reliance on agriculture fascinates archaeologists because it so profoundly affects the way people live. For one thing, whereas foragers generally need to be on the move, following the seasonal migration of game animals or the ripening of seeds and fruits, farming tends to make people settle down.[34] At least some members of the group have to stay in one place long enough to plant and tend the crops, making sure they receive sufficient water and do not become overgrown with weeds. Farming also requires that people retain enough seeds each year both to eat throughout the winter and to use for replanting the following spring. In other words, farmers need a way to store food. Together, sedentariness and storage begin to alter dramatically the kinds of dwellings people erect.

Turkey Pen Ruin.

In the Southwest, the Archaic peoples who preceded the Basketmakers subsisted primarily on grass seeds, piñon nuts, berries, small game, birds, and roots. They lived in rockshelters or constructed temporary shelters in places where they needed to camp for a while. Archaeologists often take the Great Basin Shoshoni people, who live west of the Colorado Plateau, as a historical analog for the Archaic peoples. Until the twentieth century, the Great Basin Shoshonis lived a similar lifestyle, hunting small game and gathering seeds and plants to feed themselves. If the Shoshonis are a guide, then the Archaic groups moved constantly, employing their well-developed understanding of the seasonal round of plants and animals. They accumulated little personal or family wealth but developed a rich oral tradition of stories and myths, as well as ceremonies, music, and art.[35]

Sometime between three thousand and four thousand years ago, corn agriculture began to take hold in the southern Southwest and then moved north. As Smiley demonstrated at Three Fir Shelter, corn cultivation and its attendant changes had already reached northeastern Arizona some three thousand years before the present—much earlier than was recognized even a decade ago.[36] Smiley suggests that the use of corn spread quickly throughout the region.[37] We do not yet know to what extent these early Basketmakers on the Colorado Plateau depended on corn, but the number of storage cists in their rockshelters suggests that corn made up a significant portion of the diet.

By about two thousand years ago, the Basketmakers around Black Mesa had moved out of their rockshelters and were building pithouses in the open, grouping them in what might be termed small villages. Perhaps, like their neighbors to the northeast in Grand Gulch, they derived a high percentage of their nutrition from maize. By analyzing pollen and the contents of preserved human feces, R. G. Matson and Brian Chisholm have demonstrated that this was the case at Turkey Pen Ruin in Grand Gulch as early as A.D. 1.[38] By about A.D. 200, Basketmaker II people had established residence on Cedar Mesa, where they lived in small villages in the piñon-juniper forest and dry-farmed their corn and squash.

To the east, judging from the Los Pinos phase and Durango sites, lived Basketmaker people who shared many traits with their western counterparts but whose different ways of making baskets and sandals, among other things, suggest that they had a different origin. Summarizing the archaeological findings, R. G. Matson proposes that there were two streams of Basketmaker II people, one that lived in the western part of the Colorado Plateau and another that lived in the east and apparently had not quite so great an antiquity as the westerners.[39] He suggests that this pattern might have been tied to the slow evolution of corn, over a period of as much as fifteen hundred years, from a plant requiring floodwater irrigation into a strain suitable for dry farming.[40]

But eastern or western, what were the origins of the Basketmaker II people? Matson suggests, along with archaeologists Claudia and Michael Berry, that the western branch evolved from San Pedro Archaic people who migrated into the area from the south.[41] He further offers that the eastern branch evolved in place from a northern Archaic people who adopted Basketmaker II traits from the western Basketmakers.

Such developmental models are quite tentative and depend on many shaky assumptions. Yet Matson's models give other archaeologists hypotheses to test as they pursue their own research. Matson himself, for example, along with Brian Chisholm, has noted a lack of evidence for late Archaic occupation on Cedar Mesa.[42] If correct, this observation would support the view that Basketmaker II people moved into the area with their agriculture and did not evolve from an indigenous population of Archaic people.

Further support comes from a recent attempt by Phil Geib and Dale Davidson to find evidence about the transition from the Archaic to the Basketmaker period.[43] In 1991 and 1992, they excavated an alcove in southeastern Utah called Old Man Cave, which had been disturbed by looters and revealed Basketmaker II layers on top of Archaic strata extending back nearly seventy-eight hundred years from the present. Fortunately, enough undisturbed material remained to allow the two to examine the stratigraphic layers in detail. They found that the transition had not been a gradual one. Between the last Archaic and the first Basketmaker occupation appeared several layers of sterile soil, indicating that the alcove had been abandoned by the Archaic people before the Basketmakers moved in. Although this single finding does not prove that Basketmaker II people arrived from elsewhere, it does add weight to the hypothesis.

So far, the earliest radiocarbon date for corn in Grand Gulch is about A.D. 1, obtained from samples found in the rockshelter called Turkey Pen Ruin. The absence of earlier dates for corn agriculture in Grand Gulch remains a puzzle. Did the people of Grand Gulch move in as much as a thousand years after the people of Marsh Pass, a scant one hundred kilometers to the southwest? Considering how rapidly corn agriculture spread from what is now Mexico into northern Arizona, it is hard to believe that people did not keep going a little farther north or that indigenous northern groups failed to adopt agriculture for so long. Perhaps, as Smiley suggests, archaeologists have not examined corn from the area closely enough to obtain a true picture of its range of dates.[44] Clearly, more research on the alcoves of Grand Gulch is needed. Now that the Wetherill–Grand Gulch Research Project has supplied proveniences for many of the early collections removed from Grand Gulch, it can even be hoped that corn and other organic materials from those collections will be dated to reveal new evidence for that far-reaching event, the inception of corn agriculture in the American Southwest.

ANOTHER PROMISING ARENA FOR FUTURE RESEARCH LIES IN THE BASKETMAKERS' magnificent and seemingly mysterious rock art. Everywhere in canyon country, smooth cliff faces offer vast canvases on which ancient artists could etch or paint. And paint they did, often leaving the cliff walls around their rockshelters covered with images of animals, geometric forms, and humanlike figures that now tantalize us with their elusive meaning. Slowly, mostly since the mid-1980s, anthropologists and art historians have begun to serve up some plausible interpretations of the Basketmakers' artistic legacy.

Until the 1970s, Ancestral Pueblo rock art, whether from the Basketmaker II, Basketmaker III, or later Pueblo culture, was generally neglected as a subject of serious archaeological research. If archaeologists reported pictographs (painted images) or petroglyphs (incised images) at all, they reproduced them as drawings or photographs in their reports but seldom discussed their style or content. Apparently, many archaeologists have felt unqualified to comment on or interpret artistic endeavor. Most of the thousands of rock art sites recorded in the Southwest have been documented by artists, avocational archaeologists, and other enthusiasts who developed a fascination for the subject and spent uncounted hours painstakingly photographing, drawing, and recording these sites on archaeological survey forms. Thanks to their efforts, a solid body of data now fuels the increasingly serious study of rock art panels.

It is extremely difficult to interpret another culture's iconography with confidence. Nevertheless, careful examination of rock art images in their archaeological context, along with attention to subtleties of style, execution, placement, and the associations between different images, can lead to greater understanding. For example, rock art expert Polly Schaafsma, after years of studying Ancestral Pueblo rock art along the Rio Grande, has been able to infer the movement of ideas northward from what is now Mexico into central New Mexico during early Pueblo IV times.[45] She and her archaeologist husband, Curtis Schaafsma, have also employed rock art evidence to propose that the Pueblo kachina cult moved north from Mexico to the Rio Grande pueblos, then west to the Hopi and Zuni villages.[46] Campbell Grant has analyzed the Basketmaker, Pueblo, and Navajo rock art of Canyon de Chelly in northeastern Arizona and related these images to artifacts unearthed during excavation.[47] Folklorist Jane Young has studied the rock art of Zuni Pueblo in an effort not only to probe the meaning of prehistoric symbols and rock art panels but also to examine how contemporary Zunis interpret them.[48]

Since the mid-1980s, close examination of Basketmaker rock art has also begun to yield results. By comparing images depicted on canyon walls with excavated objects, archaeologist and rock art specialist Sally Cole has shown that pictographs and petroglyphs sometimes represent artifacts unearthed at Basketmaker II sites. Cole writes: "Rock art suggests functions for . . . items of material culture that may not otherwise be apparent in the archaeological record; and in turn, archaeological materials in combination with ethnographic data provide information for the interpretation of rock art."[49]

Cole has shown, for example, that the anthropomorphic figures painted at Green Mask Alcove in Grand Gulch display jewelry similar to that found in Basketmaker burials. Some of the figures, which seem to be female, wear what appear to be belts and menstrual aprons.[50]

Drawing on ethnographic descriptions of historic Pueblo ritual items and practices, Cole has suggested that many Basketmaker II rock art panels depict shamanistic practices. For instance, a panel in Slickhorn Canyon, south of Grand Gulch, shows a figure in human form topped by the image of a duck, seemingly a headdress. Figures wearing duck headdresses are relatively common in Basketmaker II rock art and are often depicted along with other motifs that might have had ritual significance. A wooden artifact in the shape of a duck, collected by McLoyd and Graham, bears a strong resemblance to the objects that, in rock art panels, appear to constitute parts of headdresses.[51]

One of the most interesting relationships discovered between Basketmaker II artifacts and rock art has to do with the green mask that gives Green Mask Alcove its name. This well-executed image was painted in at least four colors on a carefully smoothed surface high above the current floor of the alcove. The face itself is decorated with alternating

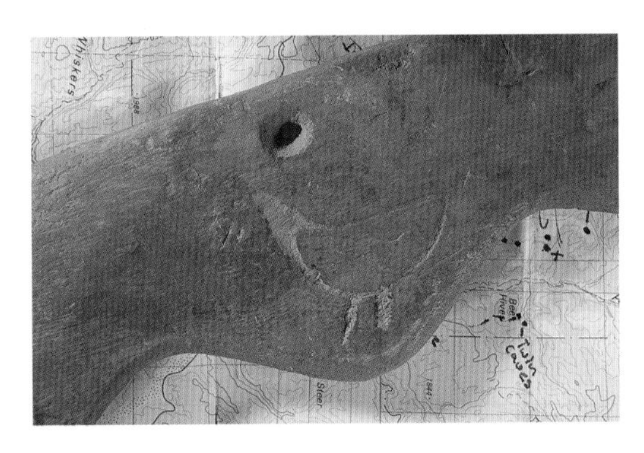

Carved wooden duck tablita from the Green collection.

Rock art panel with Green Mask, Green Mask Alcove.

horizontal bands of green and yellow. The hair, painted in red, displays two side bobs outlined in white pigment. Interestingly, it has an artifact counterpart, unearthed some fifty miles to the southwest. Kidder and Guernsey reported finding a scalp that matches this image in Kinboko Cave 1 in Marsh Pass:

> It is the entire head skin of an adult, with the hair carefully dressed. . . . The face has been colored rather elaborately; the "part" and tonsure are painted with a pasty greenish-white pigment; up the center of the "part" and across the tonsure runs a narrow streak of yellow. Just under the forehead seam there is a thin, horizontal band of red. From this to a line drawn across the face half an inch below the eyes is a zone of white. . . . Rove through two small holes in the tonsure is a narrow thong for suspension.[52]

Kidder and Guernsey also noted that the hair was bound in bobs, much like those of the Green Mask Alcove image and of images seen elsewhere in Monument Valley and Grand Gulch. The two found the scalp in a burial along with the bones of a young woman and an infant. They suggested that the scalp had once been attached to a thong around the woman's neck as a kind of trophy. According to Sally Cole, scalplike images, both pecked and painted, sometimes with a loop at the top of the head, appear in other Basketmaker II rock art. None, however, is executed with the detail of the one at Green Mask Alcove.[53] She believes that the scalp served some ceremonial function; perhaps by studying other examples of "scalps" in rock art, researchers will eventually be able to reach beyond this minimal understanding to suggest exactly what these enigmatic objects symbolized in the Basketmaker world.

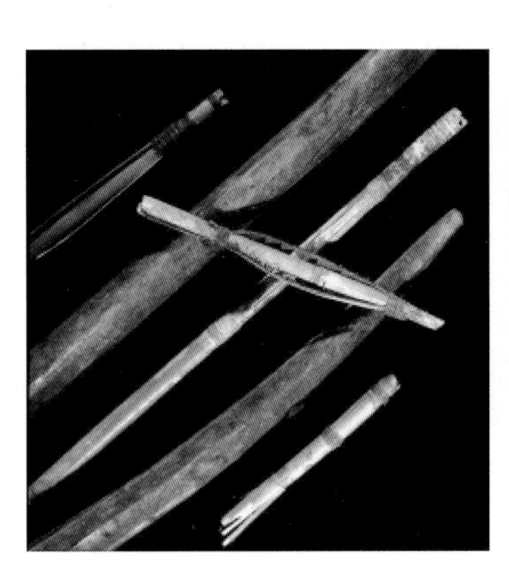

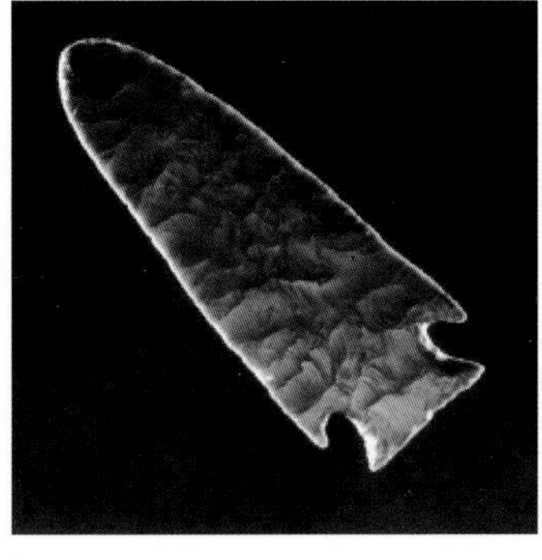

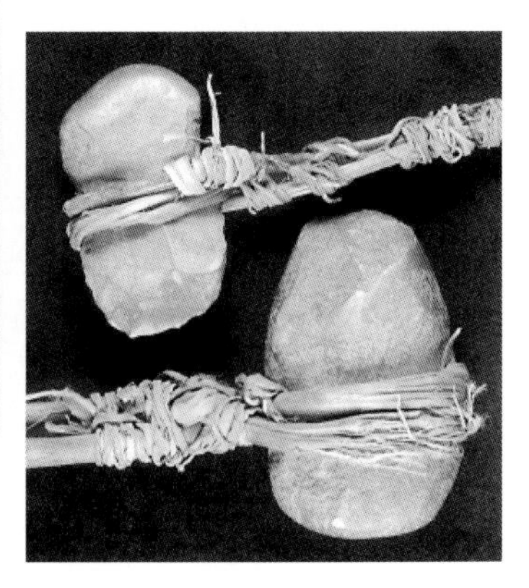

Left: Arrow shafts found by the 1897 Whitmore Exploring Expedition in Junction Ruin. Center: Chert knife blade, about 5 inches long, found lodged between the ribs of a Basketmaker skeleton in Cave 7 by members of the 1893 Hyde Exploring Expedition. Right: Two hafted axes removed by the 1893 Hyde Exploring Expedition from Cave 7 (the larger ax) and Cave 30 in Allen Canyon.

THE ANCIENT BASKETMAKERS NOT ONLY MADE ART, THEY ALSO MADE WAR. Most of the time, to be sure, they probably lived peaceful lives: their bones and desiccated bodies seldom reveal damage that cannot be explained by disease or accident. And the Basketmakers seem to have treated their dead with great esteem, preparing the bodies carefully and burying them with valued possessions. Yet archaeological evidence demonstrates that Basketmaker II people were also capable of extraordinary violence against each other. Among this evidence, some of the most compelling comes from Richard Wetherill's Cave 7.

Wetherill recognized clearly what his finds in Cave 7 meant. From the field he wrote to Talbot Hyde:

> Six of the bodies had spear heads in them, and what I consider the most valuable find in the History of America is the finding in one joint of the backbone of skeleton 103 a spear point of stone sticking into the bone at least an inch. The same thing occurs with skeleton 128 but it seems this one did not die from the wound as the cut in the outside of the bone has partially healed.[54]

Excavating the skeletons in Cave 7, the Wetherill brothers found few of the animal skins, bags, and baskets that normally accompanied Basketmaker burials. Instead, most of the artifacts associated with the buried skeletons were dart points, knife blades, and ornamental and ceremonial items small enough to be carried on a person. Although the absence of the usual burial offerings might have been the result of relatively poor preservation in Cave 7, which had greater soil moisture at Basketmaker depths than did many of the other Grand Gulch alcoves, Winston Hurst and physical anthropologist Christy Turner suspect that the absence of normal grave goods reflects the violent deaths of some of these people.[55]

Some skeletons showed evidence of having been stabbed to death, perhaps in a systematic execution; others, judging from fracture patterns on the heads, faces, and lower jaws, had been beaten around the time of death. After examining the skeletal remains, Hurst and Turner pointed out: "Head damage is . . . brutally severe. Fracture patterns indicate that both clubs and hammer-like weapons were used to beat the victims. . . . This beating may have been a form of torture. Cut marks in at least three of the studied Cave 7 males show that they were scalped as well as beaten. "[56]

Hurst and Turner also analyzed the stone points found in Cave 7 in order to try to determine whether they were predominately atlatl points, which might indicate that the people buried there had been killed in battle, or predominantly knife blades, which might signify that they had been killed at close range. From both the artifact evidence and a careful inspection of the skeletal injuries, they concluded that "there can be no doubt that a number of the victims were stabbed." Some were stabbed with bone daggers, which are driven home most effectively by using the palm of the hand, suggesting that these people might have been executed rather than killed in battle.

Males outnumber females in the Cave 7 collection by three to one, and only 15 percent of the skeletons are children. Typically, in large prehistoric burial samples, females roughly equal males, and children roughly equal adults. These observations add weight to Hurst and Turner's hypothesis that the Cave 7 burials represent a Basketmaker II group in which some of the women and children were taken captive and the rest massacred along with the men. Turner and Hurst examined the skeletons for signs of cannibalism but found none.

Were massacres and executions common in Basketmaker times, or was the slaughter in Cave 7 a tragic exception to a normally peaceable way of life? We do not yet know. One reason is that until recently, except for Christy Turner and a few others, archaeologists working in the Southwest virtually ignored evidence of prehistoric violence. Remarkably, Hurst and Turner found that although textbook accounts of the discovery of the Basketmakers referred to the Wetherills' finds in Cave 7 and cited either Richard Wetherill's letters or his one article describing the find, not a single one mentioned the condition of the skeletons. Perhaps Turner and Hurst's research will prompt more archaeologists to ask, "How did the Basketmaker people treat each other?" Perhaps it will help spark a constructive debate over the "dark side" of Ancestral Pueblo life.

As we write this book, the first one hundred years of Basketmaker research are drawing to a close. What, all told, have archaeologists learned about these ancient people? Some questions will never be answered by any amount of excavation. Because the Basketmakers left no written records, for example, we will never know what language or languages they spoke. We can surmise that they held beliefs about the world, told stories, and developed ceremonies around the sacred aspects of their lives, but the contents of their myths and rituals will always remain a mystery. We can imagine that they loved one another, shared joys and expectations, heartaches and failures, and feared hunger, injury, and death. Yet we can only speculate about how they expressed these emotions. At the same time, a century of research has forged a great deal of knowledge that can be summarized with confidence.

First, we know that the Basketmakers were farmers. Their horticulture distinguished them sharply from their predecessors, the Archaic peoples. Regardless of whether they moved into the Southwest from elsewhere, bringing agriculture with them, or evolved in place out of local Archaic groups, the Basketmakers cultivated corn and squash. Like their descendants, the

Pueblo dwellers, the Basketmakers fitted their agricultural techniques to the local environment—floodwater farming where it was possible, dry farming where it was not.

Relatively early in their history, the Basketmakers began to grow sufficient corn to depend on it for more than half of their diet. In the spring, they planted corn seeds deep in the soil to take advantage of the winter's moisture stored there. The corn they planted was far different from the hybrid varieties grown commercially today. It was short, bushy, and produced ears about six inches long with twelve to fourteen rows of kernels.[57] In normal years, the corn would sprout and grow throughout the dry month of June, then start to mature when the July rains came. The Basketmakers probably weeded between the emerging plants with simple digging sticks, and they may have carried water to them in pitch-lined baskets. To process the corn for eating, they ground the dried kernels on stone slabs, or metates, using a smaller handstone, or mano, as the grinding tool. The cornmeal could readily be cooked in stews or mixed with water and baked on hot, flat stones as corncakes.

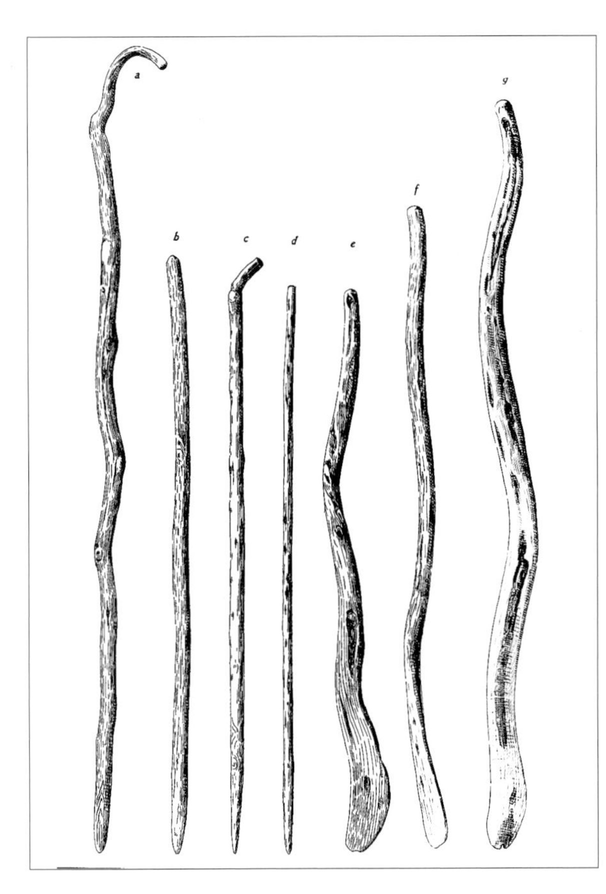

Wooden planting sticks from White Dog Cave and Cave 7.

Despite the Basketmakers' reliance on corn and squash, gathering and hunting never lost their importance. Both Basketmakers and later Pueblo people employed a mixed strategy for feeding themselves. They gathered acorns and nutritious piñon nuts and collected the seeds of Indian rice grass and other plants in season. Wild onions and lilies found near springs provided flavor, starches, and sources of vitamins. The people also collected and ate yucca pods and cactus fruit, and there is evidence, albeit meager, that they used leafy plants as salad greens or potherbs. The Basketmakers must have known the medicinal properties of many plants as well, and used them to treat their ailments.

The meat of wild animals seems to have formed a relatively small part of the Basketmaker diet. They probably hunted primarily in the fall and winter, when agricultural duties were over, using the atlatl to bring down larger animals such as deer, bears, mountain sheep, and mountain lions. Basketmaker II rock art commonly depicts mountain sheep and deer with an atlatl either superimposed over the animal image or placed nearby. Such images may represent a form of hunting magic, or perhaps they celebrate hunting success.

To catch rabbits or prairie dogs, the Basketmakers used nets and set snares made of fine string. Samuel Guernsey excavated a particularly fine rabbit net in White Dog Cave. Made of apocynum and looking a bit like an overlong tennis net, when fully stretched it extended about 240 feet. It was more than three and one-half feet wide, weighed twenty-eight pounds, and required about four miles of twine.[58] Such a net could have been stretched across the mouth of a small canyon and small game herded into it to be clubbed to death.

Except in winter, the Basketmakers apparently wore few clothes. Men went naked most of the time. Women wore a small apron made up of lengths of string tied to a waist band. Menstrual pads consisted of long strings of shredded yucca fiber held in place by the waistband. In cold weather both men and women wore tanned deerskins or robes woven of fur-wrapped twine. Sandals protected their feet, and in winter perhaps hide leggings warded off the snow and cold.

The Basketmakers adorned themselves with necklaces made from the seeds of hackberry and juniper, or from shell, bone, and stone. Chokers of leather or fiber string were sometimes hung with stone and shell pendants. Morris and Burgh discovered a particularly beautiful necklace in one of the rockshelters they excavated north of Durango, Colorado. It was made of elongated lignite beads and pink and gray shale beads strung on a string made of five two-ply strands of human hair.[59] Many of the Basketmakers' shell beads and ornaments were made from olivella shells, and others from abalone—both of which came as trade items from the West Coast or the Gulf of California. Far from living in isolation on the Colorado Plateau, the Basketmakers had contact with other prehistoric peoples in surrounding territories.

For shelter when away from home gathering plants or hunting, Basketmaker foragers likely constructed temporary shelters out of whatever materials lay at hand. For more permanent shelter near their agricultural fields, they depended on pithouses to protect them from the severest weather and to store precious foodstuffs.

The builders would first dig a shallow, roughly circular pit, normally from one to three feet deep and up to thirty feet across. After smoothing the floor of the pit, they plastered it with a layer of mud to form a hard surface. To roof the structure, they might set four poles upright in the pit floor, connecting them to each other at the top with smaller, horizontally placed poles, creating a log superstructure. Additional logs laid against the horizontal poles from outside the pit formed sloping walls, while other logs laid across the horizontal poles formed the roof.

Olivella shell necklace.

Alternatively, as Morris and Burgh found, the walls might be built from logs piled one upon the other and held in place by adobe mud. As they laid additional logs on the foundation, the builders gave them an inward slant, gradually shrinking the opening until they could lay logs and brush across it to form a roof. Finally, in either case, the builders would seal the entire structure with adobe mud to create a watertight skin.

Into the pithouse floor the Basketmakers dug a heating pit and some storage cists to hold the food they wished to preserve. Rather than build a fire, which would require ventilation, the people apparently brought in rocks that had been heated in a fire pit outdoors and laid them in the heating pit. A large rock holds a considerable amount of heat and could warm even a large pithouse. Basketmaker beds seem to have been simple nests of grass or leaves.[60]

The earliest Basketmaker II people constructed widely dispersed pithouses either on open valley slopes or on the floors of canyon alcoves and rockshelters. Later, families apparently lived in loose clusters of pithouses near their agricultural fields—what one might call proto-villages. For example, as many as ten of the pithouses Morris and Burgh excavated at Talus

Different types of Basketmaker cists.

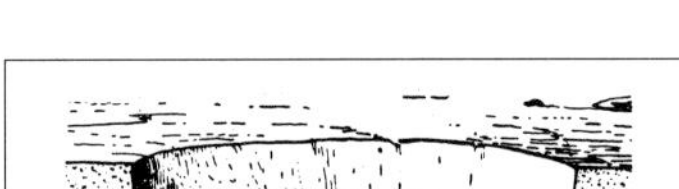

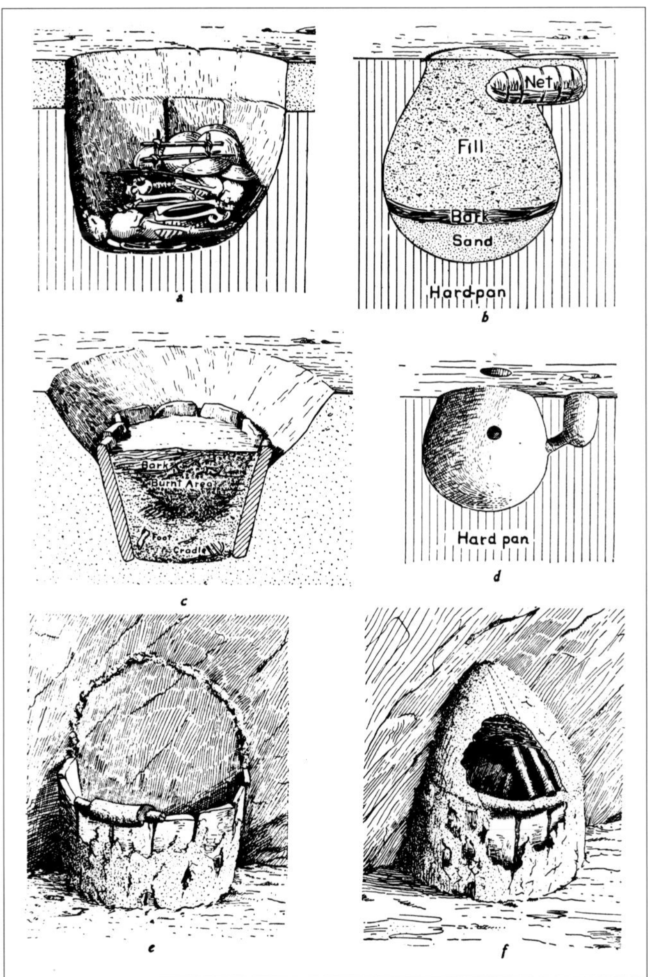

Village near Durango were contemporaneous, suggesting that they functioned as a village of families farming the rich soil along the Animas River.[61] Eventually, as the population grew and what we know as the Basketmaker II period evolved into Basketmaker III, the small proto-villages became larger and more orderly.

Just how Basketmaker villages evolved is the subject of current research. Karen M. Dohm, for example, has examined clusters of Basketmaker II pithouses on Cedar Mesa—groups of dwellings within sight and sound of one another—in an attempt to determine whether they might have functioned as early villages.[62] She concludes that the Basketmaker II people who settled Cedar Mesa had a preference for living near one another in similar pithouses that tend to be oriented in the same general direction. Dohm suggests that these loose communities of pithouses display certain elements of village structure that became more formalized later in the Pueblo period.

From the baskets, woven bags, and other implements the Basketmakers left behind, we know that they appreciated artful design. Even the most utilitarian items intended for collecting, hauling, and storing foodstuffs display a well-developed sense of pattern and symmetry.

If the Basketmakers spent much of their time just keeping alive, they also apparently found time to play. In Arizona, Kidder and Guernsey unearthed a number of game pieces made of bone. White Dog Cave provided several examples, of which three included pieces grouped together in sets of seven.[63] At Talus Village and the Falls Creek rockshelters, Morris and Burgh excavated ninety-seven items that they identified as gaming pieces.[64] Each piece was marked on one side, either in a regular pattern or at random. McLoyd and the Wetherills found similar gaming pieces. It seems that the Basketmakers, like people the world over, enjoyed games of chance.

Today, it sometimes seems a matter of chance whether future generations of archaeologists will have Basketmaker sites to analyze at all. As more and more visitors flock to enjoy the Southwest's scenic canyons and to marvel at the standing signs of Ancestral Pueblo survival skills, archaeological sites are beginning to show all the hallmarks of an endangered species. Archaeologists will continue to invent new techniques for distilling information from prehistoric remains, if only the remains themselves can now be preserved.

Vandalized site in southeastern Utah, the ancient building remains torn apart by looters.

7/The Future of the Past

In Grand Gulch we are moving into an era of managed remoteness, of planned romance. I think that is probably how it has to be if we are to preserve the qualities of the area at all in an increasingly mobile and exploitative society. The challenge is to have effective management that does not itself overwhelm the values it is designed to protect.

—William D. Lipe,
"Grand Gulch: Three Days on the Road from Bluff"

It was nearly noon in Grand Gulch, and the hot August sun was beginning to wilt the two Bureau of Land Management (BLM) rangers who had just hiked in along Kane Gulch. The sky shimmered blue overhead; in the west, puffy cumulus clouds had begun to build. Susan Ellison and Kathleen Collins had just entered the main canyon on routine foot patrol.

Up ahead, the two could see the wide alcove that shelters Turkey Pen Ruin, where the sandstone overhang offers ample cover from the sun. A frequent stop for the many hikers who pass through Grand Gulch, Turkey Pen Ruin contains a structure that today looks like the remnants of a pen; in fact it is the bare stick framework of a small jacal structure from which most of the adobe has fallen away. Because Turkey Pen Ruin is identified on some maps as a major archaeological site, attracting the curious, the BLM rangers made it a point to assess the ruin's condition whenever they could.

At this hour, the deep shade in the back of the alcove seemed hospitably inviting. If they had any luck at all, the dry breeze that sweeps along the wall of the alcove would cool them while they checked the cliff dwellings inside. As soon as they climbed the shallow slope out of the sandy wash, they stopped, sun and sweat instantly forgotten. The site looked as if it had been bombed. About a third of it was covered with potholes and littered with artifacts, both ancient and modern. As the rangers later reported:

> Digging appeared to have been done sometime during the past few days. . . . Litter around the holes was new—five soda cans, three empty cigarette packs, two food tins, a paper bag with one full can of soda, and wrappers from fruit pies.
>
> Small artifacts were found scattered about the site. These include a bone awl, pieces of rope, bits of turkey feather blankets, feathers (possibly turkey), pieces of rabbit fur and deer hides, sandal pieces, small pieces of baskets, and very few potsherds.[1]

It was Sunday, August 19, 1979. Before returning to their office in Monticello, Utah, the two rangers took notes, photographed the damage, and gathered evidence. Among other things, they were able to record a few clear footprints. The report they wrote began a frustrating criminal investigation lasting more than three months.

The Grand Gulch Primitive Area is public land, administered by the BLM for hiking and sightseeing. It received the designation "primitive area" in 1972; since then no bicycles or motorized vehicles have been allowed in. The natural resources and archaeological sites are protected by a host of federal laws that prohibit digging or collecting of any sort unless it is carried out by qualified persons under permit for research purposes. At the time Ellison and Collins discovered evidence of looting in Turkey Pen Ruin, however, the archaeological sites were protected only by the very weak Antiquities Act of 1906 and by more general laws prohibiting theft of government property.

Turkey Pen Ruin is an important site. Originally dug by McLoyd and Graham in 1891 and by the Wetherills in 1894 and 1897—well before passage of the Antiquities Act—the alcove contains evidence of having been lived in, perhaps continuously, from Basketmaker II times through the Pueblo III era.[2] Despite extensive digging a century ago, in 1974, when the BLM first hired professional archaeologists to survey Turkey Pen Ruin, major portions of the site were still untouched. Some archaeologists believed that if Turkey Pen Ruin were systematically excavated over several years, it "could give an unparalleled reconstruction of Anasazi subsistence and environmental relationships."[3]

Unfortunately, the looting that Ellison and Collins discovered had churned up several previously pristine areas. The rangers hoped that catching the looters would stop the digging and that a conviction would serve as an object lesson for others.

Digging for artifacts on public lands has been illegal since the passage of the 1906 Antiquities Act. Its penalties, however, never posed much deterrent to determined pothunters. Under the act, courts could impose only misdemeanor charges and fines of up to five hundred dollars or ninety days in prison or both. Furthermore, the difficulty of establishing guilt beyond a reasonable doubt on sites as isolated as those in Grand Gulch had long frustrated managers of public lands.[4] But in the early fall of 1979, new legislation that was just making its way through Congress raised some hope of putting the looters in jail.

Ancestral Pueblo pottery unearthed and destroyed by illegal bulldozer excavations.

ALTHOUGH THE TWO RANGERS HAD GATHERED A LOT OF USEFUL EVIDENCE, INCLUDING photographs of shoe prints and objects that might hold incriminating fingerprints, they had no way to identify the looters. All the BLM staff could do was to continue visiting the area and watch for more site destruction. They did not have to wait long. On September 11, only three weeks after the first report of looting, archaeologist Bill Haase visited the site to repair some of the damage. Instead, he found evidence of more digging:

> Over one hundred pot holes were dug in one of the rooms, a kiva and the midden area, some were dug to a depth of over three feet. . . . [T]he shovels used by Pot-Hunters were cached behind a granary wall. Because of the care taken to hide the shovels, it is possible that the vandals intended to return.[5]

A disturbed archaeological site invites more digging. Haase not only did his best to collect more evidence but also filled in the worst of the holes. First, he cut plastic sheeting and covered the bottom of the hole, weighting down the corners with stones. The plastic would indicate to future archaeologists where the disturbance had ended. Then he carefully shoveled the ashy gray soil that had been dug from the hole back into it and covered it with the yellowish sandy soil typical of the local surface. Finally, he carefully raked the surface to restore as much as he could of the original floor contour.

Although BLM employees expected the diggers to return, with many thousands of acres of land to manage in southeastern Utah they could hardly maintain constant surveillance of Turkey Pen Ruin. They were not surprised to hear on October 27 that the looters had struck again. A Taos, New Mexico, woman reported to ranger Donna Sakamoto that she had been camping the previous night near Turkey Pen Ruin when two white males approached her campfire. After chatting with her for a while, they left. Later in the night she heard sounds from the direction of Turkey Pen that sounded like someone digging.

This time the BLM office in Monticello contacted special agent Clarence "Duke" Thompson at the BLM's Utah headquarters. He inspected the site with Sakamoto on November 1. They found extensive damage, including twenty-six new holes and additional trash. Some of the trash was the plastic that Haase had placed in the bottoms of the earlier pits. Before they left the site, the two attempted to fill in the holes once again. Interviews with the Taos camper and with individuals in nearby Bluff, Blanding, and Natural Bridges National Monument, who might have noticed unusual activity in the area, yielded little useful evidence.

Site visits on November 11 and 15 revealed still more digging, for a total of five separate, documented incidents of looting. The footprints in the ruin and the type of litter the vandals left were becoming familiar to the investigators, but they still had no firm leads on the criminals.

Then, on the evening of November 16, they got a break. Jerry Ballard, a BLM recreation planner, saw a small car pass him coming down Harmony Flat Road from the direction of Turkey Pen Ruin. After jotting down the car's license plate number, he headed back to where the car had been parked. There he found fresh tennis shoe tracks matching those found in Turkey Pen Ruin, leading toward Fortress Canyon, a northern tributary of Grand Gulch. Now the BLM knew the route the looters were taking to reach the site.

Not long afterward, following a snowfall, Donna Sakamoto noticed vehicle tracks along Harmony Flat Road. She immediately called Ballard for help, and the two investigated. About three and a half miles down the road, they found a four-wheel drive Ford van with Utah plates backed up into the trees. No one was around. Through the van window the two could see a pack of Marlboro cigarettes and a Pepsi-Cola can, both brands that had been found among the modern garbage left at the site. Two sets of footprints led from the van toward Fortress Canyon.

As they investigated the evidence in and around the van, two men approached. According to a later newspaper report, "one of the individuals was carrying a shovel. When the individuals saw the BLM vehicle, they turned around and went back into the trees."[6] A few minutes later one of the men reappeared and walked toward the van. "He was wearing coveralls, hard hat, and miner's lamp, and was covered with dirt."[7] The two BLM employees questioned the man and learned his name, but they got little other information except that he and the other suspect had been "working all night." Ballard took pictures of him, his boots, and his van. After the suspect drove off, Sakamoto followed him in the BLM vehicle while Ballard tracked the other man on foot. He found only the spot where the van had stopped along the road to pick up the missing collaborator.

The next day, Ballard, accompanied part of the way by Thompson and Sakamoto, followed the footprints from where the van had been parked into Turkey Pen Ruin. Six inches of snow on the trail made tracking easy. Predictably, he found signs of recent digging. The looters had even burned one of the prehistoric kiva roof beams in a fire. Among the excavation debris Ballard found filters for protective breathing masks, a broken shovel, and assorted litter including Pepsi cans and an empty Marlboro cigarette pack.[8]

This evidence completed part of the case. The BLM investigators had been lucky in spotting the men after a snowfall, when their footsteps linked them directly to the scene of the crime. They had also done a careful job of gathering evidence. In early December 1979, the United States Attorney for Utah filed a complaint in U.S. District Court against the first man, charging him with a felony violation of the Archaeological Resources Protection Act (ARPA), which had been signed into law on the last day of October.[9] The Turkey Pen case was the first one to be brought before the courts under ARPA.

In exchange for a reduction of the felony charge to a misdemeanor violation, the twenty-one-year-old man agreed to identify his accomplice. He received two years of probation and a fine of $1,500, half of which was suspended. He was also instructed to complete high school. The second man was charged with both a felony violation of ARPA and the destruction of government property.[10] He pleaded not guilty, but the jury convicted him of the second charge. He was sentenced to three years in jail and fined $750, although his jail sentence was later reduced to three years of probation.

The second looter was found not guilty of the ARPA violation, largely because the indictment had charged him with digging in a "midden," a term not specifically defined in the law. It refers to a trash dump—a common location of Ancestral Pueblo burials and the preferred target of experienced pothunters. The National Park Service had not yet issued ARPA regulations that would define such terms and relate them to the legislation.[11]

Despite the government's failure to achieve a conviction under ARPA, this case showed prosecutors that they could still accomplish much of the intent of ARPA by using other provisions of federal and state law.[12] To the determined BLM employees, getting any conviction at all seemed a colossal success. Yet considering the damage the two men had caused to an irreplaceable site, their sentences appear extraordinarily light.

Recently dug potholes in a badly looted site.

IN THE SOUTHWEST, THE MEN, WOMEN, AND CHILDREN WHO DIG SITES TO FIND ARTIFACTS have long been called "pothunters"—they dig to find prehistoric pots and other artifacts for their personal collections or to sell. Pothunters seldom make any attempt to observe or record site information. Because the term *pothunter* does not distinguish between legal and illegal collecting, the descriptive terms "artifact hunter" and "looter" are becoming more widely used by officials.[13]

Artifact hunters search for surface items or dig on private land with permission of the landowner. Sometimes they keep careful notes of their excavations, although more often they do not. Looters dig illegally, whether on public or private land. They have every incentive not to record site information; possession of written records might make it easier for law enforcement officials to gain convictions. What makes artifact hunting and looting objectionable is that in the process, these activities destroy information in the site for everyone else.

Artifacts alone, of course, can reveal much about prehistoric life. For example, close studies of stone arrowheads, spear points, and knife blades enable archaeologists to learn about the ways such implements were manufactured and used. But artifacts make up only the tip of the information iceberg. Few people realize that the unseen world of the site may tell us more about prehistoric life than do the artifacts.

As the science of archaeology matured, archaeologists developed methods to extricate information from nearly every cubic inch of a site.[14] Spatial relationships among artifacts, for example, and the associations between artifacts and site features such as house floors, roofs, storage cists, and hearths, are vital to understanding patterns of prehistoric behavior.

At Basketmaker II habitation sites on Black Mesa, archaeologist Susan Bearden looked at the way animal bones, chipped stone, and tool fragments appeared in association with each other and with dwelling features. This analysis enabled her to detect areas where prehistoric people had performed certain types of work.[15] In a burial site excavated on Black Mesa, a metate uncovered next to the bones of a young child was found to show little wear, suggesting that it had been manufactured specifically as a burial offering. Had this site been severely disturbed or carelessly excavated, archaeologists might never have recognized that common household items could be manufactured intentionally as burial offerings.[16]

Even the soil may contain important clues. While the prehistoric inhabitants of Grand Gulch went about their daily chores, the wind deposited seeds, leaves, and pollen grains on the ground, and these became buried in stratified layers right along with the artifacts. Some plant remains are so small they cannot be seen with the naked eye. But when separated from the sand and clay and highly magnified, they disclose a great deal about what the climate was like in the past and what foods were available to the site's inhabitants. When the soil layers bearing the plant remains can be dated by radiocarbon or tree-ring methods, then these microscopic indicators provide a record of climate change and how humans have reacted to it. Such information grows increasingly relevant as climate scientists struggle to understand the warming of the world's climate and how plants and animals might respond to this and other environmental changes.

Recent research at Turkey Pen Ruin illustrates the kinds of damage looters can do. Under certain conditions, the dry climate of the Southwest will preserve human feces, or coprolites, for a long time. Found in a site's superimposed soil layers along with pollen, potsherds, and animal bones, coprolites offer immediate evidence of what people ate and what diseases they suffered from. As we mentioned in chapter 6, R. G. Matson and Brian Chisholm were able to analyze coprolites from a Turkey Pen Ruin midden to show that the Basketmaker people of Grand Gulch obtained a high percentage of their nutrition from maize. They gathered the material that provided these findings from stratigraphic layers in Turkey Pen Ruin in 1972.

The looters' digging in 1979 so disturbed this same midden that it mixed Pueblo trash with the much earlier Basketmaker refuse. If Matson and Chisholm tried to carry out their analysis today, the task would be much more difficult, if not impossible. They—and the rest of the public—would be left merely with tantalizing hints of an important finding about Basketmaker II farming practices and nutrition.

The Turkey Pen Ruin case, which received coverage in the Salt Lake City and local papers, probably helped to deter some looters, by at least a modest amount. Among other things, the conviction put potential looters on notice that the federal government was becoming more serious about prosecuting cultural resource crimes. Yet the relative openness with which the two men continued their digging, despite clear evidence that the BLM knew what they were doing, demonstrates how little respect they had for the law or for the BLM's capacity to enforce it.

The two were participating in an activity with a long history in southeastern Utah. Collectors in the United States and abroad have promoted a growing market for baskets, pottery, and other prehistoric artifacts. Because the looters working over Turkey Pen Ruin were digging in the midden rather than adjacent to the Pueblo structures, we surmise that they were looking for Basketmaker objects—the baskets, blankets, jewelry, furs, hides, clothing, and wooden implements commonly associated with burials. Basketmaker artifacts are especially prized by looters because they command premium prices from collectors. Looters often sell artifacts to dealers, who then tack on a high markup before marketing them to collectors in the United States and around the world. Many looters dig archaeological sites for fun and adventure. A few also dig to augment their own collections.

In southeastern Utah, the practice of looting grew partly from the desire of museum directors to expand their collections. Andrew Kerr, for example, a Harvard-trained associate professor at the University of Utah in Salt Lake City and chairman of the Department of Anthropology in the 1920s, amassed an impressive collection of Ancestral Pueblo pots from the mesas and canyons near Blanding, Utah. Between 1924 and 1929, Kerr hired local people to show him where to dig. Through their efforts he managed to collect some fifteen hundred pots and many other artifacts from both public and private lands.

Unfortunately, Kerr's documentation was no better than Charles McLoyd's three decades earlier, and the sources of most of these artifacts cannot be identified more precisely than as a drainage or a mesa. Kerr apparently kept no notes himself and did not train his excavators to take notes.[17] Kerr's encouragement of local digging on public as well as private land contributed to the widespread acceptance of artifact hunting and looting in the area.

Building rubble at a looted site.

The Turkey Pen Ruin case raises serious questions about what some have called "the future of the past"—our willingness and ability to protect archaeological sites for the pleasure and knowledge of our children and grandchildren. The destruction of this site is hardly unique; many similar incidents occur on public and private land throughout the United States each year. People who remove artifacts from public lands literally rob the rest of us twice—first of the artifact and then of the information the artifact and the site could have provided. Some sites are vandalized simply for amusement. It is now extremely rare to find the remains of an Ancestral Pueblo dwelling, whether on federal, state, or private land, that has not been disturbed or vandalized by looters or thoughtless, uninformed persons.

Historians and prehistorians often call archaeological sites, historic structures, artifacts, and rock art by the term "historic cultural resources," which is generally shortened to "cultural resources."[18] As the name implies, they are sources of information about the human past, and they are finite in number. They are also nonrenewable: once they are gone, they cannot be replaced. How can we protect the extraordinary cultural resources that lie in Grand Gulch and elsewhere on the Colorado Plateau? What tools are available? How can we put them to use productively?

IT WAS EARLY NOVEMBER 1993, AND THE BLM'S KANE GULCH RANGER STATION AT the primary entrance to Grand Gulch was closed for the season. Doors were sealed, the electrical generator turned off, horse troughs placed upside down. A well-traveled white van bearing California plates and a dozen high-school students ground to a stop in the gravel parking lot. Two young teachers climbed out and opened the side door, setting their grateful charges free to stretch their legs and prepare for the coming hike. Soon, backpacks, food, camp stoves, water, and bedrolls were pulled from the rear of the van, sorted, and spread on the gravel. The instructors went over the hiking rules and discussed clothing, water treatment, and waste disposal.

A student checked the ranger station for information about Grand Gulch. She saw only a faded message on a chalk board and a prominently placed sign telling visitors where to leave the five-dollar entry fee. Nothing else to assist the hikers could be found—no map, no tips about where to camp, no information about where there might be water or what hazards might be encountered. Shrugging, the student returned to the van, slipped on her backpack, and joined the others to begin the hike. The students had come to learn about Grand Gulch and to experience its archaeology firsthand, yet they received little help from the Bureau of Land Management.

Days later the students met Fred Blackburn and other members of the Wetherill–Grand Gulch Research Project, who were in the Gulch to record inscriptions. A few minutes of conversation with the students revealed that neither they and nor their instructors understood much about the archaeological sites they had seen. The students were bright and well educated and seemed to practice good behavior toward the natural environment, but they did not know how to treat the archaeological remains or how to integrate what they could learn from them into their approach to the environment. In many ways they were typical Gulch visitors—schooled in protecting the environment but relatively uninformed about archaeological sites and how to treat them.

Above: The interior of Battle Cave c. 1895, showing the results of early pothunting.
Below: The same site today, now totally looted.

Perceiving their interest, Fred interpreted the area for them. To an attentive audience he related some of the Gulch's natural and human history and explained how to treat the archaeological remains with care and respect. Students and teachers alike seemed grateful for the opportunity to learn more about the canyons and how to lessen their impact on archaeological sites.

For centuries the remoteness of Grand Gulch and other canyons of the Colorado Plateau protected both archaeological sites and the environment from major damage. Now, well-paved roads take ever more visitors into the area each year. The worst harm visitors do to prehistoric sites is by intentional looting or vandalism, but much injury takes place when people who do not know any better climb on unstable walls, stand on ancient roofs, or just walk through the fragile ruins.

Three special characteristics set the Colorado Plateau apart from other places. First, the high desert climate preserves cultural resources to an extraordinary degree. The material remnants of Ancestral Pueblos, Navajos, Utes, explorers, adventurers, cowboys, and pioneers can still be read today with remarkable clarity. Second, the largest landowner in the area is the federal government, with millions of acres under its control. The Bureau of Land Management, the National Park Service, the Bureau of Indian Affairs, the Bureau of Reclamation, the National Forest Service, the Department of Energy, and the Department of Defense administer these federal lands in trust for all citizens.

Third, the region supports a high proportion of American Indians. Apache, Navajo, Pueblo, and Ute Indians live there, descendants of the land's original inhabitants. Members of these tribes are joined by a rich cultural mix of people of European backgrounds, many of whom can trace their roots in the region back a century or more. The ancestry of many Hispanic residents of the Colorado Plateau extends to the seventeenth century. All three characteristics create special opportunities for documenting American prehistory and history through archaeology, but they pose unique challenges as well.

Federal and state agencies have formal responsibility for protecting most of the land. Among other things, they are charged with protecting cultural resources from damage caused by natural forces such as erosion, fire, and flooding or by grazing, mining, recreational use, development, looting, and vandalism.

The illegal digging that harmed Turkey Pen Ruin, like the looting of many other sites throughout the region, reflects the difficulties and frustrations state and federal land managers face in attempting to carry out their responsibilities. They have millions of acres to protect but never enough money or staff to do the job. Off-road vehicles and the desire to see remote territory make the back roads and trails of the Southwest irresistible to thousands of visitors and local people. Furthermore, the brisk market in stolen artifacts gives many people incentive to dig regardless of legal penalties. In a more chilling development, some looted artifacts have recently begun to show up in connection with drug raids, along with cocaine and stolen weapons.

Three sets of tools are available for protecting cultural resources: local, state, and federal laws, land management strategies, and education. Federal and state laws against removing artifacts from public lands can, as we have seen, be hard to enforce. Land management policy—deciding who gets to use the land and for what purposes—is always a compromise among competing demands. Even at their best, laws and policies will remain ineffective unless the public is better informed about why there is value in preserving archaeological sites. That requires steadfast educational efforts and the will to investigate and prosecute cultural resource crimes. In the Southwest, open land is too vast and personnel too few to make much difference in how archaeological sites are treated unless a wider public learns both why it should preserve its heritage and how to do it.

FEDERAL LAW SUPPLIES THE FRAMEWORK FOR PROTECTING CULTURAL RESOURCES. As far back as the early 1890s, citizens of Colorado clamored for protection of the cliff dwellings on the Mesa Verde. Watching Gustaf Nordenskiöld take Mesa Verde artifacts back to Europe awoke a few people to the loss they faced with continued digging in the ruins.[19] T. Mitchell Prudden noted in 1896 that soon after the artifacts in the cliff dwellings became widely known, local people, too, began to organize Sunday outings to collect Pueblo artifacts.[20]

Gradually, pressure built from archaeologists, public officials, and just plain citizens to make Mesa Verde a state or national park. Thanks to the persevering efforts of concerned people like Colorado Springs resident Virginia McClurg, two bills were introduced in Congress: a bill to make Mesa Verde the nation's first national park set aside for the protection of antiquities, and a general one to preserve archaeological sites. After much wrangling over both, in 1906 Congress finally passed the Antiquities Act, which was signed into law on June 8 by President Theodore Roosevelt, a historian and ardent conservationist. Three weeks later, Roosevelt signed the bill making Mesa Verde a national park.

Section 1 of the Antiquities Act makes it an offense to remove artifacts from public lands without permission. Section 2 authorizes the president to declare "historic landmarks, historic and prehistoric structures, and other objects of historic or scientific interest that are situated upon the lands owned or controlled by the government of the United States to be national monuments." Section 3 allows for the granting of excavation and collection permits for qualified scientific purposes, and Section 4 provides for the creation of uniform rules and regulations.[21]

Because penalties under the act are small and establishing guilt beyond a reasonable doubt is difficult, arrests and convictions have been few.[22] Moreover, some people even now simply do not take the removal of artifacts from public lands seriously, much less consider it stealing. Indeed, memoranda in Department of Interior files document incidents of looting on public lands by employees of various federal agencies in the 1940s, 1950s, and 1960s.[23] Although looters and collectors constitute a small minority of the total population, even these few can quickly destroy a large part of the country's heritage.

To cope with the potential loss of our history, Congress has since passed additional laws for managing and preserving historic cultural resources. The most important one is the National Historic Preservation Act of 1966 (NHPA).[24] NHPA created a legal and administrative apparatus for identifying, evaluating, and protecting historic cultural resources. Among other things, NHPA established the National Register of Historic Places, which has become an effective tool for identifying properties of historical importance and guarding them against urban development, road building, and other forms of "progress." A historic building on the National Register is less likely to be razed to make way for a shopping mall.

The Archaeological Resources Protection Act of 1979 (ARPA)—amended in 1988—gave the protection of cultural resources a boost by prescribing relatively strong penalties for looting and vandalism. As the Turkey Pen Ruin case illustrated, ARPA made a big difference in the ability of federal law enforcement officers to prosecute such cases.[25]

The latest major federal law imparts even stronger protection to Indian burials. The Native American Graves Protection and Repatriation Act of 1990 (NAGPRA) makes it a felony to traffic in Native American human remains and burial artifacts. The first offense is a misdemeanor or felony misdemeanor, punishable by up to a year in prison and a $100,000 fine. Subsequent offenses are felonies that carry penalties of up to five years in prison and fines of up to $250,000 for each offense.[26] NAGPRA also mandates that certain American Indian remains and cultural items stored in museums throughout the country be repatriated to the tribes.[27] The law attempts to undercut the market in Indian grave goods and cultural treasures, especially items that have sacred significance, by making it possible to prosecute dealers and collectors as well as looters.

What distinguishes NAGPRA from other federal statutes is that its jurisdiction extends beyond federal lands to cover Indian burials of any age, along with funerary artifacts and sacred cultural objects, whether they are found on state, local, or even private land. Nor do the items need to cross state lines to be subject to federal law. Although as we write, the law is too new for us to predict whether it will indeed reduce the incidence of looting on public and private lands, it delivers a clear warning to potential destroyers of Indian burial sites. NAGPRA's reach is broad and its penalties strong.[28]

Local and state laws, too, protect archaeological sites and artifacts in parks and other public lands.[29] Many states have enacted laws protecting graves on both public and private land.[30] Regulations generally require the excavator to notify state officials about the grave and to call in qualified archaeologists to examine the human remains. If the remains are Indian, they automatically fall under the jurisdiction of NAGPRA, and the appropriate Indian tribe must be involved in disposing of the remains and any associated artifacts.

Nevertheless, federal records show that laws alone are insufficient to stem continuing site damage. The National Park Service (NPS) estimates that between 1985 and 1987, 1,720 violations of laws protecting cultural resources took place on federal and Indian lands—an estimate that likely represents only a small fraction of the total number. A mere 11 percent of these cases resulted in a citation or arrest.[31]

Even so, that 11 percent reflects a major increase in arrests over previous experience. Slowly, the number of historic resource cases ending up in court is growing. As a result, the National Park Service, the Bureau of Land Management, the National Forest Service, and other agencies have instituted programs to educate public lands managers, attorneys, and judges about the nature of cultural resource crimes. State and local groups, as well as national organizations such as the Society for American Archaeology and the Society for Historical Archaeology, have also supported educational programs.

These efforts have begun to spark greater awareness of the problem and greater willingness to enforce the law when cases reach the courts. Yet to make these laws effective, the general public, cultural resource managers, and legal experts all need to appreciate both legal prohibitions and penalties and to support enforcement of the law with greater resolve.

A recently pothunted site in Grand Gulch.

Campfire built by a hiker in an Ancestral Pueblo dwelling.

TAKE AWAY ALL THE LOOTERS AND VANDALS, AND THE GREATEST THREAT TO archaeological sites is still with us. Visitation by people who enjoy dramatic scenery and find fascination in remnants of human history is growing steadily all across the Southwest, and Grand Gulch is no exception.

The question of how to manage the natural and archaeological resources of southeastern Utah first became an issue for the BLM in the 1960s, when the rising popularity of outdoor recreation began to bring hikers and guided horse riders into canyon country.[32] Earlier, Grand Gulch and Cedar Mesa had served primarily as pasture for the area's cattle ranchers. Grazing allotments were handled by the U.S. Grazing Service, the predecessor of the Bureau of Land Management. When the BLM was formed in 1946, it simply continued devoting the land to grazing. There was no reason not to; until the 1960s, only a handful of visitors a year ventured into the Gulch, usually in the care of the few local guides.[33]

Between 1960 and 1972, access to the Grand Gulch plateau improved immensely. In an effort to increase access to Lake Powell after the Glen Canyon dam was completed, the state of Utah paved the dirt and gravel roads into the area from Blanding, blasting a route through Comb Ridge, east of Grand Gulch. With better roads, archaeological sites on the Grand Gulch plateau became dramatically more reachable.

In 1972, the Department of Interior designated Grand Gulch and most of the land adjacent to it the Grand Gulch Primitive Area. It set aside the primitive area for nonvehicular recreation such as hiking and camping, two rapidly growing uses of public lands. Cattle grazing and mining were excluded—a major step for the BLM. As decreed in the Federal Land Policy Management Act of 1976, which guides the BLM, "public lands will be managed in a manner that will protect the quality of scientific, scenic, historical, ecological, environmental, air and atmospheric, water resources, and archaeological values . . . and will provide for outdoor recreation."[34]

In 1991, the number of registered visitors to Grand Gulch climbed to more than forty-five hundred, an increase of 50 percent from five years earlier.[35] During the mid-1970s, when visitation was much lower, the agency was able to assign six rangers to patrol Grand Gulch, assist visitors, keep out livestock, and help archaeologists clean up vandalized sites. It even established a small ranger station at Kane Gulch, along state route 261, the major entry point into Grand Gulch.

By the time Turkey Pen Ruin was looted in 1979, the BLM had already decided to remove three rangers from the area and assign them to other tasks.[36] By 1986, the agency had eliminated its last permanent position in the Gulch area and begun staffing the Kane Gulch ranger station only seasonally—a decision that reflected not only reduced funding but also management priorities that tended to downplay the importance of cultural resource preservation.

Patrol of the Gulch protects visitors and archaeological sites alike. Rangers on regular duty can alert hikers to springs that have dried up, tell them where water can still be found, and warn them about places at risk of flash flooding. They can help deter intentional wrongdoing simply by being around, and they have a chance to discover looting before the trail grows cold.

If the Kane Gulch Ranger Station were staffed at all times, the BLM could offer visitors information that might reduce much of the inadvertent damage inflicted on the archaeological resources. For example, a few years ago, a hiker sought shelter from the cold in a shallow alcove. He built a small fire and pulled some sandstone slabs from the soil to make a fire circle. Sadly, in doing so he unknowingly disturbed a Basketmaker grave. Trying to be environmentally responsible, he even cleaned up carefully the next morning and scattered the ashes—contaminating the upper layers of the site with recent organic matter. Had he been told that camping in the alcoves was forbidden, and why, he might have found a different place to bed down.

Just as visitors and archaeological sites need protection, so does the natural environment. Southeastern Utah is home to rare and unusual plants that over millennia have adapted to survive only in certain small pockets within a precarious environment. Monkey flower, canyon orchid, cave primrose, and ancient relict stands of aspen are among the species at risk in Grand Gulch. Whole colonies can be wiped out by a few well-placed acts of collection and vandalism.

The designation of Grand Gulch as a primitive area in the middle of a much larger BLM multiple-use area illustrates the difficult choices that must be made about public lands. For the Gulch, federal policymakers have opted to favor recreation. No vehicles are allowed; both individual hiking and camping and group trips with horses or llamas require a permit and a fee. Elsewhere in its domain, the BLM faces tougher decisions over use. Although it must protect the natural and archaeological resources of all its lands, the BLM is also charged with managing commercial uses such as logging, grazing, and mining. In the fragile environment of southeastern Utah, grazing often causes erosion of the canyons.[37] Oil and gas exploration and drilling open the land not only to large work crews but later to others who use the improved roads they build.

As BLM officials try to balance commerce with history, they cannot treat all sites as equally important but must gauge their relative significance to decide which ones will receive protection. The federal budget will never be large enough to save every site. Only strong public support for archaeological protection can turn back a century of loss of irreplaceable resources.

IN OUR VIEW, THE ONLY WAY WE AMERICANS WILL BEGIN TO PRESERVE ARCHAEOLOGICAL sites is to increase people's appreciation of history in much the same way the environmental movement has heightened the public's understanding of how to use our lands, lakes, and rivers. By making ordinary citizens aware of environmental damage and how it affects their lives, natural history writers, educators, biologists, and geographers have sensitized us to the steady loss of our quality of life. Americans began to have better environmental preservation when thousands of people in communities everywhere started to take responsibility for their own local environment. In a similar way, the preservation of the historical record is up to us all. Those who care about preserving America's historic and prehistoric legacy must begin to share their views with others.

When Europeans arrived on the shores of North America, they generally treated the indigenous populations as "other," not quite human. Most Europeans regarded the land as wilderness, despite clear evidence that it was inhabited and used. Indians were just in the way. Few took the time to learn Indian languages or Indian ways. Yet the few who did found foods, medicines, and ideas that have benefited the entire world. Corn, potatoes, beans, chocolate, and many other Indian foods were adopted by Europeans and exported to the Old World, where in time they revolutionized the world's gustatory habits.[38] Iroquois ideas about a union of states made their way into the United States Constitution.[39]

The handling of Native American archaeological remains and grave sites echoes the Eurocentric focus of mainstream society. Rather than being treated with respect, Indian sacred sites have more often been looted. Religious objects, both prehistoric and recent, have been taken. As Douglas Cole discovered when he examined the role of museums in collecting Northwest Coast Indian artifacts, even respected anthropologists allowed little to stand in the way of their drive to accumulate objects of ethnological interest. Franz Boas, the grand old man of Northwest Coast anthropology, declared that "stealing bones from a grave was 'repugnant work' and even prompted horrid dreams, but 'someone had to do it.'"[40]

Boas justified his grave robbing in the interest of science. At the time, it was scientifically fashionable to measure the size of the skull to determine brain capacity, so skulls were especially prized.[41] One wonders how he might have felt about someone robbing the graves of his own relatives. As historian James Riding In has protested, referring to the desecration of Indian graves, "archaeology, a branch of anthropology that still attempts to sanctify this tradition of exploiting dead Indians, arose as an honorable profession from this sacrilege."[42]

People who want to preserve the record that American history has left on the landscape need to promote a new ethic, one that accords the richness of Native American prehistory and history the respect it deserves. Americans need to look back not to revel in some distorted vision of a "golden age" but to add to their understanding of the whole American experience.

Ultimately, we need a broader, more inclusive definition of what it means to be human and cultured. Archaeology discloses the enormous range of human experience through time, and it can help foster in Americans of all ethnic backgrounds a sense of continuity and community in history. The archaeological profession, too, will have to change its position regarding the treatment of Indian remains if it is to contribute to a broadening of perspective.[43] When viewed through the widest lens, American history is not the history of Europeans in the New World, on the one hand, and American Indians, on the other, but rather of how humans of every origin have interacted with each other and with the land that makes up this continent.

Changing people's behavior toward historic sites requires not just a new rationale for valuing cultural resources but, in very practical ways, education. Sometimes education is as simple as telling visitors what to avoid doing and why. For example, we think those historic signatures that proved so critical in tracing the explorers' routes in the canyons are being effaced by hikers who believe them to be recent graffiti. Members of the Wetherill–Grand Gulch Research Project worked with the BLM to design a brochure for hikers explaining why the signatures are valuable. Unfortunately, the brochure is no longer available to hikers, and the historic signatures continue to be removed.

A great deal more than brochures could be written for the public, however, if archaeologists saw education as the responsibility we believe it should be. For most archaeologists, fieldwork, analysis, and the interpretation of data are what count. Many view the writing of formal reports and papers as a necessary evil required for professional advancement or to get the next contract or grant. Often such reports are poorly written and saturated with jargon.

Sadly, archaeologists have few incentives to share their research with the public by writing interesting articles and books that might inspire enthusiasm in a wide range of readers. Among other tasks, they need to counteract the popular, superficial notion of archaeology as treasure hunting that is promulgated by adventure films such as the Indiana Jones movies of the 1980s and by documentaries of treasure salvage in the Spanish galleons sunk off the Caribbean coasts.

Another route to expanding the public's appreciation of cultural resources takes people right into an archaeological dig. In the Southwest, institutions like the Crow Canyon Archaeological Center and the Kelly Place in Cortez, Colorado, the Four Corners School of Outdoor Education in Monticello, Utah, the Canyonlands Field Institute in Moab, and the White Mesa Institute in Blanding, Utah, offer programs in which participants help excavate, map, and document archaeological sites. These programs have their counterparts throughout the country; Earth Watch is one of the best known.

Federal agencies such as the National Forest Service, the Bureau of Land Management, and the National Park Service also conduct programs that involve government employees and the general public in preservation. Among other things, these programs show how individuals can make a difference in their own communities. They are fun, too.

It is critically important that educational programs reach children. The BLM administrations of Utah and Colorado, with active support from the central office in Washington, D.C., have recently worked with state historic preservation offices and schools to develop archaeological units that teachers can take into elementary school classrooms.[44] This effort has now spread to other states. Articles in *Science and Children,* published by the National Science Teachers Association, provide information for students and resources for teachers on archaeology as well as other fields of science.

Years ago we began to see that because of the close interdependence between preservation of cultural remains and preservation of the environment, both might be achieved by teaching people to approach the rural Southwest as a vast outdoor museum.[45] Since 1979, we have been conducting exploration seminars that introduce people to the variety and beauty of the outdoor museum on the Colorado Plateau. The seminars last from two to six days and generally focus on a research project. For example, we might use the opportunity to search for additional historic signatures or to examine Ancestral Pueblo sites for their possible astronomical orientations.[46]

The outdoor museum program provides education, interpretation, and, we hope, enjoyment. Participants range from teenagers to seniors in their seventies. We camp out in the open, far from the telephone and TV set, and experience firsthand what it is like to get up at sunrise or scurry for cover from a midnight rain shower. On long hikes, participants learn to make do with water dug up from a sandy wash or taken from slime-covered potholes. Under these conditions, visitors gain greater appreciation for what Ancestral Pueblo life must have been like. We also examine the conflicts inherent in managing the outdoor museum and explore the effects of high visitation, excessive grazing, and the policies by which federal and state agencies treat the resources under their control. Such discussions ultimately go beyond government programs to the importance of individual stewardship in protecting archaeological resources.

Similarly, indoor museums, through their collections and displays, serve the education cause. On the Colorado Plateau, museums such as Edge of the Cedars State Park and Museum in Blanding, Utah, the BLM's Anasazi Heritage Center in Dolores, Colorado, and the Museum of Northern Arizona in Flagstaff play a critical role because they serve the local community and potentially can have a large impact on local attitudes.

ONE OF THE THRILLS OF GRAND GULCH IS TO HIKE THERE ALONE OR WITH A few friends and experience the raw beauty of towering sandstone walls against thick stands of cottonwood, hackberry, piñon, and juniper. Another is to come across whole sandstone panels that the Basketmakers and later Pueblo people used as canvases for their artistry. A sense of the sacred and of deep meaning still comes through. Yet another pleasure is to discover a small stone and adobe granary tucked away on a precarious ledge high above the canyon floor and wonder how anyone ever reached such an inaccessible spot.

Moments like these still abound in Grand Gulch, but the wistful words of archaeologist William Lipe that began this chapter are even truer today than they were in 1980. Increased visitation and reduced BLM presence have contributed to a steady degradation of archaeological sites and a loss of quality in the outdoor experience. People are literally loving Grand Gulch to death. Unless the Gulch is managed more effectively, the wonder of the canyon's beauty and the thrill of discovery will be lost to future generations. Ultimately, land managers, concerned members of the public, and the legal community must all work together to protect the Gulch's natural and cultural resources.

Although successful preservation depends on creating an effective partnership, in Grand Gulch and most of southeastern Utah the Bureau of Land Management must provide the leadership. Of the BLM offices in the Four Corners states, the Colorado BLM has so far set the standard in preserving historic resources by operating the Anasazi Heritage Museum and by assuming a relatively strong stance toward protecting archaeological sites. The Utah BLM took steps in the direction of preservation and education by its prosecution of the Turkey Pen Ruin looters and its funding of the book *Anasazi Basketmaker: Papers from the 1990 Wetherill–Grand Gulch Symposium*. At the same time, BLM offices in southeastern Utah are unable to keep up with the growing threats to the many archaeological sites under their jurisdiction.

As recently as 1988, a committee of the U.S. Congress complained that the BLM had, overall, a poor record of archaeological protection and even of reporting incidents of looting and vandalism. "BLM's archaeological law enforcement program is weak all over the four-state area. There seems to be a fundamental unwillingness by BLM managers to commit resources to

A Mesa Verde–style corrugated pot found—and left—in situ in southeastern Utah.

archaeological protection."[47] Although the BLM of southeastern Utah manages vast tracts with extremely high densities of archaeological sites, it has allocated few personnel for archaeological resource protection. We have anecdotal evidence that in the past, BLM staff have sometimes not followed proper investigatory techniques in looting and vandalism cases and have ignored both the BLM's own guidelines and federal law.

If the Bureau of Land Management is to fulfill its obligations to preserve archaeological resources, it will have to change its practices. We have several suggestions for more effective management of Grand Gulch and Cedar Mesa. Most of them, of course, can be countered with the complaint that there is not enough money to fund them and that it is important to continue to reduce the federal deficit. Yet the choice of whether or not to protect the irreplaceable resources of southeastern Utah is just that—a choice of funding priorities rather than a matter of total dollars.

Carrying out these suggestions would primarily require some shifting of funds from other areas within BLM. Federal fees for grazing, mining, and other commercial uses of the land could be raised, and volunteers could be used creatively. Perhaps if the BLM began to treat Grand Gulch and other canyons under its management as components of an outdoor museum, it would make greater strides in preserving the area for future generations. Here are our suggestions.

- Provide a permanent staff presence in and near Grand Gulch. Rather than reduce its presence in and around the Gulch, the BLM should increase it. This was also the primary recommendation of the previously mentioned report by the House Committee on Interior and Insular Affairs.

- Conduct thorough surveys to document and record the archaeological and natural resources of southeastern Utah. In order to manage archaeological sites effectively, the BLM needs to know what sites are there and what condition they are in. In addition, the BLM should survey the flora and fauna of its lands to determine what primary species are present and how best to protect threatened species.

- Do a thorough survey of the rock art. As Sally Cole's research has shown, the pictographs and petroglyphs of Grand Gulch are a potentially important source of information.[48] With increased visitation, the fragile paintings and rock peckings will degrade much faster than they have until now. Because of the popular appeal of rock art, documenting this resource could be carried out by teams of lay persons with proper training and supervision, as has already been done for some of the Grand Gulch rock art panels.[49]

- Develop additional educational materials. The BLM needs to tell the geological and cultural history of the Gulch. It should also find simple ways to explain to people the inadvertent damage they can do and how to prevent it. The BLM could increase its work with volunteer groups and with local organizations such as the White Mesa Institute, the Crow Canyon Archaeological Center, the Four Corners School, and the University of Colorado Center in Cortez to develop suitable educational materials for both adults and children. The Public Education Committee of the Society for American Archaeology has established a clearinghouse for sharing information about educational programs. Its resources could be used by BLM state offices throughout the Colorado Plateau.

■ Put up descriptive panels. At the head of the trail at Kane Gulch, the BLM could set up several attractive displays giving important information about the Gulch and perhaps offering a small selection of brochures in protected receptacles. Among other things, the displays could warn of potential damage to endangered species. Although not everyone entering the Gulch will stop to read a descriptive panel, many will, and such displays could increase the safety of hikers.

■ Fund research on museum collections from southeastern Utah. The Wetherill–Grand Gulch Research Project and subsequent work have produced a great deal of information about sites and artifacts that could be put to good use in studying museum collections. Much could be accomplished with even limited funding. More importantly, BLM interest might encourage the university community to become more involved in research on the collections.

■ Stabilize the major sites. Archaeological sites need to be maintained and stabilized, particularly those that receive regular human traffic. Damage needs to be repaired promptly in order to prevent accelerated deterioration. During the 1970s, the University of Utah stabilized some sites in Grand Gulch. Stabilization is expensive, yet such work needs to continue, especially as visitation increases. In addition, evidence of looting at sites needs to be repaired in order to discourage further digging and make it harder for looters to recognize and attack pristine areas.

■ Involve the public. Because of the work of the Wetherill–Grand Gulch Research Project, as well as a 1993 *Smithsonian* article about the Wetherills and publicity over the BLM's poor management of grazing allotments in southeastern Utah, public concern has increased over preserving the resources of Grand Gulch and other canyons.[50] The BLM could boost its ability to manage the area's historic cultural resources by involving the public in the process. Many people who spend much of their time in Grand Gulch have ideas about how to improve the conservation of both cultural and natural resources. The BLM could make valuable use of their considerable collective expertise.

■ Ask existing educational and tour groups to give something back to the maintenance of Grand Gulch. Both nonprofit educational organizations and profitmaking tour operators lead groups into the Gulch. They could be encouraged to involve their participants in helping the BLM manage the Gulch more effectively. Such groups could regularly report on the condition of archaeological sites, help with archaeological surveys, and do many of the other tasks required in improving the management of Grand Gulch.

Even if all these suggestions were put into effect, a big concern would remain: What is the best balance between the public's right to experience the canyons' treasures and the need to protect them? The very popularity of Grand Gulch contributes to its eventual degradation. As we are aware from personal experience, even our efforts to tell the story of Grand Gulch add to the problem. If you as a reader are disposed to visit the Gulch after reading this book, we have augmented visitation and thereby hastened the degradation of resources. We have seen this happen at Hovenweep National Monument in Colorado, where Ray Williamson's research on Ancestral Pueblo astronomy helped stimulate visitation in the 1980s and 1990s—so much so that visitors have stripped at least one site of most of the potsherds and stone implements that once covered the ground.

An undisturbed Ancestral Pueblo site.

Preserving the future of the past is not a job only for Southwesterners; it is a national challenge. Vandalism and inadvertent damage to historic sites and landscapes are problems every community in the United States faces to some degree. Nor is preservation merely the province of bureaucrats. Those of us who genuinely care about historic or scenic places must think hard about the part we all play in overwhelming the landscape we love. Unless managers of historic properties and ordinary citizens together find effective ways to counteract and deter the destruction of our national heritage, it will slip inexorably away.

NOTES

CHAPTER 1: THE BEGINNING

1. Nels C. Nelson, "Cartier Expedition Notes," New York Museum of Natural History Archives, 1920, p. 4.

2. Archaeologists have appropriated the term *Anasazi*, the Navajo name for the ancient Pueblo peoples, to denote the ancestors of the modern Pueblos. Some Pueblo people dislike the Navajo word because it can be translated as "ancient enemy." Understandably, they prefer their own terms for their ancestors. Hopis, for example, would prefer that archaeologists use the Hopi word *Hisatsinom* to refer to the Hopis' ancestors. Because it and comparable terms for the ancestors of other Pueblo tribes do not convey the appropriate generality, we prefer the less tribe-specific term *Ancestral Pueblo* and have used it throughout this book.

3. Charles Cary Graham, "Diary." Published in Helen Sloan Daniels, *Adventures with the Anasazi of Falls Creek*, p. 10.

4. William Lipe, "Grand Gulch: Three Days on the Road from Bluff," p. 54.

5. Ann Hayes, "Trip Diary," November 1986.

6. *Outdoor museum* is a term coined by Fred Blackburn to capture the quality of the natural and cultural resources of the Colorado Plateau and how one might approach them. See Ray A. Williamson and Fred M. Blackburn, "An Approach to Vandalism of Archeological Resources," pp. 49–58.

7. Ann Zwinger, *Wind in the Rock*, p. 7.

8. Platte Lyman, "Journal," December 1, 1879. Quoted in David E. Miller, *Hole-in-the-Rock Expedition*, p. 168.

9. T. Mitchell Prudden, *On the Great American Plateau*, p. 10.

10. See Jerold G. Widdison, *The Anasazi: Why Did They Leave? Where Did They Go?*

11. The Pecos Conference—still held every year—is a two-day meeting at which Southwestern archaeologists gather to share informally their latest research. For a description of the first conference and the developmental sequence it produced, see Alfred V. Kidder, "Southwestern Archaeological Conference."

12. Francis E. Smiley, "The Agricultural Transition in the Northern Southwest: Patterns in the Current Chronometric Data."

CHAPTER 2: ON THE TRAIL OF THE BASKETMAKERS

1. Benjamin Alfred Wetherill, *The Wetherills of Mesa Verde*, p. 110.

2. Ibid., p. 110.

3. Ibid., pp. 124–25.

4. Al Wetherill was moved by the discovery of the baby to write a short poem, which appears in *The Wetherills of Mesa Verde*, p. 115:

> Ode to the Baby Mummy
>
> Greetings, child of an ancient race
> How little is told by thy baby face
> Of children's joys and a mother's tears
> All lost now for a thousand years.
>
> Thy once bright eyes beheld great things
> Thou hope of parents that childhood brings
> Yet thou, with others of thy race,
> Were doomed to pass; leave but a trace.
>
> None there are who can thy story tell.
> All are where thou didst dwell.
> All voices stilled; all lips are sealed,
> Forever closed and unrevealed.

5. Nordenskiöld signed the Alamo Ranch register on July 2. The Wetherills had many visitors during this period, and they all signed the register, which has become a historical research tool of great importance.

6. Alice Eastwood and Al Wetherill were good friends. Wetherill wrote about their experiences collecting botanical specimens in southwestern Colorado and southeastern Utah, when he served as Miss Eastwood's guide. See Wetherill, *The Wetherills of Mesa Verde*, pp. 195–213.

7. Gustaf Nordenskiöld, *The Cliff Dwellers of the Mesa Verde.*

8. Frank McNitt, *Richard Wetherill: Anasazi,* p. 42.

9. Nordenskiöld's exit from the United States was not without its difficulties, as several citizens of Durango attempted to prevent him from taking his collection out of Colorado. When it was discovered that no law prevented the removal of artifacts from the state, the authorities had to dismiss the complaint. The incident helped awaken local citizens to the need to preserve such remains and led to Mesa Verde's being made a national park some fifteen years later, in June 1906.

10. Nordenskiöld, *The Cliff Dwellers of the Mesa Verde,* p. 21.

11. See Robert Lister's "Interpretative Foreword" in Nordenskiöld, *The Cliff Dwellers of the Mesa Verde,* p. 33.

12. Nordenskiöld's collection now resides in the National Museum in Helsinki, Finland. Nordenskiöld's family were Finns who had emigrated to Sweden. The collection had been bought by a family friend, another Swedish Finn, Dr. Herman Fritjof Antell. Antell willed this collection and others to the people of Finland.

13. Wetherill, *The Wetherills of Mesa Verde,* p. 125.

14. Ibid., p. 126.

15. Ibid., p. 126.

16. Charles Cary Graham's diary was first published by Helen Sloan Daniels in her book *Adventures with the Anasazi of Falls Creek,* pp. 9–15; unfortunately, it does not include copies of the drawings. The original of the diary was believed lost. In April 1991, members of the Wetherill–Grand Gulch Research Project relocated the original in the possession of the explorer's grandson, Charles S. Graham. Unless otherwise noted, references to the diary are to the original, of which Mr. Graham kindly made a photocopy for project use.

17. Graham's diary as reproduced in Daniels, *Adventures with the Anasazi of Falls Creek,* p. 10.

18. Salt Cave is known today as Split Level Ruin because of the shape of the Ancestral Pueblo dwelling in the cave.

19. Graham called this cart a woodrack: it was a four-wheeled extendable wagon of a type often used to carry logs.

20. The artifacts were probably exhibited at the court house. Later, the newspaper *Great Southwest* reported on April 27, 1893: "A collection of Cliff Dwellers relics, property of Chas. McLoyd, will be on exhibition in a few days in the rooms at the Court House." On April 18, 1893, *Great Southwest* reported that several men, including Charles McLoyd and J. Howard Graham, had formed the Durango Archaeological and Historical Society.

21. The extensive archaeological and ethnographic collections now held by the Field Museum were purchased in large part with a one-million-dollar donation made in 1894 by entrepreneur and philanthropist Marshall Field. See Ann Hayes, "One Hundred Years in the Life of the C. H. Green Collection," pp. 121–28.

22. The so-called Brunot Treaty with the United States government was negotiated with Chief Ouray of the Utes by Felix Brunot, chief of the Indian commissioners. See Charles S. Marsh, *People of the Shining Mountains: The Utes of Colorado,* p. 75.

23. Although much of the public record reflects little sympathy for the condition of the Utes, confined on their reservation and often starving for lack of game, some settlers expressed concern over their plight. "Those Indians are now in a starving condition and Chief Ignacio says he will starve to death before he will go to the old agency [in Ignacio, Colorado] for rations. And we believe that he will do so, as he never breaks his word. He is an Indian Chief that comes up to the ideal of a noble Indian as pictured by [James Fenimore] Cooper in his novels" (Minutes of the Durango Board of Trade for January 2, 1896).

24. Both of these quotations appear in Duane A. Smith's *Rocky Mountain Boom Town.*

25. For an account of the Mormon settlers' trek, see David E. Miller's *Hole-in-the-Rock.*

26. Miller, *Hole-in-the-Rock,* pp. 5–6.

27. T. Mitchell Prudden, "A Summer among Cliff Dwellings," p. 55.

28. For a history of Durango, see Smith's *Rocky Mountain Boom Town.*

29. This was the Cumbres and Toltec line, which still operates during the summer months between Chama, New Mexico, and Alamosa, Colorado.

30. Fred M. Blackburn, interview notes, September 26, 1995. Emerald Patrick died in late December 1995.

31. Other expedition members were Bob Allan, H. R. Ricker, F. E. Leeka, D. W. Ayres, and Dr. L. W. Churd.

32. This was the female mummy pictured in the catalog, carrying the improbable caption "Woman mummy, 6 feet 2 inches high."

33. For an account of the Green collection and of Green's attempts to sell it, see Hayes, "One Hundred Years in the Life of the C. H. Green Collection."

34. Hayes, "One Hundred Years in the Life of the C. H. Green Collection."

35. C. H. Green, "Catalogue of a Unique Collection of Cliff Dweller Relics," 1892, p. 18. Apparently the photographer was F. E. Leeka, from Durango.

36. John Wetherill to Mr. Howard, University Museum, University of Pennsylvania, March 25, 1930. University of Utah Archives, Acc. 308.

37. Ann Phillips, "Archaeological Expeditions into Southeastern Utah and Southwestern Colorado between 1888–1898 and the Dispersal of the Collections."

38. *The Illustrated American* exerted a major influence in alerting the public to the archaeological remains to be found in the Southwest and elsewhere in North America.

39. Originally loaned to the University Museum at the University of Pennsylvania by C. D. Hazzard, who purchased it from McLoyd in 1892, the collection was purchased for the museum by Phoebe Hearst in 1896. She retained 250 items, later giving them to the Lowie Museum of Anthropology at the University of California, Berkeley (now the Phoebe A. Hearst Museum of Anthropology).

40. Warren K. Moorehead, untitled article, Section H in *Proceedings of the American Association for the Advancement of Science,* 1892, p. 292.

41. Warren K. Moorehead, "The Great McLoyd Collection," *The Illustrated American,* August 20, 1892, p. 23.

42. M. Edward Moseley seems to have been the first person in this century to credit McLoyd and Graham with recognizing the existence of a culture different from the cliff dwellers. See Moseley's "The Discovery and Definition of Basketmaker: 1890 to 1914."

43. Moorehead, "The Great McLoyd Collection," p. 25.

44. Hazzard Collection Catalog, 1892, p. 15, and Item number I-15.

45. We searched for Moorehead's expedition notes, hoping that they would shed more light on this issue and on the sites he visited. Unfortunately, they had been destroyed in a fire that struck the archival collection at the Phillips Andover Academy.

Chapter 3: The Wetherills in Grand Gulch

1. Richard Wetherill to Talbot Hyde, December 17, 1893. Quoted in McNitt, *Richard Wetherill: Anasazi,* p. 65.

2. For several years, we had only circumstantial evidence of John Wetherill's trip into Grand Gulch with Charles McLoyd. In June 1993, however, Fred Blackburn discovered a Wetherill signature in Cut-In-Two Cave (Cave 19 of the 1894 Hyde Exploring Expedition) dated January 10, 1893. In April 1995, Winston Hurst discovered a second "John Wetherill 1893" carved in an ax groove down-canyon from Cut-In-Two Cave.

3. Green gave lectures on his collection, illustrating them with lantern slides.

4. Moorehead, "The Great McLoyd Collection," p. 23.

5. D. W. Ayres signed the Alamo Ranch ledger on April 19 and June 23, 1892. In 1892 Ayres assisted with the excavation of Step House in Mesa Verde for the state of Colorado. He was compiling what came to be known as the Wilmarth collection, after A. F. Wilmarth, who was in charge of the excavations.

6. Frank McNitt wrote that Lang's early trip into the Gulch induced McLoyd to explore there; see *Richard Wetherill: Anasazi,* p. 55. We have no firm evidence of such a trip by Lang. Utah resident John Scorup has found a Lang signature dating as early as 1888 south of the San Juan, but none has yet turned up north of the San Juan in Grand Gulch or elsewhere.

7. McNitt, *Richard Wetherill: Anasazi,* p. 55.

8. The Hydes signed the Alamo register on August 12, 1892.

9. Wetherill, *The Wetherills of Mesa Verde,* pp. 124–25.

10. Frederick Ward Putnam, "On Methods of Archaeological Research in America."

11. Although Miss Cowing had visited the Wetherills in Mancos three times, her relationship with Richard Wetherill never came to more than friendship.

12. Richard Wetherill to Talbot Hyde, fall 1893.

13. They may have traveled part of the time along Butler Wash, which runs parallel to Cottonwood Wash just to the west of it.

14. Harry French to Jesse Nusbaum, November 11, 1947.

15. French to Nusbaum, November 22, 1947.

16. Richard Wetherill to Talbot Hyde, Bluff, Utah, December 21, 1893.

17. Richard Wetherill to Talbot Hyde, February 4, 1894.

18. Richard Wetherill to Talbot Hyde, March 1894.

19. Charles Amsden, *Prehistoric Southwesterners from Basketmaker to Pueblo,* p. 44.

20. See, for example, James H. Knipmeyer, "Some Historic Signatures of the Four Corners Region," pp. 33–40.

21. This workshop was led by instructors Jimbo Buikerood and Ed Young.

22. Richard Wetherill, field notes of the Hyde Exploring Expedition, 1894. In "Wetherill Collection of Miscellaneous Documents about the First and Second Wetherill Collections," Accession 1895-34 and 1897-45. Anthropology Archives of the American Museum of Natural History, New York City.

23. The Grand Hotel, approximately one-half mile south of Polly's Island, is now called Wrong Side Ruin because it lies on the opposite side of the canyon from most of the other villages.

24. Richard Wetherill, field notes of the Hyde Exploring Expedition, 1894, in the American Museum of Natural History.

25. They also referred to Turkey Pen Ruin as McLoyd Cave, perhaps because McLoyd had signed his name on the back wall of the small dwelling there.

26. James Ethridge's signature appears at Double Cave in Butler Wash, dated March 14, 1894.

27. Richard Wetherill, 1893–94 catalog notes.

28. Richard Wetherill to Talbot Hyde, Bluff, Utah, March 28, 1894.

29. Poncho House received its current name from S. J. Guernsey, who excavated there several years later.

30. In his 1966 edition of *Richard Wetherill: Anasazi,* Frank McNitt wrote of the Hyde collection: "Most of these relics now lie uncrated and in storage, but a number are displayed in the Southwest Hall as the 'First Wetherill Collection.'" In 1989, members of the Wetherill–Grand Gulch Research Project visited the American Museum of Natural History to study and photograph the Hyde collection and found that it had been uncrated and cataloged and was in relatively good condition.

31. The Wetherills took B. T. B. Hyde into Grand Gulch in the summer of 1894, to show him the sites from which they had collected artifacts during the Hyde Exploring Expedition.

32. McNitt, *Richard Wetherill: Anasazi,* p. 153.

33. Richard Wetherill to Talbot Hyde, October 31, 1896. Wetherill subsequently learned that the Field Museum would be visiting other canyons, and not Grand Gulch.

34. McNitt, *Richard Wetherill: Anasazi,* p. 153.

35. An Ethridge signature in Grand Gulch from December 1896 was at first a bit confusing to the project team, because there is clear evidence that the full party for the Whitmore Exploring Expedition left Mancos for Grand Gulch in January 1897. We speculate that Ethridge was sent ahead to reconnoiter.

36. McNitt, *Richard Wetherill: Anasazi*, p. 154.

37. Kathryn Gabriel, ed., *Marietta Wetherill: Reflections on Life with the Navajos in Chaco Canyon*, pp. 66–67.

38. Ibid., pp. 68–69. Photographs of the Princess verify Marietta's description. Indeed, if a mummy could look alive, the Princess did.

39. McNitt, *Richard Wetherill: Anasazi*, p. 157–58.

40. Richard Wetherill, introduction to his field notes, 1897.

41. Alfred Vincent Kidder, *An Introduction to the Study of Southwestern Archaeology*, p. 161.

Chapter 4: Archaeology in Reverse

1. David Hurst Thomas to Fred Blackburn, February 18, 1987.

2. Julia Johnson, "The History of the Wetherill–Grand Gulch Research Project," p. 30.

3. Fred Blackburn had first met Anibal Rodríguez on his initial trip to the American Museum of Natural History in 1983, when Rodríguez gave him invaluable help in searching the museum for Grand Gulch artifacts.

4. See Ray A. Williamson, *Living the Sky: The Cosmos of the American Indian*, chapter 4.

5. The Museum of the American Indian came into existence in 1916. Until 1922, when the museum building was opened, Heye's collections were stored in various places in New York and at the University of Pennsylvania Museum.

6. Viewing these artifacts at the Museum of the American Indian, project members noted that the original American Museum of Natural History numbers had been obliterated and replaced by numbers that fit the system used by the Museum of the American Indian, sometimes severing the connection to specific entries in Wetherill's catalog.

7. George Pepper to G. B. Gordon, September 2, 1908.

8. James Smith to Julia Johnson, August 15, 1988.

9. See, for example, Douglas Cole, *Captured Heritage: The Scramble for Northwest Coast Artifacts.*

10. Phillips, "Archaeological Expeditions," pp. 115–17.

11. Winston Hurst to Julia Johnson, October 18, 1988.

12. David Hurst Thomas to Fred Blackburn, October 31, 1988.

13. "Reverse Archaeology Group Traces Indian Artifacts and Museums Back to Source," *Boulder Daily Camera*, September 21, 1989; "Tracking the Anasazi," *Deseret News*, June 25, 1989.

14. Edge of the Cedars State Museum in Blanding, Utah, however, has since secured funding to upgrade its staff and facilities to allow for retention of artifacts acquired locally in southeastern Utah.

15. In 1892, D. W. Ayres had excavated Step House with Richard Wetherill. The artifacts they unearthed make up the Wilmarth collection of the Colorado Historical Society.

16. Helen Sloan Daniels, *Adventures with the Anasazi of Falls Creek*, p. 9.

17. Funding for this trip was provided by Santa Fe resident Roe Lovelace through the Wetherill Projects Fund at the University of Colorado Center in Cortez. Sandy Zimmerman graciously provided lodging at her house and offered to guide Fred and Winston through the city.

18. Many of Al Wetherill's reminiscences appear in his autobiography, *The Wetherills of Mesa Verde.*

19. It was a joy to work with the papers and photographs because Wren Wetherill had so carefully organized, labeled, and boxed them. Later, the Wetherill–Grand Gulch Research Project paid for stabilizing and conserving the map and for acid-free file folders to help Tom and his family curate their historic collection.

20. William C. Allen to Henry Conrad, September 9, 1896.

21. We believe this to be the first time a Basketmaker mummy has been radiocarbon dated.

22. David Roberts, "'Reverse Archaeologists' Are Tracing the Footsteps of a Cowboy-Explorer."

23. Note written by Paul S. Martin, January 30, 1930, on an untitled, typewritten catalog of an unknown collection, Anthropology Archive Accession no. 1468, Field Museum of Natural History, Chicago, 1897–98.

Chapter 5: Rediscovering Cave 7

1. Jesse L. Nusbaum, "The Basket Makers of the San Juan River Basin." Manuscript, Jesse Nusbaum Papers, National Anthropological Archives, Smithsonian Institution, Washington, D.C., no date. See also Nusbaum to Dr. Herbert E. Gregory, April 4, 1950, Nusbaum Collection, Museum of New Mexico Archives, Santa Fe.

2. W. H. French to Jesse L. Nusbaum, November 22, 1947, Anthropological Department Archives, American Museum of Natural History, New York.

3. Richard Wetherill to Talbot Hyde, December 17, 1893.

4. John Wetherill to Al Wetherill, 1930.

5. McNitt's notes for his book on Richard Wetherill, as well as many other materials about the Southwest, are archived at the New Mexico State Archives and Records Center, Santa Fe.

6. Warren K. Moorehead, who investigated the alcove in the summer of 1892, gave it the name Giant's Cave.

7. The oral history interview with Albert R. Lyman was conducted by Gary Shumway and Stanley Bronson on August 23, 1973.

8. Albert R. Lyman, "History of San Juan County, 1879–1917," undated manuscript in the collection of Edge of the Cedars State Park, Blanding, Utah. The incident is cited by Winston B. Hurst and Christy G. Turner II in "Rediscovering the 'Great Discovery': Wetherill's First Cave 7 and Its Implications Regarding Basketmaker Violence," pp. 150–51.

9. One set of glass plate negatives is in the possession of the American Museum of Natural History in New York. The University of Pennsylvania has only prints from the second set; apparently the glass plate negatives to that set of prints are lost.

10. Richard Wetherill's notes say only "small house 200 yards south of Cave 7." The Wetherill–Grand Gulch team had not found much significance in the notation. This experience points up one of the frustrations of historical

research. What seems both extremely obvious and vitally important to later research is accorded little import by the original observer. The search might have ended much sooner had Richard Wetherill happened to emphasize the existence of this distinctive small ruin overlooking the head of the canyon.

11. Christy G. Turner II, personal communication. Turner's analysis of the skeletal remains is reported in Hurst and Turner, "Rediscovering the 'Great Discovery.'" The article also contains a partial analysis of some of the artifacts of Cave 7.

12. From an article in the *Archaeologist,* vol. 2, pp. 154–55, 1894. This article, signed simply "H.," was probably written by Talbot Hyde from notes provided by Richard Wetherill.

13. Christy G. Turner II, "Taphonomic Reconstruction of Human Violence and Cannibalism Based On Mass Burials in the American Southwest," pp. 219–40.

14. Daniels, *Adventures with the Anasazi of Falls Creek.*

15. Graham may have signed McLoyd's name in some alcoves during the period when McLoyd was injured and could not explore.

16. The Jail House site acquired its name from the fact that some of the adobe from a jacal wall has fallen away, leaving just the wooden latticework that reinforced the adobe. Seen from a distance, the effect looks rather like bars.

17. The signature has since been obliterated, probably by hikers intent on removing graffiti.

18. C. H. Green, "Catalogue of a Unique Collection of Cliff Dweller Relics," p. 7. Green numbered the site "Cliff House 33," as it was the thirty-third cliff dwelling he had explored on his June 1891 visit to Grand Gulch.

19. C. H. Green, "Catalogue of a Unique Collection of Cliff Dweller Relics," p. 19.

20. Charles McLoyd and C. C. Graham, "Catalogue and Description of a Very Large Collection of Prehistoric Relics Obtained in the Cliff Houses and Caves of Southeastern Utah," 1892. Manuscript, Harvard University, Cambridge, Massachusetts.

21. Catalog of the McLoyd-Graham Collection, a portion of the Hazzard Collection at the University of Pennsylvania Museum of Anthropology and Archaeology.

22. Quoted from McLoyd's 1894 catalog by M. Edward Moseley in "The Discovery and Definition of Basketmaker: 1890 to 1914," p. 144.

23. Moseley, "The Discovery and Definition of Basketmaker: 1890 to 1914," pp. 140–54.

24. Wetherill, *The Wetherills of Mesa Verde,* p. 119.

25. Eleanor Stanberry to Fred M. Blackburn, December 16, 1995.

26. Both quotations appear in McNitt's *Richard Wetherill: Anasazi,* p. 67.

27. Albert H. Schroeder, "History of Archeological Research," pp. 5–13. Schroeder was referring to Pepper's "The Ancient Basket Makers of Southeastern Utah."

28. Richard E. Fike, "Antiquities Violations in Utah: Justice Does Prevail," p. 50. Fike, of course, meant the early to mid-1890s, since, so far as we know, Richard Wetherill did not set foot in Grand Gulch until January 1894.

29. See Cole, *Captured Heritage.*

30. Nels C. Nelson, *Pueblo Ruins of the Galisteo Basin, New Mexico.*

31. Ethnographic analogy also has its pitfalls, because cultural change may cause apparently obvious evidence from the prehistoric era to be misinterpreted.

32. Richard Wetherill to T. Mitchell Prudden, 1896.

33. Fortunately, the early explorers did not take *all* the artifacts or scramble all the archaeological deposits, and significant archaeological resources still exist in the canyons. They are, however, seriously threatened by increasing visitation in Grand Gulch.

34. The difficult terrain and heavy flooding McLoyd and Graham experienced on their 1890–91 expedition dissuaded them from reentering the lower Gulch on their later trips. They found many more artifacts and easier terrain in the canyons of the Colorado River, west of Grand Gulch.

35. Richard Wetherill to Gustaf Nordenskiöld, April 13, 1894.

36. Yet only in 1978, with the passage of the Archeological Resources Protection Act (ARPA), did Congress begin to assess penalties that might deter criminal action. See Carol Carnett, "Legal Background of Archeological Resources Protection."

37. R. G. Matson, *The Origins of Southwestern Agriculture,* p. 17

Chapter 6: Basketmaker Research after Wetherill

1. Alfred Vincent Kidder and Samuel J. Guernsey, *Archaeological Explorations in Northeastern Arizona.*

2. See, however, the discussion of John Wetherill in Melinda Elliott, *Great Excavations: Tales of Early Southwestern Archaeology, 1888–1939,* pp. 196–200.

3. Byron Cummings, who taught at the University of Utah, had led one of two expeditions to Rainbow Bridge in 1909. The other was led by W. B. Douglass of the United States General Land Office. One version of the story of the first visit of white men to Rainbow Bridge is told by Frances Gillmore and Louisa Wade Wetherill in *Traders to the Navajo: The Story of the Wetherills of Kayenta.* A more detailed description can be found in Stephen Jett, "The Great 'Race' to 'Discover' Rainbow Natural Bridge in 1909," pp. 3–66.

4. Kidder and Guernsey, *Archaeological Explorations in Northeastern Arizona,* p. 83.

5. Ibid., pp. 87–88.

6. Ibid., p. 206.

7. R. G. Matson, *The Origins of Southwestern Agriculture,* p. 21.

8. Kidder and Guernsey, *Archaeological Explorations in Northeastern Arizona,* p. 206.

9. The following summary derives primarily from Kidder and Guernsey, *Archaeological Explorations in Northeastern Arizona,* pp. 155–99.

10. The cedar to which Kidder and Guernsey and local Southwesterners refer is actually a form of juniper—either the Utah or the one-seed juniper.

11. William R. Perkins, "Atlatl Weights: Function and Classification," pp. 58–61.

12. Kidder and Guernsey, *Archaeological Explorations in Northeastern Arizona,* pp. 210.

13. Amsden, *Prehistoric Southwesterners,* p. 62.

14. Samuel J. Guernsey and A. V. Kidder, *Basketmaker Caves of Northeastern Arizona: Report on the Explorations, 1916–17,* p. 110.

15. Ibid., p. 116.

16. Much of Earl Morris's archaeological work on the Basketmakers in southeastern and northeastern Utah was sponsored by the philanthropist Charles Bernheimer. Except for the account in the popular book written by Morris's first wife, Ann Axtell Morris, *Digging in the Southwest,* much of Morris's work from this period remains unpublished.

17. The discovery of these rockshelters is described by Helen Sloan Daniels in *Adventures with the Anasazi of Falls Creek,* pp. 4–8. Daniels examined the caves with friends upon hearing that they contained rock paintings.

18. For Morris's earlier work in Canyon del Muerto, see Earl H. Morris, "Mummy Cave."

19. Earl H. Morris to A. V. Kidder, March 11, 1938. Quoted in Florence C. Lister and Robert H. Lister, *Earl Morris and Southwestern Archaeology.*

20. Earl H. Morris and Robert F. Burgh, *Basket Maker II Sites near Durango, Colorado,* p. 51.

21. Jeffrey S. Dean, *Tree-Ring Dates from Colorado W, Durango Area,* pp. 26–33.

22. In 1941, W. S. Stallings, Jr., reported a date of A.D. 217 for Cave du Pont, which Jesse Nusbaum had dug in 1922. See W. S. Stallings, Jr., "A Basketmaker II Date from Cave du Pont, Utah," pp. 3–6. Later examination of the evidence, however, threw the validity of this date into doubt. See B. Bannister, J. S. Dean, and W. J. Robinson, *Tree-Ring Dates from Utah S-W, Southern Utah Area,* p. 11.

23. Earl H. Morris and Robert F. Burgh, *Basket Maker II Sites near Durango, Colorado,* p. 64.

24. Earl H. Morris to A. V. Kidder, September 29, 1937. Quoted in Lister and Lister, *Earl Morris and Southwestern Archaeology,* p. 160.

25. Morris and Burgh, *Basket Maker II Sites near Durango, Colorado,* chapter 9.

26. Frank W. Eddy, *Excavations at Los Pinos Phase Sites in the Navajo Reservoir District.*

27. Frank W. Eddy, *Prehistory in the Navajo Reservoir District, Northwestern New Mexico.*

28. William D. Lipe, "Anasazi Communities in the Red Rock Plateau, Southeastern Utah."

29. R. G. Matson notes that Lipe's discovery of habitation sites might have been partly the result of advances in archaeological method and theory. He suggests that Kidder and Guernsey's sites in Marsh Pass, for example, might well be interpreted as habitation sites if they were excavated today. See Matson, *The Origins of Southwestern Agriculture,* p. 62.

30. Matson, *The Origins of Southwestern Agriculture,* pp. 73–101. The following discussion is derived primarily from these pages in Matson's book.

31. Susan E. Bearden, *A Study of Basketmaker II Settlement on Black Mesa, Arizona: Excavations 1973–1979.*

32. F. E. Smiley, W. Parry, and G. Gumerman, "Early Agriculture in the Black Mesa/Marsh Pass Region of Arizona: New Chronometric Data and Recent Excavations at Three Fir Shelter."

33. Dennis Gilpin has reported on Basketmaker II sites on the Navajo Reservation in eastern Arizona that were uncovered during construction of an Indian Health Service water system. One of these sites yielded corn that dated as early as 1350 B.C. See Dennis Gilpin, "Lukachukai and Salina Springs: Late Archaic/Early Basketmaker Habitation Sites in Chinle Valley, Northeastern Arizona," pp. 203–18.

34. There are, of course, dramatic exceptions to the equation of foraging with mobility. For instance, in coastal areas where fish, shellfish, seaweed, fruits, and seeds are readily available, societies may be relatively sedentary even though agriculture is extremely slow to catch on. The Northwest Coast of North America and the southern California coast provide especially good examples. Indian tribes in these areas developed highly structured societies and lived in villages but had little or no agriculture.

35. The Archaic peoples, for example, created pictographs and petroglyphs and developed a distinctive rock art style. See Polly Schaafsma, *Indian Rock Art of the Southwest,* chapter 3.

36. Francis E. Smiley, "The Agricultural Transition in the Northern Southwest: Patterns in the Current Chronometric Data," pp. 165–90.

37. Francis E. Smiley, "Early Farmers in the Northern Southwest: A View from Marsh Pass," p. 253.

38. R. G. Matson and Brian Chisholm, "Basketmaker II Subsistence: Carbon Isotopes and Other Dietary Indicators from Cedar Mesa, Utah." For the analysis of coprolites, Matson and Chisholm relied on studies by archaeologists D. K. Aasen ("Pollen, Macrofossil, and Charcoal Analyses of Basketmaker Coprolites from Turkey Pen Ruin, Cedar Mesa, Utah," Master's thesis, Department of Anthropology, Washington State University, Pullman) and D. Lepofsky ("Preliminary Analysis of Flotation Samples from the Turkey Pen Ruin, Cedar Mesa, Utah," manuscript on file, Laboratory of Archaeology, University of British Columbia, Vancouver, 1986).

39. Matson, *The Origins of Southwestern Agriculture,* pp. 123–24.

40. Ibid., pp. 307–309.

41. Claudia F. Berry and Michael S. Berry, "Chronological and Conceptual Models of the Southwestern Archaic."

42. Matson and Chisholm, "Basketmaker II Subsistence," p. 446.

43. Phil R. Geib and Dale Davidson, "Anasazi Origins: A Perspective from Preliminary Work at Old Man Cave."

44. Smiley, "Early Farmers in the Northern Southwest," p. 254.

45. Schaafsma, *Indian Rock Art of the Southwest,* chapter 8.

46. Polly Schaafsma and Curtis F. Schaafsma, "Evidence for the Origins of the Pueblo Katchina Cult as Suggested by Southwestern Rock Art."

47. Campbell Grant, *Canyon de Chelly: Its People and Rock Art.*

48. M. Jane Young, "Images of Power and the Power of Images: The Significance of Rock Art for Contemporary Zunis."

49. Sally J. Cole, "Iconography and Symbolism in Basketmaker Rock Art," p. 59.

50. Sally J. Cole, "Basketmaker Rock Art at the Green Mask Site, Southeastern Utah," p. 211.

51. Ibid., pp. 207–10.

52. Kidder and Guernsey, *Archaeological Explorations in Northeastern Arizona,* pp. 190–91.

53. Cole, "Basketmaker Rock Art at the Green Mask Site," p. 216.

54. Richard Wetherill to Talbot Hyde, December 17, 1893.

55. See Hurst and Turner, "Rediscovering the 'Great Discovery,'" pp. 159, 171.

56. Ibid., p. 169.

57. Basketmaker II corn was related to the so-called Chapalote variety.

58. Guernsey and Kidder, *Basketmaker Caves of Northeastern Arizona,* p. 77.

59. Morris and Burgh, *Basket Maker II Sites near Durango, Colorado,* pp. 71–72.

60. Kidder and Guernsey, *Archaeological Explorations in Northeastern Arizona,* p. 89.

61. Richard B. Woodbury and Ezra B. W. Zubrow, "Agricultural Beginnings, 2000 B.C.–A.D. 500," pp. 43–60.

62. Karen M. Dohm, "The Search for Anasazi Village Origins: Basketmaker II Dwelling Aggregation on Cedar Mesa."

63. Guernsey and Kidder, *Basketmaker Caves of Northeastern Arizona,* p. 98.

64. Morris and Burgh, *Basket Maker II Sites near Durango, Colorado,* p. 63.

Chapter 7: The Future of the Past

1. This passage and the following account of the Turkey Pen Ruin case are taken from the BLM file on the case, from personal interviews with Kathleen Collins, and from court records.

2. McLoyd and Graham first dug in Turkey Pen Ruin on March 14–18, 1891. It was likely Cave 20 of the Hyde Exploring Expedition and Cave 4 of the Whitmore Exploring Expedition. See Fred M. Blackburn and Victoria M. Atkins, "Handwriting on the Wall: Applying Inscriptions to Reconstruct Historic Archaeological Expeditions," pp. 41–102.

3. Donald R. Keller, Richard V. Ahlstrom, and Dana Hartman, "Final Report for Surface Cleanup of Cultural Sites in Grand Gulch," p. 81.

4. In Utah, state law was not much help either. Convictions could be obtained only by catching the persons in the act. Successful prosecutions were obtained only through state Justice of the Peace courts, under state law. Violators generally received $50 to $100 fines and suspended sentences.

5. William Haase, "Turkey Pen Report," Bureau of Land Management, September 11, 1979.

6. Joseph Bauman, "Charge Filed in Damage of Anasazi Site," *Deseret News,* December 4, 1979, p. D5.

7. Ibid., p. D5.

8. As the Wetherills learned over a hundred years ago, the fine, dry dust of the alcoves quickly makes breathing difficult.

9. Public Law 96-95 (16 U.S.C. 470aa et. seq.).

10. 13 U.S.C. 1361.

11. Indeed, it took the National Park Service until 1984 to issue uniform regulations. The original act contained the significant weakness that the threshold for a felony indictment was $5,000 in damage to property. Although it is relatively easy for a determined vandal to do that much damage, it is often difficult to convince a jury that an archaeological site is worth that much. Hence, in 1988, after several years of experience with the act and the regulations, Congress amended the act to reduce the felony threshold to $500.

12. ARPA is the most sweeping of federal laws designed to protect U.S. cultural resources. Many states and local communities have used ARPA as a model for their own laws. See Carol L. Carnett, *Legal Background of Archeological Resources Protection* and *A Survey of State Statutes Protecting Archeological Resources.*

13. Sherry Hutt, Elwood W. Jones, and Martin E. McAllister, *Archeological Resource Protection,* p. 16.

14. Of course, much of the information in a given soil layer is redundant, so archaeologists generally use sampling methods that acquire information from a statistically representative sample of the site. They do this also because archaeology is itself a destructive activity. Unless a site is going to be destroyed for development or other reasons, modern archaeologists generally prefer to leave as much of the site as possible untouched for future research. Finally, systematic archaeology is labor intensive and therefore extremely expensive.

15. Bearden, *A Study of Basketmaker II Settlement on Black Mesa,* pp. 46–65.

16. F. E. Smiley, Deborah L. Nichols, and Peter P. Andrews, *Excavations on Black Mesa, 1981: A Descriptive Report,* p. 75.

17. Winston Hurst, "The Kerr Collection: An Archaeological Tale of Woe, and a Study of Burial-Associated Anasazi Ceramics from the Westwater Drainage." Manuscript, 1984.

18. The more inclusive term, *cultural resources,* includes contemporary oral, written, and material cultural items.

19. Duane A. Smith, *Mesa Verde National Park: Shadows of the Centuries,* pp. 30–32. In this book, Smith provides a detailed and engaging account of the battle to make Mesa Verde a national park.

20. Prudden, "A Summer among Cliff Dwellings," p. 552.

21. Public Law 59-209; 34 Stat. 225; 16 U.S.C. 431–33, June 8, 1906.

22. See, for example, Bruce A. Anderson, "The Antiquities Act of 1906 and Problems with the Act"; also Hutt, Jones, and McAllister, *Archeological Resource Protection,* chapter 1.

23. Carol L. Carnett, personal communication.

24. 16 U.S.C. 470.

25. Carnett, *Legal Background of Archeological Resources Protection.*

26. Native American Graves Protection and Repatriation Act, Public Law 101-601, 104 Stat. 3052 (1990), Sec. 4.

27. See *Arizona State Law Journal,* vol. 24, no. 1, 1992. The entire issue is devoted to NAGPRA and related state laws.

28. See Sherry Hutt, "Illegal Trafficking in Native American Human Remains and Cultural Items: A New Protection Tool."

29. Carnett, *A Survey of State Statutes Protecting Archeological Resources.*

30. Catherine Bergin Yalung and Laurel I. Wala, "Survey of State Reparation and Burial Protection Statutes."

31. Hutt, Jones, and McAllister, *Archeological Resource Protection,* p. 13.

32. A recent report by the Grand Canyon Trust, *Preserving Traces of the Past: Protecting the Colorado Plateau's Archaeological Heritage,* deals with these issues in great depth. It, too, finds the lack of effective cultural resource management a major obstacle in protecting cultural resources. The report places public education at the top of its priorities for action.

33. Among these guides were Carl Mahon, Pete Steele, and Kent Frost. Frost describes one of his early solo trips into the Gulch in *My Canyonlands.*

34. Federal Land Policy Management Act, 43 USC 1701, Section 102(a)(8).

35. Dale A. Davidson, "Managing Cedar Mesa: A Challenge from the Past for the Future," p. 268.

36. Ibid., p. 267.

37. In 1993, the BLM defended and lost a major lawsuit brought by environmental and wilderness groups in southeastern Utah. The court ruled that the BLM had managed grazing allotments to the east of Grand Gulch poorly.

38. For a detailed account of the spread of corn agriculture throughout the world, see Betty Fussell, *The Story of Corn.* For an account of the exchange of foods between the Old and New worlds, see Alfred W. Crosby, Jr., *The Columbian Exchange.*

39. Jack Weatherford, *Indian Givers,* chapter 8.

40. Cole, *Captured Heritage,* p. 119.

41. Such efforts were often used to attempt to demonstrate Caucasian superiority.

42. James Riding In, "Without Ethics and Morality: A Historical Overview of Imperial Archaeology and American Indians," p. 12.

43. NAGPRA is forcing such a change, whether academic archaeologists follow willingly or not. See, for example, Ellen K. Couglin, "Returning Indian Remains," *Chronicle of Higher Education,* March 16, 1994, p. A8. See also Virginia Morell, "An Anthropological Culture Shift," pp. 20–22.

44. Shelley J. Smith, Jeanne M. Moe, Kelly A. Letts, and Danielle M. Paterson, *Intrigue of the Past.* Dolores, Colorado: U.S. Department of Interior Bureau of Land Management, 1993. Contact the Heritage Education Program, Anasazi Heritage Center, P.O. Box 758, Dolores, CO 81323.

45. See Ray A. Williamson and Fred M. Blackburn, "The Living Earth and the Outdoor Museum"; also Williamson and Blackburn, "An Approach to Vandalism of Archeological Resources."

46. See Williamson, *Living the Sky.*

47. U.S. House of Representatives, Subcommittee on General Oversight and Investigations of the Committee on Interior and Insular Affairs, "The Destruction of America's Archaeological Heritage: Looting and Vandalism of Indian Archaeological Sites in the Four Corners States of the Southwest," February 1988, pp. 31–36, 60–61.

48. Cole, "Iconography and Symbolism in Basketmaker Rock Art."

49. Sally J. Cole, "Grand Gulch: The Outdoor Museum 1984." Report prepared for White Mesa Institute, Blanding, Utah.

50. For the *Smithsonian* article, see Roberts, "'Reverse Archaeologists' Are Tracing the Footsteps of a Cowboy-Explorer."

Sources

THE FOLLOWING LIST INCLUDES all the books and major articles cited in this work. In addition to the published sources listed here, we also consulted unpublished sources such as the letters, notes, and collection catalogs of Richard Wetherill and others. Copies of these documents can be found in the archives of the Wetherill–Grand Gulch Research Project, which are maintained at Edge of the Cedars State Museum in Blanding, Utah.

Amsden, Charles. *Prehistoric Southwesterners from Basketmaker to Pueblo.* Los Angeles: Southwest Museum, 1949.

Anderson, Bruce A. "The Antiquities Act of 1906 and Problems with the Act." In *Cultural Resources Law Enforcement: An Emerging Science,* second edition, edited by Dee F. Green and Polly Davis, pp. 52–54. Albuquerque: USDA Forest Service, Southwestern Region, 1981.

Atkins, Victoria M. (editor). *Anasazi Basketmaker: Papers from the 1990 Wetherill–Grand Gulch Symposium.* Salt Lake City: Bureau of Land Management, Cultural Resource Series no. 24, 1993.

Bannister, B., J. S. Dean, and W. J. Robinson. *Tree-Ring Dates from Utah S-W, Southern Utah Area.* Tucson: University of Arizona, Laboratory of Tree-Ring Research, 1969.

Bearden, Susan E. *A Study of Basketmaker II Settlement on Black Mesa, Arizona: Excavations 1973–1979.* Carbondale: Southern Illinois University, Center for Archaeological Investigations, Research Paper no. 44, 1984.

Berry, Claudia F., and Michael S. Berry. "Chronological and Conceptual Models of the Southwestern Archaic." In *Anthropology of the Desert West: Essays in Honor of Jesse D. Jennings,* edited by C. J. Condie and D. D. Fowler, pp. 253–327. Salt Lake City: University of Utah Anthropological Papers no. 110, 1986.

Blackburn, Fred M., and Victoria M. Atkins. "Handwriting on the Wall: Applying Inscriptions to Reconstruct Historic Archaeological Expeditions." In *Anasazi Basketmaker: Papers from the 1990 Wetherill–Grand Gulch Symposium,* edited by Victoria M. Atkins, pp. 41–103. Salt Lake City: Bureau of Land Management, Cultural Resource Series no. 24, 1993.

Carnett, Carol L. *Legal Background of Archeological Resources Protection.* Technical Brief no. 11, Archeological Assistance Division, National Park Service, September 1991.

——*A Survey of State Statutes Protecting Archeological Resources.* Preservation Law Reporter, Special Report, and Archeological Assistance Study, no. 3. Washington, D.C.: National Trust for Historic Preservation and U.S. Department of Interior, National Park Service Cultural Resources Archeological Assistance Division, August 1995.

Cole, Douglas. *Captured Heritage: The Scramble for Northwest Coast Artifacts.* Seattle: University of Washington Press, 1985.

Cole, Sally J. "Iconography and Symbolism in Basketmaker Rock Art." In *Rock Art of the Western Canyons,* edited by J. S. Day, P. D. Friedman, and M. J. Tate, pp. 59–85. Denver: Denver Museum of Natural History and Colorado Archaeological Society, 1989.

——"Basketmaker Rock Art at the Green Mask Site, Southeastern Utah." In *Anasazi Basketmaker: Papers from the 1990 Wetherill–Grand Gulch Symposium,* Victoria M. Atkins, ed., pp. 193–221. Salt Lake City: Bureau of Land Management, Cultural Resource Series no. 24, 1993.

Crosby, Alfred W., Jr. *The Columbian Exchange.* Westport, Connecticut: Greenwood Press, 1972.

Daniels, Helen Sloan, ed. *Adventures with the Anasazi of Falls Creek.* Durango, Colorado: Fort Lewis College Center of Southwest Studies, Occasional Paper no. 3, 1976.

Davidson, Dale A. "Managing Cedar Mesa: A Challenge from the Past for the Future." In *Anasazi Basketmaker: Papers from the 1990 Wetherill–Grand Gulch Symposium,* Victoria M. Atkins, ed., pp. 265–71. Salt Lake City: Bureau of Land Management, Cultural Resource Series no. 24, 1993.

Dean, Jeffrey S. *Tree-Ring Dates from Colorado W, Durango Area.* Tucson: Laboratory of Tree-Ring Research, University of Arizona, 1975.

Dohm, Karen M. "The Search for Anasazi Village Origins: Basketmaker II Dwelling Aggregation on Cedar Mesa." *Kiva,* vol. 60, no. 2, 1994, pp. 257–76.

Eddy, Frank W. *Excavations at Los Pinos Phase Sites in the Navajo Reservoir District.* Santa Fe: Museum of New Mexico Papers in Anthropology, no. 4, 1961.

——*Prehistory in the Navajo Reservoir District, Northwestern New Mexico.* Santa Fe: Museum of New Mexico Papers in Anthropology, no. 15, parts 1 and 2, 1972.

Elliott, Melinda. *Great Excavations: Tales of Early Southwestern Archaeology, 1888–1939.* Santa Fe: School of American Research Press, 1995.

Fike, Richard E. "Antiquities Violations in Utah: Justice Does Prevail." In *Cultural Resources Law Enforcement: An Emerging Science,* 2d ed., compiled by Dee F. Green and Polly Davis, pp. 49–51. Albuquerque: USDA Forest Service Southwest Region, 1981.

Frost, Kent. *My Canyonlands.* New York: Abelard-Schuman, 1971.

Fussell, Betty. *The Story of Corn.* New York: Alfred A. Knopf, 1992.

Gabriel, Kathryn (editor). *Marietta Wetherill: Reflections on Life with the Navajos in Chaco Canyon.* Boulder, Colorado: Johnson Books, 1992.

Geib, Phil R., and Dale Davidson. "Anasazi Origins: A Perspective from Preliminary Work at Old Man Cave." *Kiva,* vol. 60, no. 2, 1994, pp. 191–202.

Gillmore, Frances, and Louisa Wade Wetherill. *Traders to the Navajos: The Story of the Wetherills of Kayenta.* Albuquerque: University of New Mexico Press, 1953.

Gilpin, Dennis. "Lukachukai and Salina Springs: Late Archaic/Early Basketmaker Habitation Sites in Chinle Valley, Northeastern Arizona." *Kiva,* vol. 2, no. 4, 1994, pp. 203–18.

Graham, Charles Cary. "Diary." Original in possession of Charles Graham, Houston, Texas. Copy in possession of Fred M. Blackburn. Published as "Charles Cary Graham's Explorations" in *Adventures with the Anasazi of Falls Creek,* Helen Sloan Daniels, ed., pp. 9–15. Durango, Colorado: Fort Lewis College Center of Southwest Studies, Occasional Paper no. 3, 1976.

Grand Canyon Trust. *Preserving Traces of the Past: Protecting the Colorado Plateau's Archaeological Heritage.* Flagstaff, Arizona: Grand Canyon Trust, 1994.

Grant, Campbell. *Canyon de Chelly: Its People and Rock Art.* Tucson: University of Arizona Press, 1978.

Guernsey, Samuel J., and Alfred V. Kidder. *Basketmaker Caves of Northeastern Arizona: Report on the Explorations, 1916–17.* Papers of the Peabody Museum of American Archaeology and Ethnology, vol. 8, no. 2, 1921.

H. [Talbot Hyde]. "Recent Finds in Utah." *The Archaeologist,* vol. 2, 1894, pp. 154–55.

Hayes, Ann. "One Hundred Years in the Life of the C. H. Green Collection." In *Anasazi Basketmaker: Papers from the 1990 Wetherill–Grand Gulch Symposium,* Victoria M. Atkins, ed., pp. 121–28. Salt Lake City: Bureau of Land Management, Cultural Resource Series no. 24, 1993.

Hurst, Winston B. "Photograph of Richard Wetherill and Utes in Camp." *Blue Mountain Shadows,* vol. 11, Winter, 1992.

Hurst, Winston B., and Christy G. Turner II. "Rediscovering the 'Great Discovery': Wetherill's First Cave 7 and Its Implications Regarding Basketmaker Violence." In *Anasazi Basketmaker: Papers from the 1990 Wetherill–Grand Gulch Symposium,* Victoria M. Atkins, ed., pp. 143–91. Salt Lake City: Bureau of Land Management, Cultural Resource Series no. 24, 1993.

Hutt, Sherry. "Illegal Trafficking in Native American Human Remains and Cultural Items: A New Protection Tool." *Arizona State Law Journal,* vol. 24, no. 1, 1992, pp. 135–50.

Hutt, Sherry, Elwood W. Jones, and Martin E. McAllister. *Archeological Resource Protection.* Washington, D.C.: Preservation Press, 1992.

Jett, Stephen C. "The Great 'Race' to 'Discover' Rainbow Natural Bridge in 1909." *Kiva,* vol. 58, no. 1, 1992, pp. 3–66.

Johnson, Julia. "The History of the Wetherill–Grand Gulch Research Project." In *Anasazi Basketmaker: Papers from the 1990 Wetherill–Grand Gulch Symposium,* Victoria M. Atkins, ed., pp. 13–28. Salt Lake City: Bureau of Land Management, Cultural Resource Series no. 24, 1993.

Keller, Donald R., Richard V. Ahlstrom, and Dana Hartman. "Final Report for Surface Cleanup of Cultural Sites in Grand Gulch." Bureau of Land Management Contract #52500, Museum of Northern Arizona, Department of Anthropology, 1974.

Kidder, Alfred Vincent. *An Introduction to the Study of Southwestern Archaeology.* New Haven: Yale University Press, 1962 [1924].

——"Southwestern Archaeological Conference." *Science,* vol. 66, 1927, pp. 489–91.

Kidder, Alfred Vincent, and Samuel J. Guernsey. *Archaeological Explorations in Northeastern Arizona.* Washington, D.C.: Bureau of American Ethnology Bulletin 65, 1919.

Knipmeyer, James H. "Some Historic Signatures of the Four Corners Region." In *Anasazi Basketmaker: Papers from the 1990 Wetherill–Grand Gulch Symposium,* Victoria M. Atkins, ed., pp. 31–40. Salt Lake City: Bureau of Land Management, Cultural Resource Series no. 24, 1993.

Lipe, William D. "Anasazi Communities in the Red Rock Plateau, Southeastern Utah." In *Reconstructing Prehistoric Pueblo Societies,* edited by W. Longacre, pp. 84–139. Albuquerque: University of New Mexico Press, 1970.

——"Grand Gulch: Three Days on the Road from Bluff." In *Camera, Spade, and Pen,* edited by Marc Gaede and Marnie Gaede, pp. 52–59. Tucson: University of Arizona Press, 1980.

——"The Basketmaker II Period in the Four Corners Area." In *Anasazi Basketmaker: Papers from the 1990 Wetherill–Grand Gulch Symposium,* Victoria M. Atkins, ed., pp. 1–10. Salt Lake City: Bureau of Land Management, Cultural Resource Series no. 24, 1993.

Lister, Florence C., and Robert H. Lister. *Earl Morris and Southwestern Archaeology.* Albuquerque: University of New Mexico Press, 1968.

McNitt, Frank. *Richard Wetherill: Anasazi.* Albuquerque: University of New Mexico Press, 1966.

Marsh, Charles S. *People of the Shining Mountains: The Utes of Colorado.* Boulder, Colorado: Pruett Publishing Company, 1982.

Matson, R. G. *The Origins of Southwestern Agriculture.* Tucson: University of Arizona Press, 1991.

Matson, R. G., and Brian Chisholm. "Basketmaker II Subsistence: Carbon Isotopes and Other Dietary Indicators from Cedar Mesa, Utah." *American Antiquity,* vol. 56, no. 3, 1991, pp. 444–59.

Miller, David E. *Hole-in-the-Rock.* Salt Lake City: University of Utah Press, 1966.

Morell, Virginia. "An Anthropological Culture Shift." *Science,* vol. 264, April 1, 1994, pp. 20–22.

Morris, Ann Axtell. *Digging in the Southwest.* New York: Doubleday, 1933.
Morris, Earl H. "Mummy Cave." *Natural History,* vol. 42, 1938, pp. 127–38.
Morris, Earl H., and Robert F. Burgh. *Basket Maker II Sites near Durango, Colorado.* Washington, D.C.: Carnegie Institution of Washington, Publication 604, 1954.
Moseley, M. Edward. "The Discovery and Definition of Basketmaker: 1890 to 1914." *Masterkey,* vol. 40, no. 4, 1966, pp. 140–54.
Nelson, Nels C. *Pueblo Ruins of the Galisteo Basin, New Mexico.* Anthropological Papers of the American Museum of Natural History, vol. 15, 1914.
Nordenskiöld, Gustaf. *The Cliff Dwellers of the Mesa Verde.* Reprint. Glorieta, New Mexico: Rio Grande Press, 1979.
Pepper, George H. "The Ancient Basketmakers of Southeastern Utah." Supplement to *American Museum Journal,* vol. 2, no. 4, Guide Leaflet no. 6, April 1902.
Perkins, William R. "Atlatl Weights: Function and Classification." *Bulletin of Primitive Technology,* vol. 1, no. 5, 1993, pp. 58–61.
Phillips, Ann. "Archaeological Expeditions into Southeastern Utah and Southwestern Colorado between 1888–1898 and the Dispersal of the Collections." In *Anasazi Basketmaker: Papers from the 1990 Wetherill–Grand Gulch Symposium,* Victoria M. Atkins, ed., pp. 103–20. Salt Lake City: Bureau of Land Management, Cultural Resource Series no. 24, 1993.
Prudden, T. Mitchell. *On the Great American Plateau.* New York: G. P. Putnam's Sons, 1906.
——"A Summer among Cliff Dwellings." *Harper's New Monthly Magazine,* vol. 95, September 1896, pp. 55–62.
Putnam, Frederick Ward. "On Methods of Archaeological Research in America." Baltimore: Johns Hopkins University Circular, 1885.
Riding In, James. "Without Ethics and Morality: A Historical Overview of Imperial Archaeology and American Indians." *Arizona State Law Journal,* vol. 24, no. 1, pp. 11–34.
Roberts, David. "'Reverse Archaeologists' Are Tracing the Footsteps of a Cowboy-Explorer." *Smithsonian,* December 1993, pp. 28–39.
Schaafsma, Polly. *Indian Rock Art of the Southwest.* Albuquerque: University of New Mexico Press, 1980.
Schaafsma, Polly, and Curtis F. Schaafsma. "Evidence for the Origins of the Pueblo Katchina Cult as Suggested by Southwestern Rock Art." *American Antiquity,* vol. 39, 1974, pp. 535–45.
Schroeder, Albert H. "History of Archeological Research." In *Handbook of North American Indians, vol. 9: Southwest,* Alfonso Ortiz, ed., pp. 5–13. Washington, D.C.: Smithsonian Institution Press, 1979.
Smiley, Francis E. "The Agricultural Transition in the Northern Southwest: Patterns in the Current Chronometric Data." *Kiva,* vol. 60, no. 2, 1994, pp. 165–89.
——"Early Farmers in the Northern Southwest: A View from Marsh Pass." In *Anasazi Basketmaker: Papers from the 1990 Wetherill–Grand Gulch Symposium,* Victoria M. Atkins, ed., pp. 243–56. Salt Lake City: Bureau of Land Management, Cultural Resource Series no. 24, 1993.
Smiley, F. E., Deborah L. Nichols, and Peter P. Andrews. *Excavations on Black Mesa, 1981: A Descriptive Report.* Carbondale: Southern Illinois University at Carbondale, Center for Archaeological Investigations, Research Paper no. 36, 1983.
Smiley, F. E., W. Parry, and G. Gumerman. "Early Agriculture in the Black Mesa/Marsh Pass Region of Arizona: New Chronometric Data and Recent Excavations at Three Fir Shelter." Paper presented at the fifty-first annual meeting of the Society for American Archaeology, New Orleans, 1986.
Smith, Duane A. *Rocky Mountain Boom Town.* Albuquerque: University of New Mexico Press, 1980.
——*Mesa Verde National Park: Shadows of the Centuries.* Lawrence: University of Kansas Press, 1988.
Stallings, W. S., Jr. "A Basketmaker II Date from Cave du Pont, Utah." *Tree-Ring Bulletin,* vol. 8, 1941, pp. 3–6.
Turner, Christy G., II. "Taphonomic Reconstruction of Human Violence and Cannibalism Based on Mass Burials in the American Southwest." In *Carnivores, Human Scavengers and Predators: A Question of Bone Technology,* G. M LeMoine and A. S. MacEachern, eds., pp. 219–40. Calgary: Proceedings of the Fifteenth Annual Conference of the Archaeological Association of the University of Calgary, 1983.
Weatherford, Jack. *Indian Givers: How the Indians of the Americas Transformed the World.* New York: Fawcett Columbine, 1988.
Wetherill, Benjamin Alfred. *The Wetherills of Mesa Verde: The Autobiography of Benjamin Alfred Wetherill.* Edited by Maurine S. Fletcher. Rutherford, New Jersey: Fairleigh Dickinson University Press, 1977.
Widdison, Jerold G. *The Anasazi: Why Did They Leave? Where Did They Go?* Albuquerque: Southwest Natural and Cultural Heritage Association, 1991.
Williamson, Ray A. *Living the Sky: The Cosmos of the American Indian.* Norman: University of Oklahoma Press, 1987.
Williamson, Ray A., and Fred M. Blackburn. "The Living Earth and the Outdoor Museum." In *Is the Earth a Living Organism?* James Swann, ed. Freeport, Maine: Audubon Expedition Institute, 1985.
——"An Approach to Vandalism of Archeological Resources." In *Coping With Site Looting: Southeastern Perspectives,* John E. Ehrenhard, ed., pp. 49–58. Atlanta: Interagency Archeological Services Division, National Park Service, 1990.
Woodbury, Richard B., and Ezra B. W. Zubrow. "Agricultural Beginnings, 2000 B.C.–A.D. 500." In *Handbook of North American Indians, vol. 9: Southwest,* Alfonso Ortiz, ed., pp. 43–60. Washington, D.C.: Smithsonian Institution Press, 1979.
Yalung, Catherine Bergin, and Laurel I. Wala. "Survey of State Reparation and Burial Protection Statutes." *Arizona State Law Journal,* vol. 24, no. 1, 1992, pp. 419–34.
Young, M. Jane. "Images of Power and the Power of Images: The Significance of Rock Art for Contemporary Zunis." *Journal of American Folklore,* vol. 98, 1985, pp. 2–48.
Zwinger, Ann. *Wind in the Rock.* New York: Harper and Row, 1978.

Picture Credits

The discovery and study of the Basketmakers involve the subject of Native American burials, an issue that has become extremely sensitive over the last decade. A century ago, it was common for the dominant Euro-American society to display prehistoric skeletons or even mummified bodies in exhibitions of archaeological artifacts. Many of the historic photographs that contribute to the Basketmakers' story contain images of skeletons or mummies. Although a good deal of what archaeologists know about Basketmaker culture derives from excavated burials, in this book we have strictly limited the display of human remains. Only when they are an integral part of the story have we included such images.

The authors thank the individuals, institutions, and collections listed below for their assistance in finding historic photographs and for generously allowing us to reproduce them in this book. Thanks also to Baylor Chapman for her help tracking down photos and permissions. Many of the photographs by Bruce Hucko are in the collections of the Wetherill–Grand Gulch Archives at the Edge of the Cedars Museum in Blanding, Utah. Photographs are copyright the individual photographers unless otherwise noted.

ABBREVIATIONS USED

CSS/FLC	Center for Southwest Studies, Fort Lewis College, Durango
AMNH	American Museum of Natural History, New York
DLS/AMNH	Department Library Services, American Museum of Natural History
FMNH	Field Museum of Natural History, Chicago
MARI	Middle American Research Institute, Tulane University
NGS	National Geographic Society
NMF	National Museum of Finland, Helsinki
NPS	National Park Service
NPS/MVNP	National Park Service/Mesa Verde National Park
PM/HU	Peabody Museum, Harvard University
SMLA	Southwest Museum, Los Angeles
·SRCA	State Records Center & Archives, 404 Montezuma, Santa Fe, NM
UPM	The University of Pennsylvania Museum

Cover: Basketmaker handprints at Polly's Island, Grand Gulch © Bruce Hucko; Hyde Exploring Expedition in Cave 7, December 1893, UPM neg. no. S4-139872

Back flap: Fred Blackburn photo © Terrance Moore; Ray Williamson photo by Katrina Lasko © School of American Research

Back cover: Mesa Verde canteen from Step House Ruin; plate 31 in *The Cliff Dwellers of Mesa Verde,* Gustaf Nordenskiöld (1893/1979), copy photo by Ted Rice

MAPS

14	Katrina Lasko, adapted from p. xxii, *The Anasazi in a Changing Environment*, George J. Gumerman, ed., A School of American Research Book, Cambridge: Cambridge University Press
30	Carol Cooperrider

FIGURES

ii–iii	See p. 99
v	See p. 37, bottom
vi	Fred Blackburn at Sandal House, 1993, Terrance Moore photo
2	Bruce Hucko photo
5	MARI, Pepper collection, neg. no. PS 547; inset: Bruce Hucko photo
6	Fred Blackburn photo
7	SMLA neg. no. n34,376
8	Left: Bruce Hucko photo; center: MARI neg. no. PS 589; right: AMNH acc. no. E203-7
9	Bruce Hucko photo
11	Bruce Hucko photo
12	Bruce Hucko photo
15	MARI neg. no. PS 598
17	Bruce Hucko photo
18	Bruce Hucko photo
20	Courtesy John Richardson; inset: courtesy Eleanor Stanberry
23	Top: Gustaf Nordenskiöld photo, NMF; center: SRCA/McNitt neg. no. 8615; bottom: Gustaf Nordenskiöld photo, NMF
24	NMF; inset: NPS/MVNP neg. no. 4946
29	Emerald Flint Patrick collection, courtesy Donna Becker
32	W. J. Carpenter photo, Fred Blackburn collection

33 Utah State Historical Society Photograph Archives, photo 979.2, neg. no. 15165
34 Photographer unknown, Fred Blackburn collection
35 FMNH neg. no. 63329
37 Top: FMNH neg. no. A83286; bottom: FMNH neg. no. 63228
38 Left: FMNH neg. no. 8016; inset: Bruce Hucko photo
39 FMNH, Green Collection, acc. no. 12/1162, Bruce Hucko photo
40 AMNH acc. nos. H-13529, H-13134, Bruce Hucko photo
41 Bruce Hucko photo; inset: *Illustrated American,* vol. 11, no. 129, p. 562 (1892), courtesy San Juan Historical Commission, Blanding, UT
43 FMNH neg. no. A8013
44 Bruce Hucko photo
46 FMNH neg. no. 63335
47 CSS/FLC
48 SRCA/McNitt: Wetherill Papers II
50 C. B. Lang photo, DLS/AMNH neg. no. 128415
51 Fred Blackburn photo
52 Bruce Hucko photos
55 AMNH acc. nos. H-13133, H-13476, H-13462, H-13506, H-13529, H-13411, H-13149, H-13961, H-13134, H-13560, H-13371, Bruce Hucko photo
56 Bruce Hucko photo
59 UPM neg. no. S4-140100
60 Top: DLS/AMNH neg. no. 338269; left: SRCA/McNitt neg. no. 8627
62 Fred Blackburn photo
63 MARI neg. no. PS-558
64 MARI neg. no. PS-598
65 Gustaf Nordenskiöld photo, NMF
66 NPS Chaco Canyon/AMNH
68 Bruce Hucko photo; inset: FMNH neg. no. 63329
70 Terrance Moore photo
72 Terrance Moore photo
75 AMNH, N. C. Nelson neg. no. 1428
77 Bruce Hucko photo
79 Left: Courtesy Kathryn Ayres; center: courtesy Charles Lang, Jr., family; right: Bruce Hucko photo
82 Terrance Moore photo
85 Bruce Hucko photo; inset: FMNH neg. no. 2100
87 Ira Block, NGS
88 FMNH neg. no. 2210
89 Don Eicher photo, courtesy Julia Johnson
90 Bill Harris photo
92 Bruce Hucko photo
93 AMNH burial no. 12295 (McLoyd's A-7), acc. nos. H-12510, H-12512, H-12511, H-12274, H-12285, H-12295, H-12351, H-12276. H-12188, H-12197, H-12253, H-12236, H-12239, H-12344, H-12345, H-12255, H-12475, H-12233, H-12516, H-12518, H-12522, H-12528, H-12556, Bruce Hucko photo
94 Top left: AMNH acc. no. H-12521, Bruce Hucko photo; top right: AMNH acc. nos. H-12507, H-12498, Bruce Hucko photo; bottom: AMNH acc. no. H-13476, Bruce Hucko photo
95 FMNH cat. nos. H-21530, H-21533, H-21532, H-21596, H-21531, H-21538, Bruce Hucko photo
96 Top left: AMNH acc. nos. H-12444, H-12453, H-12643, Bruce Hucko photo; top right: see page 93; bottom: AMNH acc. nos. 15719, 15710, Bruce Hucko photo
97 AMNH acc. no. H-13533, Bruce Hucko photo
98 Top: AMNH acc. no. H-13338, Bruce Hucko photo; bottom left: FMNH Green Collection, cat. no. 21693, Bruce Hucko photo; bottom right: Bruce Hucko photo
99 Bruce Hucko photos
100 Bruce Hucko photos
101 Bruce Hucko photo
102 Bruce Hucko photo
104 Scott Ortman photo
105 Bruce Hucko photos
106 Terrance Moore photo
107 FMNH cat. no. 1468
109 Bruce Hucko photo
110 UPM neg. no. S4-139872; inset: Bruce Hucko photo
111 Bruce Hucko photo
112 Left: FMNH, Green Collection, acc. no. 12/1162, Bruce Hucko photo; right: FMNH acc. no. 21384, Bruce Hucko photos
114 FMNH neg. no. 8017; inset: Bruce Hucko photo
115 Terrance Moore photo
118 UPM neg. no. S4-139899
119 DLS/AMNH neg. no. 59
122 Bruce Hucko photo
124 Plate 31a (photo) and fig. 32 (plan) in *Archaeological Explorations in Northeastern Arizona,* A. V. Kidder and S. J. Guernsey (1919), Washington, D.C.: Bureau of American Ethnology Bulletin 65, Ted Rice copy photos
127 Top: Plate 67 in A. V. Kidder and S. J. Guernsey (1919), Ted Rice copy photo; bottom left: MARI neg. no. PS 570; bottom right: plate 78b, Kidder and Guernsey (1919), Ted Rice copy photo
129 Plate 61 in A. V. Kidder and S. J. Guernsey (1919), Ted Rice copy photo
130 Fig. 52a in *Basket Maker II Sites near Durango, Colorado,* E. H. Morris and R. F. Burgh (1954), Washington, D.C.: Carnegie Institution of Washington, Publication 604, courtesy Carnegie Institution of Washington; Ted Rice copy photo
132 Fig. 58 in E. H. Morris and R. F. Burgh (1954), courtesy Carnegie Institution of Washington; Ted Rice copy photo
134 AMNH acc. no. H-13533; Bruce Hucko photo
135 Fig. 85 in E. H. Morris and R. F. Burgh (1954), courtesy Carnegie Institution of Washington; Ted Rice copy photo
136 Plate 65 in A. V. Kidder and S. J. Guernsey (1919), Ted Rice copy photo
137 Bruce Hucko photo
140 FMNH cat. no. 21543, Bruce Hucko photo
141 Bruce Hucko photo
142 Left: AMNH acc. no. H-12559; center: AMNH acc. no. H-12981; right: AMNH acc. nos. H-13035, H-13438; Bruce Hucko photos
144 Plate 37 in *Basketmaker Caves of Northeastern Arizona: Report on the Explorations, 1916–17,* S. J. Guernsey and A. V. Kidder (1921), Papers of the Peabody Museum of American Archaeology and Ethnology, vol. 8, no. 2, courtesy PM/HU, Ted Rice copy photo
145 AMNH acc. no. H-12510, Bruce Hucko photo
146 Plate 9 in S. J. Guernsey and A. V. Kidder (1921), courtesy PM/HU; Ted Rice copy photo
148 Bruce Hucko photo
150 Fred Blackburn photo
153 Bruce Hucko photo
155 Bruce Hucko photo
157 Top: FMNH neg. no. 63289; bottom: Bruce Hucko photo
161 Bruce Hucko photo
162 Bruce Hucko photo
167 Bruce Hucko photo
170 Bruce Hucko photo
171 Fred Blackburn at Sandal House, 1993; Terrance Moore photo
179 John Wetherill, 1891, Gustaf Nordenskiöld photo, NMF
183 Partially excavated jar with yucca-fiber wrapping found by the Hyde Exploring Expedition, 1893–94; UPM neg. no. S4-140119
185 See p.63

Index